The Bare Essentials
FORM B

The Bare Essentials
FORM B

FIFTH EDITION

Sarah Norton
Brian Green

THOMSON

NELSON

Australia   Canada   Mexico   Singapore   Spain   United Kingdom   United States

THOMSON
✦
NELSON

The Bare Essentials, Form B,
5th edition
by Sarah Norton and Brian Green

Editorial Director and Publisher:
Evelyn Veitch

Acquisitions Editor:
Anne Williams

Senior Developmental Editor:
Mike Thompson

Production Editor:
Natalia Denesiuk

Copy Editor and Proofreader:
Joan Rawlin

Indexer:
Edwin Durbin

Senior Production Coordinator:
Hedy Sellers

Creative Director:
Angela Cluer

Interior and Cover Designs:
Sonya V. Thursby,
Opus House Incorporated

Cover Image:
Peter Papayanakis and
Gabriel Sierra

Illustrations:
Kathryn Adams

Compositor:
Carol Magee

Permissions:
Vicki Gould

Printer:
Transcontinental Printing Inc.

National Library of Canada Cataloguing in Publication Data

Norton, Sarah, 1941–
   The bare essentials : form B / Sarah Norton, Brian Green.— 5th ed.

Includes bibliographical references and index.
ISBN 0-17-622533-1

   1. English language— Composition and exercises. 2. English language—Grammar. I. Green, Brian II. Title.

PE1408.N67   2004   808′.042
C2003-903335-X

Preface

Can more than 400,000 Canadian students and teachers be wrong? That's the number of people who have used *The Bare Essentials* since it was first published. Originally, it was a modest text that we hoped would simplify the work of both teachers and students. Our goal was to produce a book with accessible explanations, a minimum of technical jargon, a variety of exercises that would engage students while reinforcing their writing skills, and a style that would speak to students with patience, understanding, and humour. We hope you will agree that this new edition of *The Bare Essentials, Form B* follows that tradition, while at the same time providing new ideas and techniques that help students learn to write.

The Bare Essentials is intended for students taking an introductory writing skills course. Although not designed specifically as a remedial text, the book accommodates the wide range of ability typical of first-year college classes. New to this edition is a comprehensive Web site designed to support both students and teachers (**http://www.bareessentialsb.nelson.com**). Students who need more practice than is provided in the text will find additional examples, exercises, and self-scoring practice tests to help them master the material. Also featured are a write-in question-and-answer page, additional readings, and links to reference sites.

The instructors' site offers an Instructor's Manual with sample syllabuses, teaching tips, answers to the mastery tests in the text, and supplementary mastery tests for each chapter. The site also features PowerPoint slides and transparency masters, reading and reference links, and *The Essentials Test Manual* with its comprehensive diagnostic tests and pre- and post-tests for each chapter and unit. A writers' forum provides instructors with the opportunity to communicate their suggestions, questions, and criticisms directly to the authors.

In response to students' requests, we have shortened the book. In response to instructors' requests, we have increased the number of exercises overall. We have included enough exercises in each chapter to satisfy the needs of most first-year college students and then provided additional exercises on our Web site for those who need extra practice on particular points. We hope this compromise will please everyone.

Like its predecessors, this edition covers the skills that are indispensable to effective written communication: organization, syntax, grammar, spelling, punctuation, and diction. The text presents, illustrates, and tests these basic skills using examples drawn from a broad range of student experience. Many students are sceptical of the connection between what they learn in their generic composition class and what they are taught in their specific career courses, so we have provided as many links as we could between theory and practice. We acknowledge that bridging the gap requires the imagination and skill of a creative teacher, one who is prepared to devise or elicit from the class practical examples and writing assignments that demonstrate the basic rules.

Each "essential" is presented in a discrete unit. We have arranged the units in what might be called the "order of visibility" of composition errors, starting with spelling and ending with diction. The units are not interdependent, so the instructor can teach them in any order. The chapters within each unit, however, should be introduced in sequential order. The exercises within a unit are cumulative; those in later chapters often include questions that assume mastery of skills covered in earlier chapters.

Almost all of the exercises can be completed in the text, and the answers in the back of the book are easy to find. The first exercise in each chapter refers students to the page on which the answers for that chapter begin, and all exercises are numbered by chapter as well as by exercise (e.g., Exercise 12.2 refers to the second exercise in Chapter 12). Web exercises for each chapter are identified by chapter and number below the Web icons.

Students are directed to check their answers immediately after completing each exercise. If they follow this instruction, they get immediate feedback on their understanding and can review the explanation, if necessary, before proceeding. **We urge instructors to emphasize the importance of this procedure.** If students complete an entire set of exercises before checking their answers, they run the risk of reinforcing rather than eliminating the error the exercises are designed to correct.

The Bare Essentials is based on our experience that students can learn to write clear, error-free prose if they understand the principles involved, master the principles through practice, and apply the principles in their own writing. We know that students will not learn unless they want to. We've tried to help motivate them by beginning most chapters with a few words about the practical significance of the material. Complex material is presented in easy-to-follow steps. Most of each chapter is devoted to practice exercises, and students are directed to do as many as they need to master the rule. We've tried to forestall boredom by appealing to the interests of Canadian students and by incorporating in each chapter some exercises for which there is no one "right" answer. We believe tests should be teaching instruments as well as measures of knowledge, and we hope instructors will use our "suggested answers" as the basis for classroom discussion and debate.

Inside the front cover is a "Quick Revision Guide." Students can use it as a checklist to help them revise and edit their work. Instructors can duplicate the guide, attach a copy to each student's paper, and mark ✔ or ✘ beside each point to identify the paper's strengths and weaknesses. This strategy saves hours of marking time, and it also provides students with point-by-point feedback as to the adequacy of their work.

ACKNOWLEDGMENTS

We thank the 400,000 Canadian teachers and students who have been our sharpest critics and staunchest supporters. Specifically, we wish to acknowledge the contribution of Dawn Henwood, who developed many of the new exercises for this edition.

A NOTE FROM THE PUBLISHER

Thank you for selecting *The Bare Essentials, Form B,* Fifth Edition, by Sarah Norton and Brian Green. The authors and publisher have devoted considerable time and care to the development of this book. We appreciate your recognition of this effort and accomplishment.

We want to hear what you think about *The Bare Essentials, Form B.* Please e-mail your comments to us at **essentialsauthors@nelson.com.** Your comments and suggestions will be valuable to us as we prepare new editions and other books.

Introduction

Why You Need This Book

Here's what a manager with IBM Canada had to say recently about the kind of employee they look for:

> *At the entry level, we're looking for people with excellent communication skills: reading, listening, speaking, and — above all — writing. It's much more efficient for us to teach a good communicator how to code than it is to try to teach a good coder how to communicate.*

To an employer, any employee is more valuable if he or she can write well. No one can advance very far in a career without the ability to communicate clearly. It's that simple. Fairly or unfairly, no matter what field you are in, employers and others will judge your ability largely on the basis of your communication skills. If you want to communicate effectively and earn respect both on and off the job, you need to be able to write well.

That's the bad news. The good news is that anyone who wants to can achieve the standards of written English that are acceptable anywhere. All that is needed from you, really, is caring. If you care enough about what others think of you and about career advancement, then you'll make the necessary effort, whether that means consulting your dictionary, using a spell checker, revising your work, or doing all the exercises in this book twice!

How to Use This Book

In each chapter, we do three things: explain a point, illustrate it with examples, and provide exercises to help you master it. The exercises are arranged in sets that get more difficult as you go along. After some of the exercises, you will find a symbol directing you to the *Essentials* Web site (**http://www.bareessentialsb.nelson.com**), where we have provided additional exercises for students who need extra practice. By the time you've completed the last set of exercises in a chapter, you should have a good grasp of the skill.

Here's how to proceed.

1. Read the explanation. Do this even if you think you understand the point being discussed.
2. Study the highlighted rules and the examples that follow them.
3. Now turn to the exercises. If you've found an explanation easy and think you have no problems with the skill, try an exercise near the end of the set that follows the explanation. Check your answers. If you get all the sentences right, skip the rest and go on to the next point. Skip ahead only if you're really confident, though.

    If you don't feel confident, don't skip anything. Start with the first set and work through all the exercises, including those on the Web site, until you're certain you understand the point. As a general rule, getting three sets in a row entirely correct demonstrates understanding and competence.
4. **Always check your answers to one set of exercises before you go on to the next.** If you ignore this instruction, this book can't help you. Only if you check your results after every set can you avoid repeating mistakes and possibly reinforcing your errors.[1] The answers to the exercises in the text are in Appendix C at the back of the book. The exercises on the Web site are self-scoring.
5. When you find a mistake, go back to the explanation and examples and study them again. Look up additional examples for that point on the Web site. Try making up some examples of your own to illustrate the rule. If you are truly stuck, check with your instructor. Continue

---

[1] You can cheat, of course. You can check the answer to a question before doing it, or you can even look up all the answers before starting an exercise. If you do so, however, you will waste your time (because you won't learn anything) and your money (because you will prevent the book you've paid for from helping you). If, however, you use *The Bare Essentials* as it has been designed to be used, we guarantee that you will improve your writing skills.

with the exercises only when you are *sure* you understand. You can reinforce your understanding—and prepare for in-class tests—by doing the practice tests on the Student Home Page of the *Bare Essentials* Web site.

What the Symbols Mean

Some exercises in the text are followed by a Web icon and directions to go to specific supplementary exercises on the *Bare Essentials* Web site. Once you've logged on to the Web site, click on the button that says "Study Guide," then click on "Web Exercises." There you will find the numbered exercises listed in this book beneath the Web icon. Your answers are marked automatically, so you will know instantly whether or not you have understood the material.

When this symbol appears in the margin beside an exercise, it means the exercise is a mastery test—an exercise designed to check your level of understanding of the principles covered in the chapter you've just completed. The answers to these tests are not in the back of the book; your instructor will provide them.

We've used this symbol to highlight writing tips, helpful hints, hard-to-remember points, and information that you should apply whenever you write, not just when you're dealing with the specific principles covered in the chapter containing the icon.

A Final Suggestion

On the inside of the front cover, you'll find a Quick Revision Guide. Use it to help you revise your papers before handing them in. This book is meant to be a practical tool, not a theoretical reference. Apply the lessons in all the writing you do. Explanations can identify writing problems and show you how to solve them; exercises can give you practice in eliminating errors; but only writing and revising can bring real and lasting improvement.

Contents

UNIT 1

Spelling

Three Suggestions for Quick Improvement

Of all the errors you might make in writing, spelling is the one that is noticed by everyone, not just English teachers. Misspellings can cause misunderstandings, as when an English teacher promised his students a course with "a strong *vacational* emphasis." (Those students who weren't misled wondered what he was doing teaching English.)

They can also cause confusion. Take this sentence, for example:

Mouse is a desert with a base of wiped cream.

It takes a few seconds to "translate" the sentence into a definition of *mousse,* a *dessert* made with *whipped* cream.

Most often, though, misspellings are misleading; they spoil the image you want to present. You want to be seen as intelligent, careful, and conscientious. But if your writing is riddled with spelling errors, your reader will think you are careless, uneducated, or even stupid. It is not true, by the way, that intelligence and the ability to spell go hand in hand. It is true, however, that most people think they do. So, to prevent misunderstanding, confusion, and embarrassment, it is essential that you spell correctly.

There are three things you can do to improve your spelling almost instantly.

1. Buy and use a good dictionary.

A dictionary is a writer's best friend. You will need it every time you write, so if you don't already own a good dictionary, you need to buy one. For Canadian writers, a good dictionary is one that is Canadian, current, and reasonably comprehensive. The *Gage Canadian Dictionary,* available in an inexpensive paperback edition, is a convenient reference. It is the dictionary on which the examples and exercises in this chapter are based. Also recommended are the *Canadian Dictionary of the English Language* (Nelson, 1997) and, for those whose native language is not English, the *Cobuild English Dictionary* (HarperCollins, 1995). Unfortunately, no comprehensive Canadian dictionary is available on the Internet.

A good dictionary packs an astonishing amount of information into a small space. Thus, for each entry, you will find some or all of the following:

1. Spelling (if there are two or more acceptable spellings, the most common one is normally given first);
2. Syllables (to show you where hyphens can go if you need to break a word at the end of a line);
3. Pronunciation (if there is more than one acceptable pronunciation, the most common one is listed first);
4. Grammatical form(s): e.g., noun (*n.*), verb (*v.*), adjective (*adj.*);
5. Any irregular forms of the word, such as the plural form of a noun or the past tense and past participle of a verb;
6. Usage restrictions: e.g., slang, informal, archaic, offensive;
7. Definition(s) of the word (the most common meanings are given first, followed by the technical or specialized meanings), together with phrases or sentences illustrating how the word is used;
8. Idioms using the word;
9. Origins of the word (etymology);
10. Other helpful information: e.g., homonyms (words that sound the same as the entry word); synonyms (words that are similar in meaning to the entry word); antonyms (words opposite in meaning); and special variations in grammar, spelling, pronunciation, and usage.

Most of your doubts about spelling can be answered if you take the time to check your dictionary. The time you spend looking up words will not be wasted; your rewards will be the increased accuracy of your writing and the increased respect of your reader.

If you wonder how it's possible to look up a word you can't spell, look at the "Guide to the Dictionary," which you'll find in the front of your dictionary. In the guide are a pronunciation key and a chart showing the common spellings for all the sounds in the English language. If you know how to pronounce a word, the chart will help you to find its spelling. Another way to find a word you can't spell is to look up a synonym—a word with a meaning similar to that of the word you want. In the dictionary entry for the synonym, you'll probably find the word you're looking for.

 The "Guide to the Dictionary" may not be the most entertaining reading you've ever done, but it will be among the most worthwhile. You will find a diagram of the kinds of information given for each word and an explanation of the abbreviations and symbols used. You will discover, for example, that you don't need to memorize long lists of irregular plurals: your dictionary gives the irregular plural for any word you look up. It also gives the irregular forms of verbs, adjectives, and adverbs. If you've forgotten how regular plurals, verbs, adjectives, and adverbs are formed, the guide gives you that information too. And it shows you how to read a dictionary entry so that you can see at a glance how to add various endings to a root word.

Take half an hour to read the guide in your dictionary; then do the following exercises. Be sure to check your answers to each set before you go on to the next. Answers begin on page 319.

Exercise 1.1

1. What is a second way to spell the word *licence*? Are the two spellings interchangeable?
2. What is another spelling of the word *theater*? What other words can you think of that end in *–er* and have alternative spellings?
3. Is *envelop* spelled correctly? Is it a noun or a verb?
4. How many correct spellings are there for the word *connection*? Which is the preferred spelling in Canada?
5. Find alternative spellings for the words *aesthetic, realize, traveler, jewelry,* and *behavior*. In each case, indicate the spelling most commonly used in Canada.

Exercise 1.2

Write the plural form of each word.

1. potato
2. series
3. basis
4. deer
5. criterion
6. focus
7. hero
8. curriculum
9. species
10. phenomenon

Exercise 1.3

Combine each root word with the ending given.

1. relay + ed
2. key + s
3. play + er
4. enjoy + ment

5. say + ing

6. entry + s

7. mercy + less

8. daisy + s

9. merry + ment

10. cursory + ly

After you have checked your answers to this exercise, go back and look closely at the questions. What do the root words in questions 1 to 5 have in common? What do the root words in questions 6 to 10 have in common? How do these similarities affect the way they are spelled when an ending is added?

Exercise 1.4

Using hyphens, show where each word could be divided at the end of a line. (Some words can be divided in two or more places: *ice-break-ing*, for example.)

1. method

2. implement

3. recommend

4. resolution

5. reverse

6. iodine

7. archaic

8. teller

9. misunderstanding

10. intuition

Exercise 1.5

The following words are tricky to spell because they are not pronounced the way you might expect if you've had no previous experience with them. Look them up in your dictionary and, in the space beside each word, write out its pronunciation (the information given in parentheses immediately after the entry). Using your dictionary's pronunciation key to help you, practise sounding out each word, one syllable at a time. No answers are given for this exercise.

1. epitome

2. lien

3. circuitous

4. misanthropic

5. connoisseur

6. reconcile

7. indict

8. leukemia

9. infamy

10. leverage

2. Get help!

In addition to your dictionary, there are three other resources you can use to help you turn a misspelled mess into a perfectly spelled document.

- The spell checker in your word processing program. While far from fool-proof, online spell checkers are a reliable way to catch most typos and many misspelled words. Get into the habit of spell checking every document before you print it.
- A hand-held electronic spell checker. Conveniently pocket sized and not expensive, these devices contain a large bank of words and can provide the correct spelling if the guess you type in is not too far off. Some spell-check programs even pronounce the word for you. Ask your instructor if you can use this device (with the sound turned off, please) when you are writing in class and during exams.
- A good speller. Some people seem to have been born with the ability to spell. They're usually proud of their talent and pleased to demonstrate it, so don't be afraid to ask. The time to seek their help is at step 3 of the revision process (see pages 269–71).

3. Learn three basic spelling rules.

If you never write except with a word processor, and if you always use its spell-check function, you can skip this step and go on to Chapter 2. If, however, like most of us, your job requires you to fill out forms and occasionally to write memos, notes, and messages in longhand, you'd be wise to review these three simple rules.

English spelling is frustratingly irregular, and no rule holds true in all cases. But the three rules that follow do hold for most words. Mastering them will help you to avoid many common and potentially embarrassing errors.

Before learning the three rules, you need to know the difference between **vowels** and **consonants**. The vowels are **a**, **e**, **i**, **o**, and **u** (and sometimes **y**). All the other letters are consonants.

Rule 1
Dropping the Final *e*

The first rule tells you when to drop the final, silent *e* when adding an ending to a word.

Drop the final, silent *e* when adding an ending that begins with a vowel.

Keep the final, silent *e* when adding an ending that begins with a consonant.

Keeping the rule in mind, look at these examples:

Endings Beginning with a Vowel	**Endings Beginning with a Consonant**
-able: measure + able = measurable	*-ment:* measure + ment = measurement
-ed: live + ed = lived	*-ness:* like + ness = likeness
-er: safe + er = safer	*-ly:* safe + ly = safely
-ible: sense + ible = sensible	*-less:* sense + less = senseless
-ing: care + ing = caring	*-ful:* care + ful = careful

Exercise 1.6

In this exercise, combine each word with the ending to form a new word. When you have finished the exercise, check your answers.

1. believe + er =

2. produce + ing =

3. large + ly =

4. accommodate + ing =

5. late + ness =

6. require + ment =

7. tolerate + ed =

8. hope + ful =

9. posture + ing =

10. slice + er =

GO TO WEB

EXERCISES 1.1, 1.2

Exercise 1.7

In the following exercise, add *e* in the blank space wherever it's needed to complete the spelling. If no *e* is needed, leave the space blank.

1. bor_____ing

2. bar_____ly

3. recycl_____able

4. grad_____ing

5. inescap____able

6. complet____ness

7. pollut____ant

8. enslav____ment

9. liv____able

10. writ____ing

GO TO WEB

EXERCISES 1.3, 1.4

Exercise 1.8

Make up sentences in which you use and spell correctly the words you got wrong in Exercises 1.6 and 1.7.

EXCEPTIONS TO RULE 1

Three common words do not follow the rule.

argue + ment = argument
knowledge + able = knowledgeable
true + ly = truly

There is one more exception to rule 1: after soft *c* (as in *notice*) and soft *g* (as in *change*), keep the final, silent *e* when adding an ending beginning with *a* or *o*. Here are two examples:

notice + able = noticeable
knowledge + able = knowledgeable
outrage + ous = outrageous

Rule 2
Doubling the Final Consonant

The second rule tells you when you need to double the final consonant before adding an ending to a word.

When adding an ending that begins with a vowel (e.g., *-able, -ing, -ed,* or *-er*), double the final consonant of the root word if the word
1. ends with a single consonant preceded by a single vowel
   and
2. is stressed on the last syllable.

Notice that a word must have *both* characteristics for the rule to apply. Let's look at a few examples:

begin + er   ends with a single consonant *(n)* preceded by a single vowel *(i)* and is stressed on the last syllable *(begín)*, so the rule applies, and we double the final consonant: **beginner**

control + ed   ends with a single consonant *(l)* preceded by a single vowel *(o)* and is stressed on the last syllable *(contról)*, so the rule applies: **controlled**

prop + ed   ends with a single consonant *(p)* preceded by a single vowel *(o)* and is stressed on the last syllable (there is only one: *prop*), so the rule applies: **propped**

neighbour + ing   ends with a single consonant *(r)* preceded by two vowels *(ou)*, so the rule does not apply, and we do not double the final consonant: **neighbouring**

curl + ed   ends with two consonants *(rl)*, so the rule does not apply: **curled**

open + er   ends with a single consonant *(n)* preceded by a single vowel *(e)*, but is not stressed on the last syllable *(ópen)*, so the rule does not apply: **opener**

In words such as *equip, quit,* and *quiz,* the *u* should be considered part of the *q* and not a vowel. These words then follow the rule: *equipping, quitter,* and *quizzed.*

Note: There are a few common words ending in *l, s,* or *t* that, according to the rule, do not need a double consonant before the ending. Some examples are *cancel, counsel, focus, format, level,* and *travel.* In Canadian spelling, however, the final consonant is usually doubled: for example, *cancelled, counsellor,* and *focussing.*

The following exercises require you to combine each word with the ending to form a new word. Check your answers to each set before going on. If you make no mistakes in the first two sets, skip ahead to Exercise 1.11.

Exercise 1.9

1. plan + er
2. predict + ing
3. dig + ing
4. nail + ed
5. pop + ing

6. scan + er
7. bat + ing
8. draft + ing
9. gas + ed
10. tap + ed

GO TO WEB

EXERCISES 1.5, 1.6

Exercise 1.10

1. recur + ing
2. reveal + ing
3. debt +or
4. rain +ing
5. outrun +ing

6. befit + ing
7. grip + ed
8. reset + ing
9. nap +ed
10. regret + ed

GO TO WEB

EXERCISES 1.7, 1.8

Exercise 1.11

1. occur + ence =
2. exist + ence =

3. cohere + ence =
4. concur + ing =

5. interfere + ing =   8. depend + ence =

6. subsist + ence =   9. recur + ence =

7. differ + ence =   10. insist + ence =

When it comes to adding *-ence,* three words are especially troublesome. *Prefer, refer,* and *confer* all appear to require a doubled final consonant. But they don't because, when you add *-ence,* the stress shifts to the first syllable of the word:

prefér	preférring	*but*	préference
refér	reférring	*but*	réference
confér	conférring	*but*	cónference

Exercise 1.12

Make up sentences in which you use the words you got wrong in Exercises 1.9 through 1.11.

Rule 3
Words Containing *ie* or *ei*

There are almost a thousand common English words containing *ie* or *ei,* so remembering the rule that governs them is worthwhile. It helps to keep in mind that *ie* occurs approximately twice as often as *ei.*

The old rhyme tells you most of what you need to know to spell these words.

Write *i* before *e,* except after *c,*
or when sounded like *a,* as in *neighbour* and *weigh.*

If you remember this rhyme, you'll have no difficulty in spelling words such as *belief, piece, ceiling, receive,* and *freight.*

Unfortunately, the rhyme covers only two of the cases in which we write *e* before *i:* after *c,* and when the syllable is pronounced with a long *ā* sound. So we need an addition to the rule.

If short *ĕ* or long *ī* is the sound that is right,
write *e* before *i*, as in *their* or in *height*.

This rule covers words such as *heir, heifer, Fahrenheit, eiderdown,* and *leisure* (pronounce it to rhyme with *"pleasure"*). *Either* and *neither* can be pronounced "eye-ther" and "nye-ther," so they too require *ei*.

There are, of course, exceptions. This silly sentence contains the most common ones:

A *weird species* of *sheik seized caffeine, codeine,* and *protein.*

These exercises will help you to master *ie* versus *ei*. Fill in the blanks with *ie* or *ei*. After you finish each set, check your answers.

Exercise 1.13

1. sh____ld
2. ch____f
3. v____l
4. y____ld
5. retr____ve

6. r____ndeer
7. s____ve
8. r____gn
9. rec____pt
10. n____ce

GO TO WEB

EXERCISE 1.9

Exercise 1.14

1. My fr____nd unknowingly gave the clerk a counterf____t bill.

2. N____ther of us knows how to convert Canadian dollars to for____gn currency.

3. Larry wore a b____ge l____sure suit to his graduation party.

4. Harold perc____ved a w____rd light emanating from the closet.

5. It is conc____vable that ____ther one could do the job.

GO TO WEB

EXERCISE 1.10

There are three or four more spelling rules we could explain here, but we won't, for two reasons. First, there are many exceptions to the remaining rules for English spelling. And second, you don't need to memorize more rules if you use your dictionary and a spell checker.

2

Sound-Alikes,
Look-Alikes,
and Spoilers

Using a dictionary and a spell checker, asking a good speller for help, and applying the three spelling rules will make an immediate improvement in your writing. Following two additional suggestions will further increase your spelling accuracy, but the skills involved will take longer to master. First, learn to tell words apart that are often confused because they sound or look alike. Second, learn to spell correctly the words that most people find troublesome—words we have called spelling spoilers. A word processor will not help you with the first task, but it will with the second—so long as you always remember to spell-check your document before printing it.

Sound-Alikes and Look-Alikes

Some of your spelling troubles probably occur when you use words that either sound or look like the words you need in your sentence. A spell checker cannot help you with these words because they have two (or more) spellings, and the spelling you need to use depends on the meaning you intend. For example, as single words, *hear, our, write, meat,* and *inn* are correctly spelled. But if you combine them into a "sentence"—*Meat me write hear inn an our*—you end up with a tangle of misspellings no computer can unravel.

Careful pronunciation sometimes helps to correct this problem. For example, if you pronounce the words *you're* and *your* differently, you'll be less likely to confuse them in your writing. It's also useful to make up memory aids to help yourself remember the difference between words that sound alike but have different meanings.

accept
except

Accept means "ta**k**e." It is always a verb. *Ex**c**ept* means "**ex**cluding."

> Many people find it hard to **ac**cept praise.
> Myrna has visited every province **ex**cept Saskatchewan.

advice
advise

The difference in pronunciation makes the difference in meaning clear. *Advise* (rhymes with *wise*) is a verb. *Advice* (rhymes with *nice*) is a noun.

> Do not let anyone *advise* you before you hear your lawyer's *advice.*

affect
effect

Affect as a verb means "influence." As a noun, it means "a strong feeling." *Effect* is a noun meaning "result." If you can substitute *result,* then *effect* is the word you need. (Occasionally, *effect* is used as a verb meaning "to bring about.")

> The audience was strongly *affected* by the play's sound *effects.*
> The new premier promises to *effect* many changes.

a lot
allot

A lot (often misspelled *alot*) should be avoided in writing. Use *many* or *much* instead. *Allot* means "distribute" or "assign."

>   *many*   *much*
> He still has a~~ lot of~~ problems, but he's coping a~~ lot~~ better.
> The teacher will *allot* the marks according to the difficulty of the questions.

are
our

Are is a verb. *Our* shows ownership.

> Nelly Furtado and Alanis Morissette *are* two popular Canadian singers.
> Canada is *our* home and native land.

choose
chose

Pronunciation gives the clue here. *Choose* rhymes with *booze* and means "select." *Chose* rhymes with *rose* and means "selected."

> Please *choose* a topic.
> I *chose* filmmaking.

coarse
course

Coarse means "rough, unrefined." (Remember: the word **arse** is co**arse**.) For all other meanings, use *course*.

That sandpaper is too *coarse* to use on a lacquer finish.
This *course* is not as easy as it looks.
Of *course*, results will vary.

complement
compliment

A *complement* completes something. A *compliment* is a gift of praise.

A glass of wine would be the perfect *complement* to the meal.
Some people are embarrassed by *compliments*.

conscience
conscious

Your *conscience* is your sense of right and wrong. *Conscious* means "aware" or "awake"—able to feel and think.

After Ann cheated on the test, her *conscience* bothered her.
Ann was *conscious* of having done wrong.
Her teacher was *unconscious* of Ann's cheating.

consul
council
counsel

A *consul* is a government official stationed in another country. A *council* is an assembly or official group. Members of a *council* are *councillors*. *Counsel* can be used to mean both "advice" and "to advise."

The Canadian *consul* in Venice was very helpful.
Hugh was president of the Student *Council*.
Maria gave me good *counsel*.
She *counselled* me to hire a lawyer.

desert
dessert

A *désert* is a dry, barren place. As a verb, *desért* means "leave behind." *Dessért* is the part of a meal you'd probably like an extra helping of, so give it an extra *s*.

The tundra is Canada's only *desert* region.
As soon as our backs were turned, our lookout *deserted* his post.
This restaurant is famous for its maple *desserts*.

dining
dinning

You'll spell *dining* correctly if you remember the phrase "wining and dining." You'll probably never use *dinning*. It means "making a loud noise."

The dog is not supposed to be in the *dining* room.
After *dining* at the restaurant, the suspect boarded a bus.
The sounds from the karaoke bar were *dinning* in my ears.

does
dose

Pronunciation provides the clue. *Does* rhymes with *buzz* and is a verb. *Dose* rhymes with *gross* and refers to a quantity of medicine.

It *doesn't* matter to me who *does* the work.
The doctor prescribed another *dose* of morphine to ease the pain.

forth
fourth

Forth means "**for**ward." *Fourth* contains the number **four**, which gives it its meaning.

The volunteers went boldly *forth*.
The Raptors lost their *fourth* game in a row.

hear
here

Hear is what you do with your **ear**s. *Here* is used for all other meanings.

Do you *hear* me?
Ranjan isn't *here*.
She was *here* just a moment ago.

it's
its

It's is a shortened form of *it is.* The apostrophe takes the place of the *i* in *is.* If you can substitute *it is,* then *it's* is the form you need. If you can't substitute *it is,* then *its* is the correct word.

> *It's* hard to predict who will win the election. (*It is* hard to predict.)
> The book has lost *its* cover. ("The book has lost *it is* cover" makes no sense, so you need *its.*)

It's is also commonly used as the shortened form of *it has.* In this case, the apostrophe takes the place of the *h* and the *a.*

> *It's* been a bad month for software sales.

later
latter

***Late*r** refers to time and has the word **late** in it. *Latter* means "the second of two" and has two *t*'s. It is the opposite of *former.*

> Fran planned to meet her brother *later.*
> You take the former, and I'll take the *latter.*

led
lead

The word *lead* is pronounced "led" only when it refers to the heavy, soft, grey metal used in items such as lead bullets or leaded windows. Otherwise, *lead* is pronounced to rhyme with *speed* and is used as the present tense of the verb *to lead.* (*Led* is the past tense of the same verb.)

> When I asked her to *lead* me to the person in charge, she *led* me to the secretary.
> Your suitcase is so heavy it must be filled with either books or *lead.*

loose
lose

Pronunciation is the key to these words. *Loose* rhymes with *goose* and means "not tight." *Lose* rhymes with *ooze* and means "misplace" or "be defeated."

> A *loose* electrical connection is dangerous.
> Some are born to win, some to *lose.*

miner
minor

A ***mine*r** works in a **mine.** *Minor* means "lesser" or "not important." For example, a *minor* is a person of less than legal age.

Until child labour laws were introduced, many *minors* worked as *miners*.
Living in the country involves some *minor* inconveniences.

moral
morale

Again, pronunciation provides the clue you need. *Móral* refers to the understanding of what is right and wrong. *Morále* refers to the spirit or mental condition of a person or group.

Parents are responsible for teaching their children *moral* behaviour.
Team *morale* is so low that the coach is on Prozac.

peace
piece

Peace is what we want on **Ea**rth. *Piece* means a part or portion of something, as in "a **pie**ce of **pie**."

Everyone hopes for *peace* in the Middle East.
A *piece* of the puzzle is missing.

personal
personnel

Personal means "priv**a**te." *Personnel* refers to the group of people working for a particular employer or to the office responsible for maintaining employees' records.

Some people require more *personal* space than others.
All new *personnel* are required to attend an orientation session.
Yasmin works in the *Personnel* Office.

principal
principle

Principal means "m**a**in." A princip**le** is a ru**le.**

A *principal* is the main administrator of a school.
The federal government is Summerside's *principal* employer.
The *principal* and the interest totalled more than I could pay. (In this case, the principal is the main amount of money.)
One of our instructor's *principles* is to refuse to accept late assignments.

quiet
quite

If you pronounce these words carefully, you won't confuse them. *Quiet* has two syllables; *quite* has only one.

The church was *quiet*.
I am not *quite* sure how to get there.

stationary
stationery

Stationary means "fixed in pl**a**ce." *Station**e**ry* is writing pap**er.**

> The shop installed a *stationary* saw.
> The couple could not agree on their wedding *stationery*.

than
then

*Th**a**n* is used in comp**a**risons. Pronounce it to rhyme with *can*. *Th**e**n* refers to time and rhymes with *wh**e**n*.

> Karim is a better speller *than* I.
> I wish I had known *then* what I know now.
> Tanya withdrew from the competition; *then* she realized the consequences.

their
there
they're

Their indicates ownership. *T**here*** points out something or indicates place. It includes the word **here**, which also indicates place. *They're* is a shortened form of *they are*. (The apostrophe replaces the *a* in *are*.)

> It was *their* fault.
> *There* are many hot dog vendors on campus.
> Don't go over *there*.
> *They're* late, as usual.

too
two
to

The *too* with an extra *o* in it means "more than enough" or "also." *Two* is the number after one. For all other meanings, use *to*.

> She thinks she's been working *too* hard. He thinks so *too*.
> The *two* sisters looked like twins.
> The *two* women knew *too* much about each other *to* be friends.

were
where
we're

If you pronounce these three carefully, you won't confuse them. *Were* rhymes with *fur* and is a verb. *W**here*** is pronounced "hwear," includes the word **here**, and indicates place. *We're* is a shortened form of *we are* and is pronounced "weer."

> You *were* joking, *weren't* you?
> *Where* one kitten goes, the other will follow.
> *We're* excited about our vacation plans.

who's
whose

Who's is a shortened form of *who is* or *who has*. If you can substitute *who is* or *who has* for the *who's* in your sentence, then you have the right spelling. Otherwise, use *whose*.

> *Who's* coming to dinner? (*Who is* coming to dinner?)
> *Who's* been sleeping in my bed? (*Who has* been sleeping in my bed?)
> *Whose* paper is this? ("*Who is* paper" makes no sense, so you need *whose*.)

woman
women

Confusing these two is guaranteed to irritate your women readers. *Wo**man*** is the singular form; compare **man**. *Wo**men*** is the plural form; compare **men**.

> One *woman* responded to our ad.
> In 1918, Canadian *women* won the right to vote in federal elections.

you're
your

You're is a shortened form of *you are*. If you can substitute *you are* for the *you're* in your sentence, then you're using the correct form. If you can't substitute *you are*, use *your*.

> *You're* welcome. (*You are* welcome.)
> *Your* nephew is my cousin. ("*You are* nephew" makes no sense, so *your* is the word you want.)

In the exercises that follow, choose the correct word in each pair. If you don't know an answer, go back and reread the explanation. Check your answers after each set. Answers begin on page 321.

Exercise 2.1

1. I'd be happy to (except, accept) your invitation, (except, accept) I haven't received it yet.
2. The blue cushions (complement, compliment) the pastel wallpaper and create a (quiet, quite) atmosphere.
3. A (stationary, stationery) engine is one that is fixed in (its, it's) place.
4. Jana plans to (choose, chose) her (coarses, courses) on Tuesday.
5. After his (fourth, forth) break-in, my cousin could no longer live with his guilty (conscious, conscience).
6. (Who's, whose) the (woman, women) wearing the red dress?
7. The (two, too, to) girls left (their, they're, there) purses in the cloakroom.

8. Geoff can't (hear, here) your (advice, advise) when he has his headphones on.
9. The doctor told me the low (does, dose) would cause few side (affects, effects).
10. I saw (are, our) new neighbours quarreling in their (dining, dinning) room.

Exercise 2.2

1. The (moral, morale) among the striking (miners, minors) was very low.
2. The teacher (led, lead) the children to the two (woman, women) who were waiting for them.
3. Please hand me a (peace, piece) of lemon meringue pie, my favourite (desert, dessert).
4. Most (personal, personnel) were pleased to see the new (stationary, stationery) bike in the exercise room.
5. It would be a shame to (loose, lose) a friend over such a (miner, minor) disagreement.
6. The town (counsel, council) met in the room (where, were, we're) Queen Victoria had tea.
7. Rita was (conscience, conscious) that Ron's (complement, compliment) had made her blush.
8. The (moral, morale) of the story is that (its, it's) more blessed to give (then, than) to receive.
9. (Their, they're, there) going to join us at the station (later, latter).
10. (You're, your) brother would rather sing (then, than) dance.

GO TO WEB

EXERCISES 2.1, 2.2

Exercise 2.3

1. (Does, dose) anyone know where the corporate (stationary, stationery) is kept?
2. (Led, lead) pipes can cause (quiet, quite) a few health risks.
3. Abram is afraid he will (loose, lose) the ring he so carefully (choose, chose).
4. Over the years, Canada has sent (fourth, forth) many (peace, piece) keepers to foreign lands.
5. Despite her (personal, personnel) reservations, the (principal, principle) endorsed the new curriculum.

6. (Who's, whose) (advise, advice) will you follow?
7. First turn the key, (then, than) step on the accelerator.
8. Caleb's parents (were, where, we're) surprised to learn that (were, where, we're) getting married next week.
9. I enjoy both Mexican and Chinese cuisine, but I prefer the (later, latter).
10. The heat of the (desert, dessert) seemed to (affect, effect) my brain.

GO TO WEB

EXERCISES 2.3, 2.4

Exercise 2.4

This exercise is quite challenging. Not all of the 25 paired words in parentheses are given in the list of sound-alikes and look-alikes on pages 16–22. See how you do!

Last summer, despite my mother's (advise, advice), I decided to (adopt, adapt) a puppy. There are so many cute dogs that I found it difficult (to, too, two) decide which breed to (chose, choose). Once I visited the pound, though, I made up my mind (quiet, quite) quickly. Lucky, a wiry little dog with (course, coarse), curly fur, stole my heart.

Unfortunately, Lucky also stole gloves, socks, and almost everything (of, off) my desk (accept, except) the pencil sharpener. Obviously, in his (passed, past) life, he had been terribly neglected and, as a result, he did almost anything to attract attention. For a while, I tolerated his theft of (miner, minor) articles, but when he ate a box of expensive (stationary, stationery), I began to (loose, lose) my (patience, patients).

I took Lucky to puppy school, but the training didn't have much (affect, effect). The trainer explained that, because dogs are pack animals, Lucky would try to play the (dominate, dominant) role unless I clearly demonstrated that I was pack leader. So, as a point of (principal, principle), I made Lucky wait for his (diner, dinner) until I had finished my (desert, dessert). When we (passed, past) someone we knew on the street, I made him (heel, heal) while I chatted. Once a (weak, week), we devoted an (our, hour) to reinforcing his training.

Now Lucky has learned his (lessen, lesson) and behaves much better (then, than) he once did. Indeed, he has become such a wonderful companion that I really can't decide (who's, whose) luckier—Lucky or me.

Exercise 2.5

In the exercise that follows, cross out any incorrect spellings and replace them with the correct words.

1. Moments after it's takeoff, the plane banked to sharply to the left.
2. I certainly won't chose the one who's application was late.
3. Please check with the Personal Department before you hire legal council.
4. If he dose that again, it will effect his chances for promotion.
5. The Canada Counsel for the Arts will announce its awards latter this month.
6. When I receive a complement, I feel self-conscience.
7. Who's turn is it to find the compliment of the angle?
8. If you could remember these three simple rules, than you're spelling troubles would be over.
9. Their are many children who believe the tooth fairy will come if they loose a tooth.
10. My mother is quiet a women.

Exercise 2.6

Correct the 20 spelling errors in the exercise below.

My cousin Rita cannot except that computers can be helpful. She is so suspicious of the affects of new technology that she insists on keeping her money under her mattress, as a matter of principal. She is convinced that an automated teller machine will loose her money, so she choses not to use ATMs.

Naturally, Rita dose not trust the Internet. She is conscience of the many scams that circulate on the World Wide Web, so she refuses to here anything good about the Net. Its hard to believe how deeply she distrusts technology. She refuses to take my advise that she try an introductory coarse in computer literacy. Unfortunately, her personnel prejudice also prevents her from recieving e-mail messages from woman all over the world who want to keep in touch with her.

Her attitude may seem a miner problem, but it causes conflict in are family. My brother is a computer programmer, and he hates listening to Rita hold fourth about the evils of his profession. At our last family gathering, the two of them turned my grandmother's dinning room into a battleground. Although I haven't quiet made up my mind about computers, I know one thing: I like to enjoy my Sunday dinner in piece!

Exercise 2.7

Below is a list of word pairs that are often confused. Use each word in a sentence that clearly differentiates the word from its sound-alike or look-alike. Use your dictionary to help you. When you are finished, exchange papers with another student and check each other's work.

1. emigrate, immigrate
2. weather, whether

3. breath, breathe
4. hole, whole

5. allusion, illusion
6. cite, site
7. human, humane

8. precede, proceed
9. altogether, all together
10. insure, ensure

Your own writing is the best test of your spelling accuracy. Write ten or more sentences using the sound-alikes and look-alikes that cause you the most difficulty.

Spelling Spoilers

Here is a list of words that are frequently misspelled. Have someone dictate the list to you. Circle the ones you misspell and memorize them, a few at a time. Try to learn ten each week. Review your list often, until you have mastered every word. Making up memory aids for especially troublesome words will help you to conquer them. Here are some examples to get you started:

accommodate	It means "make room for," and the word itself makes room for two *c*'s and two *m*'s.
business	*Busi*ness is no **sin**.
environment	The word *envir**on**ment*, like the earth, has **iron** in it.
friend	He is a *fri**end*** to the **end**.
grammar	Poor *gram**mar*** will **mar** your writing.

absence	category	eighth
accommodate	clothes	embarrassed
achievement	committee	environment
acknowledge	conscious	exercise
acquire	convenience	existence
across	criticism	explanation
address	definitely	extremely
adolescence	dependent	familiar
among	desperate	February
answer	development	finally
apparent	disappear	forty
argument	disappoint	friend
beginning	discipline	gauge
business	dissatisfied	government
careful	doesn't	grammar

guarantee
guidance
height
hoping
hypocrisy

immediately
independent
indispensable
laboratory
library

license (or licence)
likely
loneliness
lonely
maintenance

marriage
mentally
necessary
ninety
ninth

occasion
occasionally

omission
opinion
opportunity

paid
parallel
perform
planned
possess

prejudice
privilege
procedure
proceed
professor

psychology
recommend
relevant
repetition
restaurant

rhythm
ridiculous
safety
schedule

secretary

separate
shining
similar
somewhat
speech

studying
succeed
surprise
technique
thorough

tragedy
truly
unnecessary
until
unusual

usually
vacuum
Wednesday
writing
written

Exercise 2.9

Make up sentences containing the words you misspelled when the list of spelling spoilers was dictated. Underline the spelling spoiler in each sentence. (If you do this exercise once a week, you will master the list very quickly.)

One final suggestion. Despite all your efforts, you may find that there are a few words you just cannot spell correctly. The solution? Write out a list of these pesky words and post it close to your computer. (It's also a good idea to tape a copy of the list onto the inside cover of your dictionary.)

Another, less satisfactory, solution is to try to avoid these words. You could check your dictionary or a thesaurus to find synonyms (different words with the same meanings) for the words you can't spell and use the synonyms instead. The main problem with this solution is that it is even more time-consuming than learning the correct spellings in the first place!

There are, however, occasions when using a synonym will help you convey more accurately the meaning you intend. Two thesauruses are available in inexpensive paperback editions: *Roget's Thesaurus* (the one in dictionary form, not the one organized by subject) and the *Collins Paperback Thesaurus* in A–Z form, which, as its title suggests, is organized alphabetically. Your word processor probably has a built-in thesaurus you can consult, but be careful; you can't choose just any word from the list that pops up when you ask for a synonym for a word you've used too frequently or one you don't feel confident is the word you need.

The information provided by a thesaurus must be used with caution. Inexperienced writers sometimes assume that long, obscure words are sure to impress their readers. In fact, the opposite is usually true. Most readers are irritated, if not confused, by unnecessarily "fancy" language. Why write "The children were enthralled by the antics of the prestidigitator" when what you mean is "The children loved the magician's act"? For more on this subject, see Unit 6.

3

Capital Letters

Capital letters should be used in a few specific places and nowhere else. Some writers suffer from "capitalitis": they put capital letters on words randomly, regardless of whether the words are nouns, verbs, or adjectives. Like "exclamatosis," "capitalitis" is a disease communicated by comic books and cartoon strips, which capitalize every word.

Not many people have this problem. If you are in the majority who generally use capitals correctly, skip this chapter and go on to something else. If you are puzzled about capital letters, though, or have readers who are puzzled by your use of them, read on.

Capitalize the first letter of a word that fits into one of these categories.

1. The first word in a sentence, in a direct quotation, or in a sentence from a quoted source:

   Please do not play games on this computer.
   The robot commanded, "Hand over the remote control."
   Writer and broadcaster Lister Sinclair claims that Canadians have one thing in common: "We all hate Toronto."

2. The names of specific persons:

   Sheila Copps   Kofi Annan

   The names of specific places:

   Baffin Island   Spring Garden Road
   Pluto   Singapore
   Canada's Wonderland   Climax, Saskatchewan

The names of specific things:

Pacific Ocean	Goods and Services Tax
Royal York Hotel	Mount Royal College
Our Lady Peace	Assiniboine River

3. The days of the week, the months of the year, and specific holidays (but not the seasons or geographic directions):

Wednesday	June
Christmas	Mother's Day
summer	north

4. The titles of books, films, television shows, newspapers, and magazines; of specific people (but not the names of their positions); and of school courses (but not subject names, unless they are languages):

The Bare Essentials, Star Wars, Friends, The Montreal Gazette
Governor General Adrienne Clarkson (*but* the governor general)
Premier Stephen Kakfwi (*but* the premier)
Mr. Rex Murphy, Ms. Sarah McLachlan
Biology 101 (*but* the biology course)
Introduction to Economics; introductory economics; the English
    language; conversational Mandarin

5. The names of specific companies, products, businesses, organizations, and departments:

Calona Winery	Kleenex, Shreddies, Jello
New Democratic Party	Human Resources Department
Maritime Life	United Church

Correct the capitalization in the sentences below. Check your answers to each set before continuing. Answers begin on page 322.

Exercise 3.1

1. rowena spent two hours waiting in line to register for introduction to Fashion Design.

2. when I worked at swiss chalet, I won the employee of the month award two months in a row.

3. april and may, the beginning of Spring, are my favourite months.

4. The minister of health plays a prominent role in the Prime minister's cabinet.

5. secret tunnels beneath moose jaw, saskatchewan, once hid a number of chicago gangsters, including al capone.

6. my wife never misses *hockey night in canada*.

7. charlottetown's *anne of green gables* is one of the longest running plays in canadian Theatre History.

8. when my sister travelled to rome, she read the *vancouver sun* every day on the internet.

9. george has been the chief financial officer of merman enterprises for more than 12 years.

10. reverend mullen was very excited to speak to the bishop in person last fall.

Exercise 3.2

1. the newcomers' club welcomes immigrants from the South to the community.

2. the meeting will be held next wednesday at the Mayor's house on clifton avenue.

3. dr. thomas assured him that grace hospital was one of the best hospitals in New brunswick for Orthopedic Surgery.

4. although I have never been very good at Math, I'm doing very well in mr. johnson's computing class.

5. karl phoned payroll services to inquire about the unexpected deduction for Dental Insurance on his last pay cheque.

6. timothy findley, author of *the piano man's daughter*, will be greatly missed by the Literary Community.

7. when he studied at wycliffe college, bishop franklin developed a passion for vietnamese food.

8. rebecca has to use soy milk on her cheerios now that she has been diagnosed with lactose intolerance.

9. the hubble telescope floats above earth and takes pictures of the moon.

10. my Cousin and I plan to attend caribana in toronto next month.

GO TO WEB

EXERCISES 3.1, 3.2

Exercise 3.3

Review the five rules of capitalization before you try this mastery test.

1. Gerald enrolled in Red river community college in the Fall of 2000.

2. Margaret Laurence's novel, *stone angel*, is a classic of Canadian Literature.

3. The Lab Assistant asked, "who broke the beaker containing dr. Philips' formula?"

4. Our french teacher and his bride spent their honeymoon touring the lake district of england.

5. Brookview public school is holding a Bake Sale next week to raise money for the cancer society of manitoba.

6. The Governor of Oregon agreed with the Senator from B.C., who argued that Democracy is better served by Canada's Parliamentary System than by the U.S. Presidential System.

7. The Bay, which began as the hudson's bay company, has roots stretching back to the days of the french fur trade.

8. Some people believe that captain kidd's Pirate treasure is buried on oak island, off the Coast of nova scotia.

9. Ernie coombs, better known as mr. dressup, entertained generations of canadian children on cbc television.

10. After earning his College diploma, Ralph studied Horticulture in his spare time and eventually started his own nursery, Ralph's rare blooms.

4

The Apostrophe

We have chosen to deal with apostrophes as a spelling problem because, unlike other punctuation marks, apostrophes are not used to indicate the relationship between the parts of a sentence. An apostrophe indicates either a relationship between two elements of a single word, in a contraction, or a relationship between one word and the word immediately following it, in a possessive construction.

Apostrophes are often misused, causing readers to be confused or amused. Sometimes you need an apostrophe so that your reader can understand what you mean. For example, there's a world of difference between these two sentences:

The instructor began the class by calling the students' names.
The instructor began the class by calling the students names.

In most cases, however, a misused apostrophe just irritates an alert reader:

Seasons greetings from the Norton's.
Were playing two game's on Sunday.
Freshly picked apple's for sale.

It isn't difficult to avoid such embarrassing mistakes. Correctly used, the apostrophe indicates either **contraction** or **possession.** Learn the simple rules that govern these two uses and you'll have no further trouble with apostrophes.

The instructor began the class
by calling the students names.

1. Contraction

You'll need to use contractions less often than possessives. Contractions lend a conversational tone to written English, and in most of the writing you do in college or on the job, you should avoid them. However, when you are writing informally, or when you are quoting someone's spoken words, you'll need to know how contractions are formed.

The rule about where to put an apostrophe in a contraction is one of the rare rules to which there are no exceptions. It *always* holds.

When two words are shortened into one, and a letter (or letters) is left out, the apostrophe goes in the place of the missing letter(s).

she is →	she's	they have →	they've
we are →	we're	there is →	there's
he had →	he'd	he will →	he'll
you would →	you'd	do not →	don't
it is, it has →	it's	will not →	won't (Note the spelling
who is, who has →	who's		variation here.)

Exercise 4.1

Place apostrophes correctly in these words, which are intended to be contractions. Notice that when an apostrophe is missing, the word often means something completely different. Answers begin on page 323.

1. cant
2. shed
3. well
4. lets
5. shell

6. wouldnt
7. wed
8. theyre
9. wont
10. hell

GO TO WEB

EXERCISES 4.1, 4.2

Exercise 4.2

Correct these sentences by placing apostrophes where they are needed.

1. Id like to see John, but hes not home today.

2. Yvette said shed wash the dishes since its her turn to do kitchen duty.

3. Dont you think we should find out if hell be coming?

4. Lets help Johann and Chris think of some fresh ideas for the project theyre starting.

5. The dialect in parts of Newfoundland hasnt changed much since the seventeenth century.

6. Theres no one whod hike the Bruce Trail with Scott.

7. Im glad to learn that youve been given the job.

8. How are we supposed to read the map if weve lost the flashlight?

9. We finally realized our mistake: wed entered the wrong password.

10. Terry wont go to the concert if her sister cant go too.

2. Possession

The apostrophe is also used to show ownership or possession. Here's the rule that applies in most cases.

1. Add *'s* to the word that indicates the OWNER.
2. If the resulting word ends in a double or triple *s*, erase the last one, leaving the apostrophe in place.

person + s = person's   man + s = man's
people + s = people's   men + s = men's
sisters + s = sisters's̸   mother-in-law + s = mother-in-law's
Socrates + s =Socrates's̸   goodness + s = goodness's̸

When you're forming possessives, you must first figure out whether the owner is singular or plural. For example:

the employee's schedule (the schedule belonging to one *employee*)
the employees' schedule (the schedule belonging to two or more *employees*)

If you remember that possession indicates *what belongs to whom,* you can figure out where to put the apostrophe by "translating" your sentence, like this:

Incorrect: Tamara wore her new pilots wings proudly.

1. Translation: the wings belong to one pilot.
2. Add *'s*:

Correct: Tamara wore her new pilot's wings proudly.

Incorrect: The doctor treated the patients burns.

1. Translation: the burns belonged to the patient? or the patients? Here's where you have to decide whether one or more than one is involved.
2. Add *'s* or *s'*:

Correct: The doctor treated the patient's burns.
                  (Only one patient is involved.)

Also correct: The doctor treated the patients' burns.
                  (More than one patient is involved.)

Possession does not have to be literal. The owner does not have to be a person or thing. Ideas or concepts can be "owners" too:

a life's work = the work of a life
a day's drive = a drive of a day
out of harm's way = out of the way of harm

There is an alternative to part 2 of the possession rule that is highlighted on page 38. Many writers prefer to keep the final *s* when it represents a sound that is pronounced, as it does in the possessive form of one-syllable words (e.g., boss, class) and of some names (e.g., Harris, Brutus). The following examples illustrate this alternative usage:

the boss's office   Ms. Harris's promotion
the class's decision   Brutus's betrayal

Note that a few words, called **possessive pronouns**, are already possessive in form and so do not take an apostrophe:

your/yours   our/ours
her/hers   their/theirs
his, its   whose

Your decision is *yours* to make, not *his* or *hers*.
Whose turn is it next: *ours* or *theirs*?

Four of these possessive pronouns are often confused with the contractions that sound like them. When you need to decide which spelling to use, separate the contraction into its two root words and try them out in the sentence. If the sentence makes sense, then the contraction is the spelling you need. If not, use the possessive.

Possessive	Contraction
its	it's = it is *or* it has
their	they're = they are
whose	who's = who is *or* who has
your	you're = you are

You'll understand the difference between these sound-alikes if you study the following examples carefully:

They're going for pizza with their friends. (*They are* going for pizza with ~~they are~~ *their* friends.)

You're losing your hair. (*You are* losing ~~you are~~ your hair.)

It's rewarding to see Canada take its place on the Olympic podium. (*It is* rewarding to see Canada take ~~it is~~ its place on the Olympic podium.

Who's been sleeping in whose bed? (*Who has* been sleeping in ~~who is~~ whose bed?)

Exercise 4.3

Make the following words possessive.

1. children
2. woman
3. the Smiths
4. computers
5. Great Lakes
6. photo
7. babies
8. strikers
9. nobody
10. Chris

Exercise 4.4

In the following exercise, make the words in parentheses possessive.

1. (Clara) new dog is just starting to lose (it) puppy teeth.

2. (Biff) favourite pastime is spending his (girlfriend) money.

3. Our (college) aim is to meet (students) social needs as well as (they) academic goals.

4. The (Sorensons) daughter is a (children) entertainer in Vancouver.

5. (Bikers) equipment is on special at (Leather Larry).

6. (Klaus) feet are so small that he has to buy (women) loafers.

7. (Calgary) reputation as an affordable city is fading now that the (city) housing costs are rising.

8. My (father) intuition told me I should screen the (Web site) images before letting my ten-year-old see them.

9. Virtue may be (it) own reward, but I won't refuse (you) offer of cash.

10. To (no one) surprise, (Queen Elizabeth) visit to Toronto attracted less attention than the (Pope).

GO TO WEB

EXERCISES 4.3, 4.4

Exercise 4.5

Correct these sentences by placing apostrophes where they are needed in contractions and possessives.

1. The Pittsburgh Penguins wouldnt have won the Stanley Cup without Mario Lemieuxs goals.

2. Our budgets so tight this year that well be spending our vacation in the back yard.

3. "Cant you come back tomorrow?" begged Gwens aunt.

4. The CDs surface was badly scratched, so its files could not be loaded into the computer.

5. Donald Sutherland, whos from St. John, New Brunswick, is one of Canadas most famous actors.

6. A patients fears can be eased by a kind nurses attention.

7. The speakers topic was way beyond our students understanding.

8. Youll notice that Key Porter Books list of authors includes Pamela Wallin and Jean Chrétien.

9. Isnt it strange that nobodys heard from Sean since he left for Ireland?

10. *Due South*s hero, Paul Gross, put the Mounties red uniform in television's limelight.

3. Plurals

Here is the last apostrophe rule.

> 3. Do not use an apostrophe to make a word plural.

The plural of most English words is formed by adding *s* to the root word: for example, *memos, letters, files*. The *s* tells the reader that the word is plural. If you add an apostrophe before the *s*, you are signalling to the reader that the word is either a contraction or a possessive. Be careful not to mislead your reader!

Incorrect: Do not use apostrophe's to make word's plural.
Correct: Do not use apostrophes to make words plural.

Exercise 4.6

Correct the misused and missing apostrophes in these sentences.

1. The Fortress of Louisbourg is one of the countrys largest historical reconstruction's.

2. The Royal Ontario Museums collection's are internationally famous.

3. Childrens wear and womens' shoes have been moved to the second floor.

4. Peter's lifes ambition was to travel across Nunavut with a team of husky's.

5. Despite what the school's have taught for year's, Alexander Graham Bell was not the telephones inventor.

6. Apostrophe's can be difficult to place when you don't know the rule's that govern their use.

7. Laura Secords most famous legacy has been a chain of candy store's.

8. The required text's for this course are *The Bare Essential's* and *Rogets Thesaurus*.

9. "Victorys mine!" claimed the wrestler, waving his arm's and jumping up and down.

10. Hedonist's are those who pursue pleasure for it's own sake.

Find and correct the 15 apostrophe errors in the following paragraph.

Josh and Patricia plan to spend they're holiday's camping in one of Banffs beautiful parks. Theyve already purchased most of their equipment, including sleeping bags, tent, folding chairs, and a portable stove. They had intended to pack lightly, but already its clear that theyll need a roof rack, if not a utility trailer, to carry all they're gear. They're budget has been stretched to the limit, and they havent even begun to shop for supply's. Clothing, food, and insect repellant will eat up whats left of their credit. Canadian's who think that campings a cheap vacation havent spent much time in the aisle's of Canadian Tire.

Before you do the mastery test, let's review what you've learned about using apostrophes.

- When contracting two words into one, put an apostrophe in the place of the missing letters.
- Watch for owner words: they need apostrophes.
- To indicate possession, add *'s* to the owner word.
- Possessive pronouns (e.g., *their, its, ours*) do not take apostrophes.
- Never use an apostrophe to form the plural of a word.

This exercise will test your ability to use apostrophes correctly: in contractions, in possessive constructions, but *not* to form plurals. Correct the 30 errors in the following sentences.

1. As Canadian's, weve long been proud of our countrys unique commitment to multiculturalism.

2. Multicultural policies' have shaped neighbourhood development and our schools curriculum's.

3. Theyve boosted tourism by creating restaurant's and entertainment, including summer festival's, such as Winnipegs Folklorama and Torontos Caribana.

4. Multiculturalism isnt just a good thing for local communities, however; recent study's suggest that its also good for Canadian business.

5. Researchers have concluded that person's from different backgrounds encourage creativity in one another.

6. If company's really want to improve they're capacity for finding innovative solutions to complex business problems, then they should hire employees from various cultural and racial group's.

7. Moreover, if the Canadian government is serious about improving Canadas ability to function in the knowledge economy, then it's immigration policies need to encourage diversity, too.

8. In todays competitive global market's, we need strategic thinkers who can bring a variety of viewpoint's to analyze a situation.

9. By making the immigration process easier for skilled immigrants', Canada could build up it's intellectual capital and improve it's position in the world economy.

10. As knowledge worker's replace industrial worker's, were going to have to stimulate diversity in order to ensure our nations survival.

5

Numbers

Numbers may be expressed as words (*one*, *four*, *nine*) or as figures (*1*, *4*, *9*), depending on the kind of assignment you are writing and what the numbers refer to. In a few circumstances, a combination of words and figures is required. In scientific and technical papers, numbers are normally given in figures; in humanities papers, numbers that can be expressed in one or two words are usually spelled out. For college papers, ask your instructor which style he or she prefers. For general purposes, including most business writing, follow the guidelines given below.

When to Use Words

1. Spell out numbers from *one* to *ten*; use figures for numbers above *ten*.

Canada has *ten* provinces and *three* territories.

If you think *13* is an unlucky number, remember that Canada has *14* legislatures, including the federal government.

There are two exceptions to this general rule.

A. Spell out any number that begins a sentence, or rewrite the sentence so that the number does not come first.

Incorrect: 30 percent of Canadians surveyed support the current government.

Correct: *Thirty* percent of Canadians surveyed support the current government.

Also correct: Of those Canadians surveyed, 30 percent support the current government.

B. When you are presenting a series of numbers, be consistent. Do not mix words and figures.

We are looking for fifteen salespeople, three accountants, and two customer service representatives. (*Not* "15, three, and two")

Only 2 of the 12 teams will proceed to the provincial championships. (*Not* "two of the 12 teams")

2. Spell out ordinals (*first, second, twenty-first*, etc.), approximate periods of time, ages, and common fractions that can be written in one or two words.

Up to its *sixth* or *seventh* month, an infant can breathe and swallow at the same time.

Approximately *thirty* years ago, Paul Henderson scored the most famous goal in the history of Canadian hockey.

While the average Canadian male can expect to live to be *seventy-five*, his wife can expect to live to *eighty-one*.

Scientists believe that most people use only about *one-tenth* of their intellectual potential.

Exercise 5.1

Applying the two highlighted rules on pages 45 and 46, correct any errors in the following sentences. Answers begin on page 325.

1. List 3 good reasons why I should consider your request for promotion.

2. For the 1st time, Gus felt confident leading the class.

3. Having spent 4 summers on Prince Edward Island, I would feel very comfortable working in the Maritimes.

4. For every 2 books you purchase, you can buy a third one for 1/2 the regular price.

5. I paused for about 15 minutes to allow twelve goslings to cross the road.

6. 7 and 5 are my favourite numbers to choose in the lottery.

7. Between the ages of 14 and 17, I lived in Taiwan.

8. At least ⅓ of the students on campus commute from the suburbs each day and another ¼ live in residence.

9. Brandon, the 1st stop on our itinerary, is the 2nd largest city in Manitoba.

10. It takes forty-three muscles to frown, but only seventeen to smile.

When to Use Figures

As a general rule, you should use figures when you are presenting complex or precise numerical information or when your sentence or paragraph contains several numbers.

3. Use figures to show dates, specific times, addresses, percentages, and exact measurements or amounts of money.

Dates	April 1, 2003, *or* 1 April 2003
Times	8:45 a.m. *or* 08:45; 7:10 p.m. *or* 19:10 (Use words with *o'clock*: e.g., *nine o'clock.*)
Addresses	3582 Windsor Street; 168 Grosvenor Road
Percentages	22 percent fat; a 1.5 percent inflation rate (Use the % sign only with figures in tables or in series: e.g., "From 1999 to 2002, our sales increased by 8%, 13%, and 19%.")
Exact measurements	2 m, 200 cm, 500 ml, 4 L, 450 g, 110 km/h, −30°C, 0.1 mm
Amounts of money	79 cents *or* $0.79, $1.98, $379.99, $200,000

Exercise 5.2

With Rule 3 in mind, correct the errors in the following sentences.

1. On April twentieth, Beth will take possession of her new house at eighteen Borden Lane.

2. At 8 o'clock in the morning, I was awakened by the sound of winds blowing at eighty km/h.

3. The final product should measure twelve cm by 22 cm.

4. Remember that 1 teaspoon is equivalent to five ml, and that one cup is equivalent to 250 ml.

5. Finally, at the age of 42, Dan was able to put a small down payment on his first home, a bungalow priced at sixty thousand dollars.

6. In early two thousand two, interest rates at the major banks dropped to less than four percent.

7. 1800 puppy mills in Quebec produce more than nine hundred thousand sickly dogs each year.

8. The temperature in Yellowknife often falls below negative forty degrees Celsius by two p.m.

9. Driving a car at ninety km/h uses about twenty percent less fuel than driving it at 105 km/h.

10. Petra's great-grandmother arrived in Lethbridge in nineteen hundred fifteen when she was only 22 years old.

When to Use Both Words and Figures

4. When one number immediately follows another, spell out the one that makes the shorter word.
5. For numbers over a million, express the number in figures and the quantity in words.

The Grey Cup is contested by *two 12-man* teams of heavily padded and helmeted warriors.

Our local car dealers sold more than *200 four-wheel* drive vehicles the day after our first big storm.

Canada's population has now topped 31 million.

Light from the most distant stars in our galaxy takes *4 billion* years to reach Earth.

The following exercises will test your ability to apply all of the rules and exceptions presented in this chapter.

Exercise 5.3

Correct any errors in the expression of numbers in the following sentences.

1. The astrologist predicted that over the next 3 years Alden's chances of getting married would be fifty-four percent, thirty-three percent, and 22 percent.

2. An adult polar bear can weigh up to three hundred forty kg, or as much as a mid-sized sedan.

3. More than 100,000,000 years ago, dinosaurs roamed Alberta's Badlands. The first fossils of these prehistoric beasts were discovered in eighteen hundred eighty four.

4. 19 of the 20 candidates were under the legal driving age of 16.

5. In the 19th century, it was common for women to wear hoop skirts that measured between 2.7 and four metres in circumference.

6. For my 18th birthday, I received a two thousand dollar cheque.

7. Karim is planning a party for his great-aunt, who will be 99 on Wednesday. 60 guests are expected to attend the celebration.

8. In 1998, over two million men and three million women attended Canadian theatres.

9. Hannah has a curfew of ten p.m., but on her prom night she stayed out until 1 o'clock in the morning.

10. To assemble the workbench, you will need thirty-two four-cm nails.

GO TO WEB

EXERCISE 5.1

Exercise 5.4

Before you tackle this final exercise, review the five highlighted rules given in this chapter. It's a good idea to write them out on a single sheet of paper and keep them before you as you go through the exercise. There are 15 errors in the following passage.

Trivial Pursuit is the ultimate board game for people from 9 to 99 who love the challenge of discovering 1000s of miscellaneous, little-known facts. One interesting piece of trivia is that the game itself was invented by 2 enterprising Canadians, Chris Haney and Scott Abbot. The friends started with a simple prototype in nineteen seventy-nine and scrambled and scraped to raise enough money to produce one thousand games two years later. The production budget was so tight that the initial artwork was created by an unknown artist who was only 18 years old and agreed to work for company shares rather than money.

When the 1st-edition sets were finally ready in 1981, they retailed in the American market at approximately thirty dollars each. This was a high cost for a board game, but Trivial Pursuit rapidly became a success in spite of its price tag, selling more than three and one half million copies in its first 5 years. The 18th-century poet, Alexander Pope, seems to have been prophetic when he wrote, "What mighty contests arise from trivial things." By 2000, nineteen years after the initial production run, Trivial Pursuit contests had become such a popular form of amusement world-wide that the game's cumulative sales totalled more than one billion American dollars. Today, the game's inventors, who each own twenty-two percent of the shares in the company they founded, are both millionaires, and Trivial Pursuit holds a spot in the Games Hall of Fame.

UNIT 2

Sentence Structure

6

Cracking the Sentence Code

There is nothing really mysterious or difficult about sentences. You've been speaking them successfully since you were two. The difficulty arises when you go to write—not sentences, oddly enough, but paragraphs. Almost all college students, if asked to write ten sentences on ten different topics, could do so without making errors. But when those same students write paragraphs, fragments, run-ons, and other sentence faults appear. These errors give the reader a poor impression of the writer.

The solution to sentence-structure problems has two parts.

Be sure every sentence you write
1. sounds right
    and
2. has a subject and a verb.

If English is your first language, your ear is probably the best instrument with which to test your sentences. If you read your sentences aloud, you may be able to tell by the sound whether they are complete, clear, and satisfactory. A complete sentence is one that makes sense by itself.

Read these sentences aloud:

Snowboarding is one of the world's newest sports.
Although snowboarding is still a young sport.

The second "sentence" doesn't sound right, does it? It does not make sense on its own and is in fact a sentence fragment.

Testing your sentences by reading them aloud won't work if you read your paragraphs straight through from beginning to end. The trick is to read from end to beginning. That is, read your last sentence aloud and *listen* to it. If it sounds all right, then read aloud the next-to-last sentence, and so on, until you have worked your way back to the first sentence you wrote.

Now, what do you do with the ones that don't sound right? Before you can fix them, you need to be able to decode each sentence to find out if it has both a subject and a verb. The subject and the verb are the bare essentials of a sentence. Every sentence you write must have both. (The only exception is a **command**, in which the subject is understood rather than expressed. Consider this command: "Do the following exercises." The subject *you* is understood.)

Finding Subjects and Verbs

A sentence is about *someone* or *something*. That someone or something is the **subject.** The word (or words) that tells what the subject *is* or *does* is the **verb.** The verb expresses an action, condition, or occurrence.

Find the verb first. One way is by finding the word whose form can be changed to indicate a change in time. Consider this sentence:

The mayor called for the vote.

The word *called* (in the past) can be changed to *calls* (present) or *will call* (future), so *called* is the verb.

Once you have found the verb, find the subject by asking *who* or *what* the verb is referring to.

Look at the following examples. We have underlined the subjects once and the verbs twice.

Jean helps me.
(Helps expresses an action and is the verb.
Who or what helps? Jean helps, so Jean is the subject.)

This new accounting program will save me hours of time.
(Will save expresses an action and is the verb.
Who or what will save? The program.)

Finding verbs is relatively easy.
(Is expresses a condition and is the verb.
Who or what is [easy]? Finding, which is the subject.)

Jacques Cartier described Canada as "the land God gave to Cain."
(Described expresses an occurrence and is the verb.
Who or what described? Jacques Cartier.)

Hint: You can test whether you've identified the subject and the verb correctly by putting them together to see whether or not they make sense. For example, "<u>Finding</u> <u>is</u>" makes sense; "<u>verbs</u> <u>is</u>" does not. "This <u>program</u> <u>will save</u>" makes sense; "This <u>new accounting</u> <u>will save</u>" does not.

Find the subject and the verb in the following sentences. Underline the subject with one line and the verb with two. Check your answers beginning on page 326. If you made even one mistake, do Web exercises 6.1 and 6.2. Be sure you understand this material thoroughly before you go on.

Exercise 6.1

1. It lives!

2. The mummy lives in a crypt.

3. The crypt is its home.

4. The cemetery's south wall contains the crypt.

5. In the movie, the mummy walks at night during a full moon.

6. Walking alone in a cemetery during a full moon is not a good idea.

7. According to the legend, the mummy never goes beyond the cemetery walls.

8. Believe me. It does.

9. Some real Egyptian mummies are on display at the Royal Ontario Museum.

10 Studying them provides insight into ancient Egyptian life.

GO TO WEB

EXERCISES 6.1, 6.2

Exercise 6.2

1. Most Canadians are concerned about nutrition.

2. Specialty health-food stores exist in almost every town.

3. Even mainstream stores offer organic produce.

4. Many people take vitamin supplements.

5. Demand for vitamin-enriched foods increases each year.

6. Each year, our consumption of pasta and cereals grows as well.

7. But we also eat more fat-filled foods like butter and cream.

8. Every Canadian eats about 9L of ice cream every year.

9. This number represents a 7 percent increase over last year's figure.

10. Lowering our fat intake is an ongoing struggle for many of us.

The subject usually comes before the verb in a sentence, but not always. Occasionally, we find it after the verb:

> Back to the refreshment stand for the fourth time <u>stumbled</u> the weary <u>father</u>.
> (Who or what <u>stumbled</u>? The <u>father</u>.)

> At the bottom of the page, in red ink, <u>was</u> my <u>grade</u>.
> (Who or what <u>was</u>? My <u>grade</u>.)

In sentences beginning with *There* + some form of the verb *to be,* or with *Here* + some form of the verb *to be,* the subject comes after the verb:

> There <u>are</u> three good <u>reasons</u> for learning to write well.
> (Who or what <u>are</u>? <u>Reasons</u>.)

> There <u>will be</u> a <u>test</u> next week.
> (Who or what <u>will be</u>? A <u>test</u>.)

> Here <u>are</u> the <u>solutions</u> to last week's problem set.
> (Who or what <u>are</u>? <u>Solutions</u>.)

In questions, the subject often follows the verb:

> <u>Are</u> <u>you</u> sure about this?　　<u>Is</u> <u>he</u> late again?
> (Who or what <u>are</u> sure? <u>You</u>.)　(Who or what <u>is</u> late? <u>He</u>.)

 But notice that, in questions beginning with *who, whose, what,* or *which,* the subject and the verb are in "normal" order:

> <u>Who</u> <u>went</u> camping?　　<u>What</u> <u>jumped</u> out of a tree?
> <u>Whose</u> <u>tent</u> <u>leaks</u>?　　<u>Which</u> <u>beetles</u> <u>bite</u>?

Exercise 6.3

In the following exercise, underline the subject in each sentence with one line and the verb with two. Check your answers before you go on.

1. The prairie grass waved in the wind.

2. Hiking is an exhilarating experience.

3. Is Kim on the invitation list?

4. Who dialed 911?

5. Drive carefully.

6. Whose gloves are lying on the radiator?

7. Which dog won the obedience trials?

8. Here is my desk.

9. Fortunately, there are two chocolates left.

10. There were once more than 20 taverns within the walls of the Fortress of Louisbourg.

GO TO WEB

EXERCISES 6.3, 6.4, 6.5, 6.6

More about Verbs

The verb in a sentence may be a single word, as in most of the exercises you've just done, or it may be a group of words. **Helping verbs** (auxiliary verbs) are often added to main verbs so that an idea can be expressed precisely. The words *shall, should, may, might, can, could, must, ought, will, would, have, do,* and *be* are helping verbs.

The complete verb in a sentence consists of the main verb + any helping verbs.

Here are a few of the forms of the verb *begin*. Notice that in questions the subject may come between the helping verb and the main verb.

You <u>may begin</u> now.
We <u>should begin</u> soon.
He <u>could have begun</u> without
  our consent.
I <u>shall begin</u> at once.
We <u>are beginning</u> at the third chapter.
<u>Did</u> you <u>begin</u> yet?

It <u>has begun</u> to rain.
She <u>will have begun</u> to worry.
I <u>am beginning</u> to feel hungry.
The project <u>should begin</u> soon.
He <u>will begin</u> later today.
We <u>should have begun</u> an
  hour ago.

One verb form *always* takes a helping verb. Here is the rule.

A verb ending in *-ing* MUST have a helping verb (or verbs) before it.

Here are a few of the forms an *-ing* verb can take:

She <u>is beginning</u> to annoy me.
<u>Are</u> you <u>beginning</u> to cry?
He <u>should be beginning</u> now.
They <u>were beginning</u> to make progress.
I <u>shall be beginning</u> a new routine.
He <u>could be beginning</u> to go bald.

Beware of certain words that are often confused with helping verbs.

Words such as *not, only, always, often, sometimes, never, ever,* and *just*
are NOT part of the verb.

These words sometimes appear in the middle of a complete verb, but they
are modifiers, not verbs. Do not underline them.

I <u>have</u> just <u>won</u> a one-way ticket to Moose Factory.
She <u>is</u> always <u>chosen</u> first.
Most people <u>do</u> not <u>welcome</u> unasked-for advice.

GO TO WEB

EXERCISES 6.7, 6.8, 6.9, 6.10

In the following exercises, underline the subject once and the complete verb twice. Correct the first set of ten sentences before you go on to the next.

Exercise 6.4

1. The prairies have fostered a vibrant artistic community.

2. The train could arrive early.

3. By graduation day, Bruce will have attended more parties than anyone else on campus.

4. Should we try bungee jumping?

5. Barb must have written her exam yesterday.

6. I have almost finished eating my muffin.

7. You should try the maple fudge!

8. Did you see the blue jay?

9. Surely peace will eventually be achieved.

10. Marvin had never intended to procrastinate.

GO TO WEB

EXERCISES 6.11, 6.12

Exercise 6.5

1. We ought to have registered early.

2. Ralph has been waiting two weeks for that phone call.

3. I have not ever travelled to the Fraser Valley.

4. How could Suzy have known about Fred's allergy to Body Shop scents?

5. They had not locked the cabin securely.

6. Why is mother hiding in the garage?

7. Because of her high marks, Kendra can attend the college of her choice.

8. Which book did you lend Monica?

9. Our friends are planning a trip to Muskoka for the fall.

10. You really should explore your Celtic roots during your stay in Cape Breton.

More about Subjects

Groups of words called **prepositional phrases** often come before the subject in a sentence or between the subject and the verb. When you're looking for the subject in a sentence, prepositional phrases can trip you up unless you know the following rule.

The subject of a sentence is NEVER in a prepositional phrase.

You must be able to identify prepositional phrases so that you will know where *not* to look for the subject. A prepositional phrase is a group of words that begins with a preposition and ends with the name of something or someone (a noun or a pronoun). Often a prepositional phrase will indicate the direction or location of something. In the phrases below, the italicized words are prepositions:

about the book	*between* the desks	*near* the wall
above the book	*by* the book	*of* the program
according to the book	*concerning* the memo	*on* the desk
after the meeting	*despite* the order	*onto* the floor
against the wall	*down* the hall	*over* a door
along the hall	*except* the staff	*through* the window
among the books	*for* the manager	*to* the staff
among them	*from* the office	*under* the desk
around the office	*in* front *of* the desk	*until* the meeting
before lunch	*inside* the office	*up* the hall
behind the desk	*in* the book	*with* a book
below the window	*into* the elevator	*without* them
beside the computer	*like* the book	*without* the software

Before you look for the subject in a sentence, cross out all prepositional phrases.

The keyboard ~~of your computer~~ should be cleaned occasionally.
What <u>should be cleaned</u>? The <u>keyboard</u> (not the computer).

~~In case of an emergency,~~ a member ~~of the class~~ should go ~~to the nearest security office for help~~.
Who <u>should go</u>? A <u>member</u> (not the class).

GO TO WEB

EXERCISE 6.13

In the following exercises, first cross out the prepositional phrase(s) in each sentence. Then underline the subject once and the verb twice. Check your answers to each set of ten sentences before going on. If you get two sets entirely correct, skip ahead to Exercise 6.9.

Exercise 6.6

1. The flock of Canada geese circled overhead.

2. John Irving is the author of *A Prayer for Owen Meany*.

3. Millions of Canadians watch American football on television.

4. The definition of high fashion varies from province to province.

5. A trend in Vancouver is not necessarily a fad in St. John's.

6. In her excitement, she sprang over the handrail.

7. Her love for him has not waned for twenty years.

8. Aren't you concerned about the state of the environment?

9. I appreciated the honesty of his response.

10. He limped slowly through the door.

Exercise 6.7

1. The stars shine down on Earth from light years away.

2. Twenty minutes of aerobic exercise about three times a week keeps me fit.

3. The crash of SwissAir flight 111 into the ocean off Peggy's Cove, Nova Scotia, reminded all of us of our mortality.

4. Escape from the Kingston Penitentiary appears to be nearly impossible.

5. The party starts in the warehouse at 5:00.

6. The article concerning pet cemeteries is reprinted in tonight's paper.

7. Several of the doctors were attending the conference for the first time.

8. The wild roses of Prince Edward Island smell sweeter than any other flowers.

9. You really should see the dentist about that loose tooth.

10. Of all the Canadian comedy shows on television, *This Hour Has 22 Minutes* is the funniest.

GO TO WEB

EXERCISES 6.14, 6.15

Contrary to your expectations and despite the rumours, your instructor does not bite.

Exercise 6.8

1. Most tourists are willing to try the local dishes, except for cod tongues.

2. By waiting on tables, babysitting, and borrowing from friends, I manage to make ends meet.

3. By lobbying the government for support, the farmers should gain greater subsidies.

4. The parcel for the manager is waiting at the front desk.

5. After cycling from one coast to the other, Philippa wrote a book about her journey.

6. The journalist's obvious bias in favour of the police made his report unreliable.

7. In *The Stone Diaries*, Carol Shields includes a great recipe for lemon pudding.

8. The forests of Temagami, in northern Ontario, form an unspoiled wilderness.

9. The book behind the dresser was covered with mould and mildew.

10. Despite its strong taste, espresso contains no more caffeine than regular coffee.

GO TO WEB

EXERCISES 6.16, 6.17

Exercise 6.9

Write ten fairly long sentences of your own. In at least three of them, place the subject after the verb. Cross out all the prepositional phrases, and underline the subject once and the complete verb twice.

Multiple Subjects and Verbs

So far, you have been working with sentences containing only one complete subject and one complete verb. Sentences can, however, have more than one subject and one verb. Here is a sentence with a multiple subject:

<u>Stanley Park</u> and <u>Wreck Beach</u> <u>are</u> two of Vancouver's popular tourist attractions.

This sentence has a multiple verb:

<u>The biker</u> <u>elbowed</u> and <u>shoved</u> his way to the candy counter.

And this sentence has a multiple subject and a multiple verb:

The <u>goalie</u> and the <u>coach</u> <u>smiled</u> for the cameras and <u>waved</u> the team flag.

The elements of a multiple subject or verb are usually joined by *and* or *or*. Multiple subjects and verbs may contain more than two elements, as in the following sentences:

<u>Clarity</u>, <u>brevity</u>, and <u>simplicity</u> <u>are</u> the basic qualities of good writing.

<u>I</u> <u>finished</u> my paper, <u>put</u> the cat outside, <u>took</u> the phone off the hook, and <u>crawled</u> into bed.

Identify the subjects and verbs in the following exercises. It's a good idea to cross out any prepositional phrases first. Underline the subjects once and the verbs twice. Be sure to underline all elements of a multiple subject or verb (there may be more than two). Check your answers to each set before continuing.

Exercise 6.10

1. The Toronto Maple Leafs and the Montreal Canadiens are traditional archrivals.

2. Whistler or Lake Louise would make an excellent vacation spot.

3. Neither Geoff nor Sue was able to attend the Roch Voisine concert.

4. During World War II, many Canadian women worked in munitions factories and nursed in military hospitals.

5. Both women and men stand to benefit from the recent changes to parental leave policies.

6. Shauna and Wes plan to marry next July.

7. Measure the ingredients carefully and mix them thoroughly.

8. Coal miners and fishermen are seeking retraining.

9. The coyote stopped in its tracks, stared at the small child beside the dumpster, then turned and loped away.

10. Students with good time management skills can research, organize, draft, and revise a first-class paper by the deadline.

GO TO WEB

EXERCISES 6.18, 6.19, 6.20, 6.21, 6.22

Exercise 6.11

Food fuels our bodies. In important ways, it also nourishes our souls, cements relationships, and provides an outlet for creative experimentation. We use food for celebrating special events. We share food with friends and even strangers. An essential ingredient in any courtship is dining together, whether at a restaurant or at the home of one of the lovers. In my family, we remember history according to certain meals. There are the cooking disasters from the early years: "Remember that soggy eggplant casserole? The dog wouldn't touch it." Then there are the more dramatic catastrophes, like the flaming mushroom soufflé. That incident required Dad's prompt use of the kitchen fire extinguisher. Finally, there are the extraordinary culinary labours of love. For a special wedding gift, Dad gave Mom a triple-layer wedding cake of his own making. On my brother's second birthday, Mom stayed up all night and baked a choo-choo train birthday cake, complete with a caboose. After my sister's first chess championship, Mom cooked a special Chinese meal from scratch. Cooking together, eating together, and cleaning the kitchen together form important rituals. Without them, we would be hungry not just for physiological nourishment but also for a sense of human community.

Here's a summary of what you've learned in this chapter. Keep it in front of you as you write the mastery test.

Summary

- The subject is *who* or *what* the sentence is about.
- The verb tells what the subject *is* or *does*.
- The subject normally comes before the verb (exceptions are questions and sentences beginning with *there* or *here*).
- The complete verb = a main verb + any helping verbs.
- By itself, a word ending in *-ing* is not a verb.
- The subject of a sentence is never in a prepositional phrase.
- A sentence can have more than one subject and/or verb.

Exercise 6.12

This challenging exercise will test your subject- and verb-finding ability. In each sentence below, first cross out any prepositional phrases, and then underline each subject with one line and each verb with two lines. Be sure to underline all elements in a multiple subject or verb.

1. For international competitions, even male swimmers shave their legs.

2. Of all the emotions, sincerity is the most difficult to mimic.

3. Talking, laughing, and nudging one another with their elbows, the girls giggled their way down the street.

4. According to Major-General Lewis MacKenzie, the former commander of Canada's peacekeeping forces in Yugoslavia, the dilapidated state of Canada's military is a national disgrace.

5. The difference between the right word and almost the right word is the difference between lightning and a lightning bug. (Mark Twain)

6. Skiing, snowboarding, and skidooing help Canadians pass the long winter.

7. Multiculturalism in Canada cannot be left to chance but must be actively fostered and pursued. (Pierre Elliott Trudeau)

8. Among the students in Irena's pottery class are a veteran of the Korean War, a homemaker with seven grown children, a middle-aged architect, and a fuchsia-haired teenager from Saskatoon.

9. After several days of negotiations, Riley sold his house and put a down payment on a condominium in Regent Park.

10. Despite her misgivings, Harriet decided to marry Stanley, move to Peachland, and set up her photography studio in her husband's hometown.

7

Solving Sentence-Fragment Problems

Any group of words that is punctuated as a sentence but does not have a subject or a complete verb is a **sentence fragment.** Fragments are appropriate in conversation and in some kinds of writing, but normally they are not acceptable in college, technical, or business writing. You've already learned how to spot a sentence fragment: read the words aloud, and check whether the subject or the verb (or both) is missing. Let's look at a few examples:

Now, as always, is greatly influenced by its willful neighbour.
(Who or what <u>is influenced</u>? The sentence doesn't tell you. The subject is missing.)

The overpass above the TransCanada Highway.
(What about the <u>overpass</u>? The verb is missing.)

The committee attempting to analyze Canada's participation in U.N. peacekeeping missions.
(Part of the verb is missing. Remember that a verb ending in -*ing* must have a helping verb in front of it.)

To help students in every lab but this one.
(Subject and verb are both missing.)

After class on Thursday.
(Subject and verb are both missing.)

Now, what do you do with the fragments you've found?

> To change a sentence fragment into a complete sentence, add whatever is missing: a subject, a verb, or both.

You may need to add a subject:

> Now, as always, <u>Canada</u> is greatly influenced by its willful neighbour.

You may need to add a verb:

> The overpass above the TransCanada Highway <u>was completed</u> last week.

You may need to add part of a verb:

> The committee <u>is attempting</u> to analyze Canada's participation in U.N. peacekeeping missions.

You may need to add both a subject and a verb:

> A <u>technician</u> <u>is</u> available to help students in every lab but this one.

And sometimes you need to add more than just a subject and a verb:

> <u>I</u> <u>will meet</u> you after class on Thurday.

Don't let the length of a fragment fool you. Students sometimes think that, if a string of words is long, it must be a sentence. This is not necessarily so. No matter how long the string of words is, if it doesn't contain both a subject and a verb, it is not a sentence. Consider this example:

> Here and there a ruddy little pond, like a pocket looking glass dropped on the prairie, with a score or so of wild ducks swimming in it, or a slight round hollow where a pond used to be, with the wild ducks flying high.

Duncan, Sara Jeannette. "The Men of Moosomin."

Do you know what's missing? Can you change the fragment into a sentence?

In the following exercises, read each "sentence" aloud. Put S before each complete sentence and F before each sentence fragment. Make each fragment into a complete sentence by adding whatever is missing: a subject, a verb, or both.

After you complete each set of ten sentences, check your answers. If you get two sets entirely correct, you may skip the rest. Answers begin on page 329.

Exercise 7.1

1. _____ Happy to hear from you.

2. _____ Large enough to fill the room.

3. _____ Consider the prime minister's new budget.

4. _____ About Tuesday's meeting.

5. _____ Pondering the consultant's advice, he left the office in a mental fog.

6. _____ On the way to Saskatchewan.

7. _____ Driving for three days.

8. _____ The acrobats juggling on the corner.

9. _____ Too tired to drive.

10. _____ No problem.

GO TO WEB

EXERCISES 7.1, 7.2

Exercise 7.2

_____ For the seventh year in a row, the Buskers' Festival taking over the downtown area. _____ Acrobats, jugglers, mimes, and musicians from all over the world. _____ Streets in the business district magically transformed into a strolling circus. _____ Try to take in at least a couple of events. _____ Especially the sword swallower from London. _____ Also entertaining is the unicyclist from Spain. _____ Careful to watch your valuables in the crowds. _____ Pickpockets being as fond of the buskers as everyone else.

GO TO WEB

EXERCISES 7.3, 7.4

Exercise 7.3

_____ Canadian singers Shania Twain and Celine Dion a lot in common. _____ Although Shania sings country music and Celine records pop songs, both are successful superstars. _____ Yet, despite the millions of records they have sold and the luxurious lifestyles their stardom provides, neither woman is a diva. _____ Coming from humble backgrounds, both still close to their families. _____ Shania, a surrogate mother for her orphaned brothers and sisters. _____ Celine in touch with her family in Quebec. _____ Finally, both new mothers who took maternity breaks from their musical careers.

Dependent Clause Fragments

A group of words containing a subject and a verb is a clause. There are two kinds of clauses. An **independent clause** is one that makes complete sense on its own. It can stand alone, as a sentence. A **dependent clause**, as its name suggests, cannot stand alone as a sentence; it depends on another clause to make complete sense.

Dependent clauses are easy to recognize, because they begin with words such as these:

Dependent Clause Cues

after	so that
although	that
as, as if	though
as long as	unless
as soon as	until
because	what, whatever
before	when, whenever
even if, even though	where, wherever
if	whether
in order that	which, whichever
provided that	while
since	who, whom, whose

Whenever a clause begins with one of these words or phrases, it is dependent.

A dependent clause must be attached to an independent clause. If it stands alone, it is a sentence fragment.

Here is an independent clause:

Marisa is bilingual.

If we put one of the dependent clause cues in front of it, it can no longer stand alone:

Because Marisa is bilingual

We can correct this kind of fragment by attaching it to an independent clause:

Because Marisa is bilingual, she has her choice of jobs.

In the following exercises, put an S before each clause that is independent and therefore a sentence. Put an F before each clause that is dependent and therefore a sentence fragment. Circle the dependent clause cue in each sentence fragment. Remember to check your answers after each exercise.

Exercise 7.4

1. _____ Although the marriage ceremony started late.

2. _____ Until I hear from Suzy.

3. _____ As soon as Herb arrives at Pearson Airport.

4. _____ Provided that your form is completed correctly.

5. _____ Whoever leaves the room last.

6. _____ After the dance is over and all the musicians are gone.

7. _____ Since Confederation.

8. _____ Where I put his car keys.

9. _____ Before the clock strikes midnight.

10. _____ Because the journalists could not understand Chrétien's English or his French.

GO TO WEB

EXERCISES 7.5, 7.6

Exercise 7.5

1. _____ Before we could get there.

2. _____ Which was filled beyond its seating capacity.

3. _____ After we talked about the various drawbacks of the plan.

4. _____ Since last summer, Camp Iona's facilities have improved.

5. _____ Even if the accused is found guilty.

6. _____ Although she is smart and capable.

7. _____ When a commodity is scarce, its market value increases.

8. _____ Whoever finds our missing puppy.

9. _____ Everyone who has a voter's registration card.

10. _____ Unless you want to wait 20 minutes for the car to defrost.

GO TO WEB

EXERCISES 7.7, 7.8

Exercise 7.6

Correct the sentence fragments in Exercises 7.4 and 7.5. Make each fragment into a complete sentence by adding an independent clause either before or after the dependent clause. Remember to punctuate correctly: if a dependent clause comes at the beginning of your sentence, put a comma after it. When you have completed the exercise, exchange it with another student to check each other's work.

Most sentence fragments are dependent clauses punctuated as sentences. Fortunately, this is the easiest kind of fragment to recognize and fix. All you need to do is join the dependent clause either to the sentence that comes before it or to the one that comes after it — whichever linkage makes better sense.

One final point. If you join your clause fragment to the independent clause that follows it, put a comma between the two clauses (see Chapter 18, page 187).

Read the following example; then read it aloud, beginning with the last sentence and working back to the first.

> Montreal is a sequence of ghettos. Although I was born and brought up there. My experience of French was a pathetically limited and distorted one.

The second "sentence" sounds incomplete, and the dependent clause cue at the beginning of it is the clue you need to identify it as a sentence fragment. You could join the fragment to the sentence before it, but then you would get "Montreal is a sequence of ghettos, although I was born and brought up there," which doesn't make sense. The fragment should be linked to the sentence that follows it.

Montreal is a sequence of ghettos. Although I was born and brought up there, my experience of French was a pathetically limited and distorted one.

Richler, Mordecai. "Quebec Oui, Canada Non!"

Exercise 7.7

Identify the sentence fragments in the paragraph below. Circle the dependent clause cue in each fragment you find. Then correct each fragment by joining it to a complete sentence before or after it—whichever makes better sense. Exercise 7.7 contains nine fragments. Check your answers on page 330.

Although Canada enjoys a temperate climate compared to the rest of the world. Complaining about the weather is a favourite national pastime. That is popular from coast to coast. Whereas Vancouver urbanites groan about the rainy weather. Saskatchewan farmers lament the prairie drought. Unless Ottawa has an abnormally mild winter. Ottawa's citizens complain. About the frigid temperatures and the nearly impassable snowdrifts. Even though we Canadians enjoy outdoor sports and activities and are known as hardy folks. We're seldom content. With whatever the weather brings us. Whether it's cold or hot. We compensate for our vulnerability. By grumbling about Mother Nature's unpredictability.

GO TO WEB

EXERCISE 7.9

Correct the fragments in Exercises 7.8 and 7.9 in any way you choose. Try to use the variety of the techniques for fixing fragments that you have learned in this chapter. When you are finished, compare your answers with our suggestions on page 330.

Exercise 7.8

Exercise 7.8 contains 11 fragments.

People say that pets and their owners tend to look alike. After a while. There is some truth to this generalization. As far as I can see. Reflecting on my own experience. I can think of several uncanny resemblances. Between pets and owners. For example, Fluffy the long-haired tabby cat. And my Aunt Ruby with her permed hair. Also, my neighbour, Joe Maxwell. Whose Rottweiler is as surly and overweight as he is. Then there is Sheena Lougheed's toy poodle. High-strung, fussy, perfectly groomed, and whiny. The mirror image of Sheena. Especially when they both wear red ribbons in their hair.

Exercise 7.9

Exercise 7.9 contains 15 errors.

My cousin, Jack, used to fix Automated Teller Machines (ATMs) for CIBC. When he was in college. He liked the job. Because he said it gave him a feeling of prestige. Wearing a beeper was part of the job. So he felt very important. As if he were a surgeon or a firefighter on call. The job had its drawbacks, however. Particularly the odd hours. Some weekends Jack had to work the 4 p.m. to 12 a.m. shift. This made it hard for him to make a Saturday night date. Let alone enjoy one uninterrupted. Not many young women have the patience to put up with leaving a movie halfway through to report to a repair site. Watch Jack and his partner fiddle with the insides of an ATM for an hour. Or more. The job presented certain risks, too. Whenever Jack opened up an ATM. He put himself in potential danger. By exposing thousands and thousands of dollars. He worked with a partner. Of course. But neither of them carried a gun. Only a pager and a cell phone. To communicate with security guards. Despite the excellent pay. I never applied to work with Jack. For me, too much responsibility and too little social life.

Exercise 7.10

As a final test of your skill in correcting sentence fragments, try this exercise. Some of the items below contain only complete sentences. Put a check mark (✔) beside them. The others contain one or more sentence fragments. Mark them with an ✗; then make each fragment into a complete sentence.

1. _____ Once a common sight every spring, the mayflower is now rarely seen in Nova Scotia's woods. Even though it is the official provincial flower.

2. _____ Now that basketball is an Olympic sport, it has become popular with Canadian youth. The Toronto Raptors have been encouraging this trend.

3. _____ Although she's tall enough and her athletic ability is above average, her chances of being selected for the team are slim.

4. _____ Customer service is one aspect of business no company can afford to ignore. When customers get angry, they take their business elsewhere.

5. _____ Her father being an owner of Roots. She had several opportunities to model for advertisements during her college years.

6. _____ During the intermission and after the show, members of the press circulating in the lobby. The show's critical success seemed likely, if not absolutely certain.

7. _____ As an employee, none of us is indispensable to the company. Although we sometimes like to think we are.

8. _____ Rick Mercer's television program, *Talking to Americans*, ridicules Americans. Who lack even basic knowledge about Canada.

9. _____ Seldom realize the danger we pose to shore birds. We often disturb their nests when we walk on sand dunes or let dogs run loose on the beach.

10. _____ The Internet was supposed to improve the availability of information for everyone. Instead, it has created a division. Between those who have access to the technology and those who don't. Resulting in what social critics call "the digital divide."

8

Solving Run-On Sentence Problems

Some sentences lack essential elements and thus are fragments. Other sentences contain too many elements or elements that are incorrectly linked together. A sentence with too much in it or with inadequate punctuation between clauses is a **run-on.** Run-ons tend to occur when you write in a hurry, without taking time to organize your thoughts first. If you think about what you want to say and punctuate carefully, you shouldn't have any problems with run-ons.

Let's look at the three kinds of run-on sentences: the comma splice, the fused sentence, and the true run-on.

Comma Splices and Fused Sentences

As its name suggests, the **comma splice** occurs when two complete sentences (independent clauses) are joined together with only a comma between them. Here's an example:

Yogurt is a healthy snack, poutine is not.

A **fused sentence** occurs when two complete sentences are joined together with no punctuation between them. For example:

Yogurt is a healthy snack poutine is not.

There are three ways you can fix a comma splice or fused sentence.

1. Use a semicolon to separate the independent clauses.

For example:

Yogurt is a healthy snack; poutine is not.

(If you are not sure how to use semicolons, see Chapter 19.)

2. Add an appropriate linking word between the two clauses.

Two types of linking words will work.

1. You can add one of these words: *and, but, or, nor, for, so,* or *yet.*

These words should be preceded by a comma. Here is an example:

Yogurt is a healthy snack, but poutine is not.

2. You can add one of the dependent clause cues listed on page 74. For example:

Although yogurt is a healthy snack, poutine is not.

3. Make the independent clauses into two separate sentences.

Yogurt is a healthy snack. Poutine is not.

Note: All three solutions to comma splices and fused sentences require you to use a word or punctuation mark strong enough to come between two independent clauses. A comma by itself is too weak, and so is a dash.

The sentences in the following exercises will give you practice in fixing comma splices and fused sentences. Correct the sentences where necessary, and then check your answers, beginning on page 331. Since there are three ways to fix each sentence, your answers may differ from our suggestions. If you're confused about when to use a semicolon and when to use a period, be sure to read pages 192–93 before going on.

Exercise 8.1

1. Sir John A. MacDonald is on the ten dollar bill Sir Wilfred Laurier is on the five dollar bill.

2. I have had many manicures, I have never had a pedicure.

3. Russell de Carle has a solo album, he still sings with Prairie Oyster.

4. Natalie prefers pickles, onions, and tomato on her hamburger, she doesn't like mayonnaise, mustard, or ketchup.

5. Yan plans to travel to Montreal this summer, she hopes to see Quebec City on the way.

6. Dwight has lived in Punkeydoodle Corners, Ontario, all his life, he never understands why people laugh when he tells them the name of his hometown.

7. Sir Isaac Brock, a hero of the War of 1812, was buried four different times.

8. Zachary will be going to college if he is accepted, his parents have more than enough money.

9. Harry Houdini was in Montreal in October 1926 and was punched by a student, he died in Detroit two weeks later, and some biographers believe his death was caused by the injury he sustained in Montreal.

10. Kenny bought me a dozen roses, I didn't tell him I'm allergic to flowers.

Exercise 8.2

1. I love soccer, I feel like Pele every time I'm on the field.

2. Francis asked me to a movie I couldn't go because my cousin had just flown in from the Yukon.

3. Quarterback Doug Flutie went to the NFL, many Canadians remember him for having led the Calgary Stampeders and the Toronto Argonauts to Grey Cup victories.

4. The rules of CFL and NFL football are different, I don't understand either game.

5. We are moving to Abbotsford next month, so we are holding a yard sale this weekend.

6. She smelled the flowers, she smiled happily, then she sneezed loudly.

7. Tomorrow we will pay off our mortgage then we can finally afford to buy some furniture.

8. Don't tell Chris where his wife has gone, she is at the mall buying his birthday gift.

9. Yasmine and David are getting married in the United Church, even though they are Jewish, no synagogues are available that day.

10. My brother's friends spilled red wine all over my white carpet, it was ruined.

GO TO WEB

EXERCISES 8.1, 8.2

Exercise 8.3

1. When our team wins, we always do our special cheer, some other teams think we are crazy.

2. The largest metropolitan area in Canada is Toronto, the second largest is Montreal, and the third largest is Vancouver, my favourite city.

3. Sally left the bank because Quebecor offered her a management position, she loves her new job.

4. Vowing to make her the happiest woman in the world, Shane asked Lana to marry him, she agreed.

5. The Taxpayer Action Movement wants Jean Chrétien to retire, I'd like him to go to the moon.

6. Frances thought her interview had gone very well, however, she wasn't offered the job.

7. There are some advantages to having a friend for a boss, there are more disadvantages.

8. The most important thing I've learned as a manager is that success depends on teamwork unless team members play the same game, the business may fail.

9. During filming of the movie, the actor worked under a pseudonym the credits of the movie don't even list him as playing the lead character.

10. After I woke up late for work, I decided to call in sick an hour later, I went to the mall and ran into my boss.

Exercise 8.4

In the exercise that follows, correct the comma splices and fused sentences any way you choose. This would be a good time to review the three ways of fixing these errors. Your goal should be to produce paragraphs in which the sentences are both correct and effective. Exercise 8.4 contains ten errors (one of which is a sentence fragment).

The most popular tourist attraction in Derby Line, Vermont, is a theatre in which audiences sitting in the United States can watch performances in Canada, this seemingly impossible feat is the result of the theatre's unique location. The building straddles the border between Vermont and Quebec a black stripe painted on the floor marks the official dividing line between the two countries. Constructed early in the last century, the building is divided not only geographically but also functionally, it is a library as well as a theatre the name of this unusual structure is the Haskell Free Library and Opera House the library is on the ground floor, the theatre is upstairs. Most of the building, including the library and the stage, is in Quebec, the entrance to the building is in Vermont.

A Canadian woman, Martha Stewart Haskell, built the structure as a tribute to her American husband, over the past 100 years, some famous troupers have performed on its stage, the first "name act" to appear was the Columbian Minstrels, who opened the theatre in 1904. Recently renovated, the Haskell Free Library and Opera House continues to provide its cross-border patrons with full library services. And first-rate theatrical performances.

GO TO WEB

EXERCISE 8.3

The Monster Run-On Sentence

In the "monster" **run-on sentence**, too many clauses and often too many words are crowded together into one sentence. There is no hard-and-fast rule about how many independent clauses you may have in a sentence, but more than three can result in a sentence that is hard to read and even harder to understand.

> There were still a dozen or so guests who remained at the party, not counting the host, but after Raoul and Su Mei left, we decided it was time to go, so we collected our coats and said goodbye to the others, and then, after driving home very cautiously at speeds not exceeding 50 km/h, we sat up drinking coffee until three o'clock in the morning discussing our host's terrible taste in friends.

Clearly, the writer who created this monster got carried away with enthusiasm and just scribbled down everything that came to mind without thinking of the reader's tolerance or patience. If you take your time and remember your readers, you probably won't make this error. If you do find run-on sentences in your writing, however, you can correct them by following two steps.

1. Cut out all unnecessary words.
2. Apply one of the three solutions to comma splice and fused sentence problems: semicolons, linking words, and sentence breaks.

To turn a monster sentence into a correct and civilized one, first read through your sentence and identify any words or phrases that are not essential to its meaning.

> *There were still* a dozen *or so* guests *who* remained at the party, *not counting the host*, but after Raoul and Su Mei left, we decided *it was time* to go, so we collected our coats and said goodbye *to the others*, and then, after driving home *very* cautiously at *speeds not exceeding* 50 km/h, we sat up drinking coffee until three o'clock *in the morning* discussing our host's terrible taste in friends.

Run-on sentences are often made worse by **wordiness** (see Chapter 30 for hints on how to eliminate unnecessary words from your writing). In the example above, the words in italics are unnecessary or redundant and should be eliminated. Here's how the sentence reads without them:

> A dozen guests remained at the party, but after Raoul and Su Mei left, we decided to go, so we collected our coats and said goodbye, and then, after driving home cautiously at 50 km/h, we sat up drinking coffee until three o'clock discussing our host's terrible taste in friends.

This version is an improvement, but it is not as clear and concise as it could be. Let's move on to step 2:

> A dozen guests remained at the party, but after Raoul and Su Mei left, we decided to go. We collected our coats and said goodbye. Then, after driving home cautiously at 50 km/h, we sat up until three o'clock drinking coffee and discussing our host's terrible taste in friends.

This version is both concise and clear.

> In the following exercises, first eliminate all unnecessary words. Then use semicolons, linking words, or sentence breaks to correct what is left.

There is more than one right way of fixing these sentences. Just make sure your corrections make sense and are easy to read. The answers provided, which begin on page 332, are only suggestions.

Exercise 8.5

1. A recent study published in *The National Post* claims that women have better general oral, written, and verbal skills than men and I just want to say to the authors of that study, "D'oh."

2. Our supervisor recently held a meeting the other day to discuss the possible reasons for our department's lack of productivity and she told us that we would continue to have these meetings daily until she finds out why we are not working at a considerably higher efficiency level.

3. There are two main reasons for my dissatisfaction with my car: the most important being the rusting of the entire undercarriage and followed by the complete disintegration of the electrical system.

4. I look back with real nostalgia on winters in the small Manitoba town where I grew up with remembering the softly falling snow, the great excitement of the year's first snowball fight, and the crunch of snow beneath my boots on those really icy cold prairie mornings, these memories prove that the mind recalls the pleasant experiences and forgets the painful ones through the years as we age.

5. Following a high-speed chase and the arrest of the car's driver, the police learned that the vehicle involved had been stolen, so they added the charge of theft to the reckless-driving charge and the driver had to spend the night in jail, there he came to realize the seriousness of his situation and finally demanded his right to call a lawyer.

Grandmother of eight makes hole in one.

GO TO WEB

EXERCISE 8.4

Exercise 8.6

Exercise 8.6 contains 20 errors.

One popular and widely practised Canadian pastime that is seldom mentioned in the media, such as television, radio, or the press, is poking fun at the regional accents that distinguish one part of the country from another, since their dialect is particularly distinctive, Newfoundlanders have long been the target of this game, however, anyone who has travelled across Canada from coast to coast quickly learns that each region or section of the country has its own characteristic linguistic features. Sometimes these features are determined by provincial or territorial borders, at other times linguistic regions transcend political and geographical boundaries. For instance, an example is the many people in the Atlantic provinces, including New Brunswick, Nova Scotia, Prince Edward Island, and Newfoundland, tend to pronounce vowel sounds with a Maritime twang, "light" sounds like "loight," for example, they also tend to soften the "th" sound in words such as "brother" or "other," which are consequently commonly pronounced as "brudder" and "udder."

Sometimes regional speech differences and variations go beyond matters of pronunciation or how people say words, and such differences produce what is called a regional dialect. In speech, for instance, many Newfoundlanders use verbs differently than do speakers of standard English they say "I wants to go shopping" instead of "I want to go shopping." Natives of the Miramichi Valley use another distinctive construction, they say "youse" instead of the standard second person plural, "you."

Pronunciation, slang, and grammatical constructions differ from region to region across Canada, we should be proud of our rich, diverse regional dialects.

Exercise 8.7

As a final test of your ability to identify and correct run-on sentence errors, supply appropriate sentence breaks to make this garble into a grammatically correct paragraph. You may need to add or delete a few words to make some of the sentences complete and clear. Correct the 10 errors in the following paragraph.

Libraries aren't just about reading anymore, instead, they function as bustling, multi-purpose community centres, when I was a child, our local library was housed in a run-down, dusty brick building it was presided over by Mr. Dryasdust, a stern elderly fellow who wore old-fashioned wire glasses and frowned severely at anyone who chewed gum or whispered, but nowadays the atmosphere is dramatically different, there are two or three young, vibrant librarians, they lead musical activities for children, teach job-search skills to adults, and host pottery classes in the evenings, and the library isn't the quiet, tomb-like place I remember rather it's a cheerful, even rambunctious place, on a typical weekday morning, you can hear the tap-tap of library patrons typing e-mail at the computer keyboards, the giggles of children playing in the toy corner.

9

Solving
Modifier Problems

The thieves were caught before much of the loot could be disposed of *by the police.*

Stamping her feet and switching her tail to brush away flies, Amy led the mare out of the barn.

For sale: A set of first-year law texts *by a needy student in almost perfect condition.*

These sentences show what can happen to your writing if you aren't sure how to use modifiers. A **modifier** is a word or group of words that adds information about another word in a sentence. In the examples above, the italicized words are modifiers. Used correctly, modifiers describe or explain or limit another word, making its meaning more precise. Used carelessly, however, modifiers can cause confusion or, even worse, amusement. Few things are more embarrassing than being laughed at when you didn't mean to be funny.

You need to be able to recognize and solve two kinds of modifier problems: **misplaced modifiers** and **dangling modifiers.**

Misplaced Modifiers

Modifiers must be as close as possible to the words they apply to. Usually, a reader will assume that a modifier modifies whatever it's next to. It's important to remember this, because, as the following examples show, changing the position of a modifier can change the meaning of your sentence.

Only I love you. (No one else loves you.)

I only love you. (I don't have any other feelings for you.)

I love only you. (You are the only one I love.)

I love you only. (You are the only one I love.)

To make sure a modifier is in the right place, ask yourself "What does it apply to?" and put it beside that word.

When a modifier is not close enough to the word it refers to, it is said to be misplaced. A **misplaced modifier** can be *a single word in the wrong place:*

The supervisor told me they needed someone who can perform statistical analysis badly.

Is some company really hiring people to do poor work? Or does the company urgently need someone familiar with statistical analysis software? The modifier *badly* belongs next to *needed:*

The supervisor told me they badly needed someone who can perform statistical analysis.

Be especially careful with these words: *almost, nearly, just, only, even, hardly, merely, scarcely.* Put them right before the words they modify.

Misplaced:	I almost ate the whole pizza.
Correctly placed:	I ate almost the whole pizza.
Misplaced:	Many nineteenth-century women nearly had babies every year between their marriage and their death.
Correctly placed:	Many nineteenth-century women had babies nearly every year between their marriage and their death.

A misplaced modifier can also be *a group of words in the wrong place:*

Scratching each other playfully, we watched the monkeys.

The modifier, *scratching each other playfully,* is too far away from the word it is supposed to modify, *monkeys.* In fact, it seems to modify *we,* making the sentence ridiculous. We need to rewrite the sentence:

We watched the monkeys scratching each other playfully.

Look at this one:

I worked for my aunt, who owns a variety store during the summer.

During the summer applies to *worked* and should be closer to it:

During the summer, I worked for my aunt, who owns a variety store.

Notice that a modifier need not always go right next to what it modifies; it should, however, be as close as possible to it.

Occasionally, as in the examples above, the modifier is obviously out of place. The writer's intention is clear, and the sentences are easy to correct. But sometimes modifiers are misplaced in such a way that the meaning is not clear, as in this example:

Alison said on her way out she would deliver the package to Hugh.

Did Alison *say* it on her way out? Or is she going to *deliver the package* on her way out? To avoid confusion, we must move the modifier and, depending on which meaning we want, write:

On her way out, Alison said she would deliver the package to Hugh.

or

Alison said she would deliver the package to Hugh on her way out.

Rewrite the following sentences, placing the modifiers correctly. Check your answers to each set before going on. Answers begin on page 333.

Exercise 9.1

1. Sylvester bathed the dog wearing his best suit.
2. I write a letter to my boyfriend who lives in England every week.
3. The blaze was put out before any damage was done by the Riverview Fire Department.
4. Shelley almost did not arrive until three o'clock in the morning.
5. You will find a parking lot in the next block with an elevator.
6. Tell me what you have read with your books closed.
7. She ate one piece of toast only this morning.
8. Elizabeth said on her way to school she would drop off her job application to Esso.
9. Unless they are Chinese or Italian, some people never go to restaurants.
10. After driving almost over me, my sister was grounded for a week.

Exercise 9.2

1. He barely kicked the ball ten metres.
2. A mechanic who looked younger than my car slightly was the only employee working in the garage.
3. My instructor told me at the end of the term I would get my marks by mail.
4. Harry caught sight of a moose and her two calves using his new binoculars.
5. I was able to loosen the clamp that held the broken cable in place with a screwdriver.

6. Six hundred thousand Canadian men nearly get a vasectomy each year.

7. Pedro married a woman with a title and a vast fortune in Wales.

8. Dressed in her Kelly Osbourne costume, Penny thought her daughter looked perfect for the Hallowe'en party.

9. The football practices have been organized for players who are not playing with a team in the summertime as a fitness program.

10. Claire arrived with her golden retriever in a summer hat.

GO TO WEB

EXERCISES 9.1, 9.2

Dangling Modifiers

A **dangling modifier** occurs when there is no appropriate word in the sentence for the modifier to apply to. That is, the sentence does not contain a *specific word* or *idea* to which the modifier can sensibly refer. With no appropriate word to refer to, the modifier seems to apply to whatever it's next to, often with ridiculous results:

(After a good night's sleep,) my teachers were impressed by my alertness.
(This sentence seems to say that the teachers had a good night's sleep.)

(Cycling close to the curb,) a minivan swerved and nearly hit me.
(The minivan was cycling close to the curb?)

Dangling modifiers are trickier to fix than misplaced ones; you can't simply move danglers to another spot in the sentence. There are two ways to correct them. One way requires that you remember the following rule.

When a modifier comes at the beginning of a sentence, it modifies the subject of the sentence.

This rule means that you can avoid dangling modifiers by choosing the subjects of your sentences carefully. All you have to do is make the subject an appropriate one for the modifier to apply to. Applying this rule, we can correct both examples simply by changing the sentences' subjects:

(After a good night's sleep,) I impressed my teachers with my alertness.

(Cycling close to the curb,) I was nearly hit by a swerving minivan.

Another way to correct a dangling modifier is to change it into a dependent clause:

After I had a good night's sleep, I impressed my teachers with my alertness.

While I was cycling close to the curb, a minivan swerved and nearly hit me.

Howling piteously, we brought the cat in from the blizzard.

Sometimes a dangling modifier comes at the end of a sentence:

A picnic would be a good idea, not having much money.

Can you correct the preceding sentence? Try it; then look at the suggestions at the bottom of the page.[1]

Here is a summary of the steps to follow in solving modifier problems.

Summary

1. Ask "What does the modifier apply to?"
2. Be sure there is a word or word group in the sentence for the modifier to apply to.
3. Put the modifier as close as possible to the word or word group it applies to.

The sentences in Exercises 9.3 and 9.4 contain dangling modifiers. Correct them by changing the subject of each sentence to one the modifier can appropriately apply to. There is no one "right" way to correct each sentence; our answers are only suggestions.

Exercise 9.3

1. Leaving the theatre, it had gotten dark.

2. Reading a novel, her dog cuddled on Emma's lap.

3. Swerving to miss the cyclist, the tree was hit.

4. Before taking a grammar quiz, dangling modifiers should be reviewed.

5. After finding a four-leaf clover, it went into my diary, to be pressed and dried.

6. Hanging in the Avenida Art Gallery, Frank Buchwitz is the photographer.

---

[1] Here are two suggested corrections:
1. Add a subject: Not having much money, I thought a picnic would be a good idea.
2. Change the dangler to a dependent clause: Since *I didn't have much money*, I thought a picnic would be a good idea.

7. After criticizing both my work and my attitude, I was fired.

8. Not having practiced beforehand, our performance was a dismal failure.

9. Hoping to miss the rush-hour traffic, the car was warmed up and ready to go before 7:00 a.m.

10. Driving down the Trans-Canada Highway, the road kill sickened me.

Exercise 9.4

1. Before vacuuming the floor, the furniture should be dusted.

2. Setting the oven on high, the chicken cooked quickly.

3. Before calling you, *Chicago* had already started.

4. After changing the tire, the jack should be released.

5. The next question is whether to order beer or soft drinks, having decided on pizza.

6. Having completed the beginning, the ending is the second most important part of the essay.

7. Staring into the black night, the wolf's howl terrified me.

8. Pulling out of the driveway, the rose border smelled lovely.

9. While taking a bath, a mouse jumped on the counter.

10. Littering on the road, the Mounties stopped the bicycle campers.

Exercise 9.5

Correct the dangling modifiers in Exercise 9.3 by changing them into dependent clauses.

Exercise 9.6

Correct the dangling modifiers in Exercise 9.4 by changing them into dependent clauses.

Driving through Banff, a moose blocked the road.

Correct the misplaced and dangling modifiers in Exercises 9.7 and 9.8 in any way you choose. The answers on pages 335–36 are only suggestions.

Exercise 9.7

1. Just before leaving Shoppers Drug Mart, my cell phone rang.

2. The mosquitoes became annoying sitting on the back porch.

3. While watching *Royal Canadian Air Farce*, the television suddenly went off.

4. Startled by the telephone, the razor cut Derek's chin.

5. While swinging away from the pitch, a ball hit the batter.

6. At the age of four, my mom taught me to drive a tractor.

7. While sitting outside the Swiss Chalet, my brother drove by and waved.

8. Bryan Adams is acclaimed for his skillfully choreographed performances, his sensitive lyrics, and his original compositions from Vancouver to Halifax.

9. As a college student constantly faced with new assignments, the pressure is sometimes intolerable.

10. Being horribly hung over, the only problem with a free bar is knowing when to quit.

---

1. Marilyn plans to prepare an olive and onion appetizer for her guests soaked in vodka.
2. Above my desk is a photo of my baby hanging by a blue ribbon.
3. As a dog allowed to run freely, we are concerned that it may be run over.
4. She gave the oranges to the customer wrapped in newspaper.
5. Joseph and Karyn miss the smell of the sea being from Nova Scotia.
6. Seth was nearly rejected by every girl in Guelph.
7. Riding home on the subway, my wallet was stolen.
8. Obviously having drunk too much, I drove Biff to his apartment, made him a pot of coffee, and called his mother.
9. While walking to school, a large tree fell and injured three children.
10. I told my mother I had almost attended all my classes this term.

GO TO WEB

EXERCISES 9.3, 9.4

Now test your mastery of modifiers. Correct the errors in this final exercise.

1. The book explains how to get what you want clearly.
2. After three years at Red Deer College, a full-time job sounded exciting.
3. My wedding dress almost fits as well as it did the day we married.

4. As a doctor at Windsor Regional Hospital, the days are long and exhausting.

5. Rotting slowly over the years, the villagers no longer drive cars or bicycles over the bridge.

6. Having tested positive for alcohol, the RIDE patrol arrested our designated driver.

7. Entering the theatre, the music was overwhelming.

8. Thinking about the number of alcohol-related accidents, the police should be encouraged, not condemned, for their increasingly strict enforcement of the impaired-driving laws.

9. Sitting at the table, the steak and lobster were waiting for us.

10. My five-year-old nephew would like to have his dad visit the class as the most popular child in daycare.

10

The Parallelism Principle

When writing about items in a series, you must be sure all the items are **parallel**; that is, they must be written in the same grammatical form.

> Wilderness camping requires us to study maps, check our gear, and hard training.

The items in this series are not parallel. Two of the items are infinitives (*to study,* [*to*] *check*), but the third ends in *-ing* and is a noun phrase. To correct the sentence, you must make all the items in the series take the same grammatical form — either

> Wilderness camping requires us *to study* maps, [*to*] *check* our gear, and [*to*] *train* hard. (all infinitives)

or

> Wilderness camping requires *studying maps*, *checking gear*, and *training hard*. (all noun phrases)

Correct faulty parallelism by writing all items in a series in the same grammatical form.

One way to tell whether all the items in a series are parallel is to write the items in list form, one below the other. That way, you can make sure that all the elements are the same — that they are all single words, or all phrases, or all clauses.

Not Parallel	Parallel
My brother is *messy, rude,* and *an obnoxious person.*	My brother is *messy, rude,* and *obnoxious.*
(This list has two adjectives and a noun phrase.)	(This list has three adjectives.)
I support myself by *delivering pizza, poker,* and *shooting pool.*	I support myself by *delivering pizza, playing poker,* and *shooting pool.*
(This list has two phrases and one single word as objects of the preposition *by*.)	(This list has three phrases as objects of the preposition *by*.)
Jules wants a job that *will interest him, will challenge him,* and *pays well.*	Jules wants a job that *will interest him,* [*will*] *challenge him,* and [*will*] *pay him well.*
(This series of clauses contains two future tense verbs and one present tense verb.)	(All three subordinate clauses contain future tense verbs.)

As you can see, achieving parallelism is partly a matter of developing an ear for the sound of a correct list. Practice and the exercises in this chapter will help. Once you have mastered parallelism in your sentences, you will be ready to develop ideas in parallel sequence and thus to write clear, well-organized prose. Parallelism, far from being a frill, is a fundamental characteristic of good writing.

In the following exercises, correct the sentences where necessary. As you work through these exercises, try to spot faulty parallelism and correct it from the sound of the sentences before you examine them closely for mistakes. Check your answers to each set of ten before going on. Answers begin on page 336.

Exercise 10.1

1. The minimum requirements for survival are food and a roof over your head.

2. I like to run in Waterton Lakes National Park, hike along the Bruce Trail, and swimming in English Bay.

3. Elsie wants both love and to keep her freedom.

4. Carefully and with grace, Bonita descended the stairs in her satin gown.

5. We can either drive to Summerside, or we could fly to Tucson.

6. Haley spent the day watching the whales and visited the tourist shops.

7. I opened my eyes and discovered a cast on my arm, a brace on my leg, and headache.

8. A teacher's main responsibilities are to educate students and ensuring their safety.

9. If I can't be an RCMP officer, I want to be a chef or funny.

10. The best thing I ever did was get married and having children.

GO TO WEB

EXERCISES 10.1, 10.2

Exercise 10.2

1. Our team is quick, strong, and does have skill, despite its losing record.

2. This term, our art class includes drawing, how to paint, and to sculpt.

3. While our guests chatted about the Sarah Harmer concert, Lauren and I made the salad, grilled the hamburgers, and the table was set.

4. The most common ways to catch a cold are to share someone else's food or drink, to be sneezed on, and don't wash your hands.

5. You can invite the boys to the taping of *Gabereau* by phoning them, or you could email them if you'd like.

6. I have to complete three projects for my literature classes: writing a research paper on T.S. Eliot, to read three Canadian novels, and act in a Shakespeare play.

7. Thursday night the Hamilton Chamber of Commerce hosted a dinner attended by trustees, the people in management, and employees.

8. Kwok is a good leader: charismatic, fearless, has strong principles, and speaks articulately.

9. The literal meaning of the word "flog" is "to beat." Figuratively, it means to promote something, selling something aggressively, or sell illegally.

10. Pigs not only require a lot of attention, but caring for them is expensive and you get tired.

GO TO WEB

EXERCISES 10.3, 10.4, 10.5, 10.6

Exercise 10.3

Make the following lists parallel. In each case, there's more than one way to do it because you can make your items parallel with any item in the list. Therefore, your answers may differ from ours. Here's an example:

Incorrect:	stick handling . . . score a goal
Correct:	stick handling . . . goal scoring
Also correct:	handle the stick . . . score a goal

1. Incorrect: Chinese   from Canada   of U.S. origin

   Correct:

2. Incorrect: brushing   to rinse   floss

   Correct:

3. Incorrect: sensitive   responsive   easy to talk to

Correct:

4. Incorrect: original   functional   full of ingenuity

Correct:

5. Incorrect: valueless   without meaning   uninteresting

Correct:

6. Incorrect: hot chocolate   reading a bedtime story   having my back rubbed

Correct:

7. Incorrect: achieve my career goal   finding true love   world traveller

Correct:

8. Incorrect: handsome   wit   kind

Correct:

9. Incorrect: being a pharmacist   work as a doctor   nursing

Correct:

10. Incorrect: efficient   always on time   paying attention to organization

Correct:

Exercise 10.4

Create a sentence for each of the parallel lists you developed in Exercise 10.3.
Example: His stick handling was adequate, but his goal scoring was pitiful.

Exercise 10.5

Correct the faulty parallelism in the following paragraphs. Exercise 10.5 contains ten errors.

One of the frustrating things about living in Canada is that there is little choice about which airline to use when you want to see friends, relatives, or a business trip. As a sales representative for a national company, I often have to travel within Canada, the United States, and Hong Kong. Ever since Air Canada became a monopoly, I have often found myself swearing under my breath when faced with their limited flight options. It's true that a few discount airlines, such as WestJet and Jetsgo, are now available, but their schedules tend to be erratic. For instance, a budget airline might fly from Regina to Calgary only on Tuesday mornings and in the afternoons on Thursdays. But these flights are often delayed because of low priority on the runways.

As a business traveller, I need an airline I can count on because I have appointments to keep and deadlines. Also, budget airlines do not provide cell phones at every seat, and seats wide enough to fit my large frame. Furthermore, in-flight service is hardly existent. I'm used to being offered food, beverages, headsets, and having a choice of reading materials. Budget airlines provide none of these things. Instead, you have to bring your own lunch, and don't forget your magazines and newspapers. I'm already carrying a laptop, a briefcase, not to mention my sample case, and a carry-on! How am I supposed to add lunch to this burden, let alone reading material?

I will, however, give budget airlines credit for one thing: they don't lose my luggage as often as Air Canada does, even when I check in late or forgetting to label one of my bags.

Exercise 10.6

As a test of your ability to correct faulty parallelism, revise the following sentences.

1. Every time I go home to New Brunswick, there are three things I never fail to do: eat lobster, visiting Magnetic Hill, and fiddle playing with my granddad.

2. Maritime music is my favourite because it reminds me of home: it makes me want to dance a jig, and reflecting my Irish roots.

3. This tourism guide to vacations in the Yukon Territory invites us to "Plan [our] holiday to include sleigh races, hunting, and skis."

4. When I located my birth mother in Alaska, I found out she was born in Yellowknife, sending me to New Brunswick, and moving to Juneau after I was born.

5. Today's TV shows feature explicit sexuality, violence, and have characters who are superficial.

6. My dog is smelly, eats anything in sight, and is a loud barker.

7. Most first-year students want to meet new friends, survive financially, and passing their courses—not necessarily in that order.

8. Our current member of Parliament is arrogant, speaks too loudly, is ignorant, and insincere; the one before her was timid, ignorant, and quiet.

9. After my first year as a full-time teacher, I could classify students into three categories: the confident, those who had no confidence, and some did not even care.

10. Recording endless numbers of faulty sentences for his students to correct is a sacrifice of Professor Green's blood, makes him perspire, and causes him to cry.

Exercise 10.7

For each of the topics in this exercise, list five descriptive features in grammatically parallel form. Here is an example for the topic "life guard":

Single Word	Phrase/Clause
bronzed	has a tan
young	is youthful
athletic	flexes muscles
watchful	scans the waves
courageous	dives in after the helpless swimmer

1. your supervisor or colleague

2. a job applicant

3. a teacher or counselor

4. Nelly Furtado or another popular musician

5. a museum or library

Exercise 10.8

Write a piece of correspondence on a topic of your choice or on one your instructor assigns. When you have completed a first or, preferably, a second draft, read it over carefully. While your spell checker may have corrected some of your errors, remember that no program can flag your use of a correctly spelled wrong word: for example, *accept* instead of *except*, *their* when you mean *they're*, or *than* when the meaning requires *then*. Check your sentence structure by reading your work aloud from the last sentence back to the first. Be especially alert for errors in modifiers and parallelism. Here are some topics you may wish to consider for this assignment.

1. Write a letter to your municipal representative recommending an improvement that should be made to your neighbourhood. Indicate the specific ways that the improvement could benefit the community.

2. Write a letter of recommendation to a prospective employer for a friend who has used your name as a character reference. Outline your friend's specific strengths, using examples to support your recommendation.

3. Write a memo to one of your instructors requesting an extended deadline on a current assignment. Provide substantial reasons for your request.

4. Write to one of your former instructors or employers requesting permission to use that person's name as a reference in your current job search. Explain the responsibilities of the position you are applying for and outline what you have been doing since this instructor/employer last supervised you.

5. Write a letter to the dean of student services recommending that the college you attend establish a carpooling program, a day care centre, or another similar program. Indicate specific benefits that such a program could provide.

11

Refining
by Combining

To reinforce what you've learned about sentence structure, try your voice and your hand (preferably with a pencil in it) at sentence combining. You've rid your writing of fragments; you've cast out comma splices; you're riding herd on run-ons. But you may still find that your sentences, although technically correct, are choppy or repetitious. And you may be bored with conveying the same idea in the same old way. Sentence combining will not only confirm your mastery of sentence structure but also enable you to refine and polish your writing.

What is sentence combining? Sometimes called sentence generating or embedding, **sentence combining** is a technique that enables you to avoid a choppy, monotonous style while at the same time producing correct sentences.

Let's look at two short, technically correct sentences that could be combined:

Our paper carrier collects on Fridays.

Our paper carrier delivers the *Winnipeg Free Press* on Saturdays.

There are several ways of combining these two statements into a single sentence.

1. You can connect them with an appropriate linking word, such as *and, but, or, nor,* or *for.*

Our paper carrier delivers the *Winnipeg Free Press* on Saturdays <u>and</u> collects on Fridays.

2. You can change one of the sentences into a subordinate clause.

Our paper carrier, <u>who delivers the *Winnipeg Free Press* on Saturdays</u>, collects on Fridays.

On Fridays, our paper carrier collects for the *Winnipeg Free Press*, <u>which she delivers on Saturdays</u>.

<u>Although she delivers the *Winnipeg Free Press* on Saturdays</u>, our paper carrier collects on Fridays.

3. You can change one of the sentences into a modifying phrase.

(Having collected her money on Friday,) our paper carrier delivers the *Winnipeg Free Press* on Saturday.

On Fridays, our paper carrier collects for the *Winnipeg Free Press*, (a Saturday paper.)

4. Sometimes it is possible to reduce one of your sentences to a single-word modifier.

On Fridays, our paper carrier collects for the (Saturday) *Winnipeg Free Press*.

In sentence combining, you are free to move parts of the sentence around, change words, add or delete words, or make whatever other changes you find necessary. Anything goes, so long as you don't drastically alter the meaning of the base sentences. Remember that your aim in combining sentences is to create effective sentences—not long ones. Clarity is essential, and brevity has force. Here's another example to consider.

Correct but stilted sentences conveying an idea:

David Suzuki is a scientist.
He is Canadian.
He is an advocate for the environment.

Correct and smooth sentences conveying the same idea:

David Suzuki is a Canadian scientist who is an advocate for the environment.

David Suzuki, a Canadian scientist, is an advocate for the environment.

An advocate for the environment, David Suzuki is a Canadian scientist.

The skills that you learn by combining sentences identify you as a perceptive and sensitive writer. They are useful not only in writing and speaking but also in reading, listening, and problem solving.

In the following exercises, try your answers aloud before you write them. (You may want to scan the punctuation information in Unit 4 before you tackle these exercises.)

Exercise 11.1

Combine the following sentences, using the cues in parentheses as your guide to linking the sentences. Answers begin on page 337.

1. Rapunzel pulled up her hair.
   The prince was in the tower. (when)

   _____

   _____

2. The new Thai restaurant is popular.
   Their food is inexpensive. (and)

   _____

   _____

3. I enjoy many aspects of small-town life.
   I miss Vancouver's coffee shops. (but)

   _____

   _____

4. The supervisor hired Roger for the forestry job.
   There were better qualified candidates for the job. (even though)

   _____

   _____

5. Kate Nelligan has never played a major Hollywood role.
   Kate Nelligan is a well-established actor. (although)

   _____

   _____

6. Kim Campbell came to power as prime minister in 1993.
   In 1993, the backlash against feminism was in full swing. (just when)

   _____

   _____

7. The Mermaid Theatre is based in Nova Scotia.
   The Mermaid Theatre is a puppeteer troupe.
   Mermaid Theatre tours Canada and the United States. (that)

   _____

   _____

8. The Calgary Stampede is an exciting event.
   The Calgary Stampede draws thousands of spectators every year. (that)

   _____

   _____

9. The audience obviously enjoyed Paula's peculiar brand of humour.
   The audience frequently interrupted Paula's performance with applause. (-ing)

   _____

   _____

10. Not many Americans choose to spend their holidays in Canada.
    The value of the Canadian dollar makes vacationing in Canada a real bargain for Americans. (even though)

    _____

    _____

Exercise 11.2

Using dependent clause cues (see p. 74) and the transitions listed on page 193, combine the following sentences into longer, more interesting units. *Hint:* Read each set of statements through to the end before you begin to combine them, and try out several variations aloud or in your head before writing down your preferred solution. Then compare your answers with our suggestions on page 338.

1. Fred is not at Castle Frank station.
   We should call the restaurant.
   Fred works at the restaurant.

   _____

   _____

   _____

2. Most people like chocolate.
   Inez does not like chocolate.
   Inez is allergic to chocolate.

   _____

   _____

   _____

3. The two lovers held hands.
   The lovers walked up and down Lovers' Lane.
   It was time for them to part for the night.

   _____

   _____

   _____

4. The clock in the Peace Tower had struck six times.
   We took our skates off.
   We went home.

   _____

   _____

   _____

5. Margot cannot come to class today.
   Margot has a toothache.
   Margot has to see her dentist.

   _____

   _____

   _____

6. Tom Thomson was a famous Canadian painter.
   Tom Thomson was an enthusiastic canoeist.
   Tom Thomson disappeared mysteriously during a canoeing trip.

   _____

   _____

   _____

7. Please serve something besides pickerel.
   Some of us hate pickerel.
   We can still enjoy our dinner.

   _____

   _____

   _____

8. The loon's call startled the tourist.
   The loon's call echoed.
   The loon's call was sudden.
   The tourist ran inside the hotel.

   _____

   _____

   _____

9. Terence can register for classes in the fall.
   He pays his tuition on time.
   He passes all his current courses.

   _____

   _____

   _____

10. The Northern Lights danced across the sky.
    The Northern Lights looked like fireworks.
    The scientific name for the Northern Lights is *aurora borealis*.

_____

_____

_____

Exercise 11.3

This set of exercises is more challenging. In some questions, you may need to combine the given statements into two, three, or more sentences. Again, be sure to read through all the statements in each question to identify related ideas before you begin revising. Turn to page 338 to compare your sentences with our suggested revisions.

1. The Canada Games are held every two years.
   The Canada Games take place in different cities.
   The Canada Games create great national pride.
   The first Canada Games were held in 1967.

2. The Miramichi River is located in northern New Brunswick.
   The Miramichi River is famous for its salmon.
   The Miramichi River attracts many people interested in fly fishing.
   The people come from all over the world.

3. Writer's block is the inability to generate ideas on paper.
   Writer's block can be a paralyzing experience.
   It can be difficult to overcome.
   Freewriting can help overcome writer's block.
   Dictating into a tape recorder can help overcome writer's block.
   Asking questions of your topic can help overcome writer's block.

4. Prince Edward Island is now connected to Nova Scotia.
   It is connected by Confederation Bridge.
   Confederation Bridge is 12.9 km long.
   Prince Edward Island is much more accessible than it used to be.
   Formerly, the island could be reached only by ferry.

5. The World Wide Web is a boon to researchers.
   It provides information rapidly.
   It provides a wealth of information.
   It is accessible 24 hours a day.
   It is important to evaluate the content of a Web site.
   It is important to note the source of a Web site.
   Not all Web sites offer reliable information.

6. *Harry Potter* is a children's book.
   Harry Potter has become an international phenomenon.
   The author of *Harry Potter* even gave a public reading at Toronto's Skydome.
   Harry Potter has sparked the imaginations of millions of young readers.
   Harry Potter has been critically acclaimed.
   Harry Potter has been denounced.
   Some religious conservatives claim *Harry Potter* encourages Satanism.

7. Margaret had several errands to complete.
   She walked to the bank.
   She deposited her pay cheque.
   She walked home.
   She discovered she had left her wallet at the automatic teller machine.
   She returned to the bank.
   She asked a teller about her wallet.
   The teller returned Margaret's wallet.
   Margaret gave the teller a big hug.

8. Cross-cultural communication can be challenging.
   Cultures do not agree on the use of hand gestures, for one thing.
   A polite signal in one culture can be offensive in another culture.
   American President George Bush discovered this.
   He gave the "V" for victory sign with his pointer and middle fingers.
   He was visiting Australia.
   Australians consider the "V" an obscene gesture.

9. The study of a musical instrument teaches many things.
   It teaches self-discipline.
   It teaches listening skills.
   It teaches history.
   The study of a musical instrument offers many rewards.
   It provides entertainment.
   It provides a sense of accomplishment.
   More people could study musical instruments.
   Their quality of life would be enhanced.

10. The maid is on vacation.
    The chef is ill.
    The Rolls is in the shop for maintenance.
    It has been an unbearable day.
    Everything has gone wrong.
    On the financial front, the news is no better.
    My accountant tells me I have to pay taxes.
    I had to pay taxes last year.
    The stock market is down.

My tailor has cancelled this afternoon's appointment.
I'm even out of champagne.
Life is hardly worth living.

After you have combined a number of sentences, you can evaluate your work. Read your sentences aloud. How they sound is important. Test your work against the following six characteristics of successful sentences.

Summary

1. **Meaning:** Have you said what you mean?
2. **Clarity:** Is your sentence clear? Can it be understood on the first reading?
3. **Coherence:** Do the parts of your sentence fit together logically and smoothly?
4. **Emphasis:** Are the most important ideas either at the end or at the beginning of the sentence?
5. **Conciseness:** Is the sentence direct and to the point? Have you cut out all redundant or repetitious words?
6. **Rhythm:** Does the sentence flow smoothly? Are there any interruptions in the development of the key idea(s)? Do the interruptions help to emphasize important points, or do they distract the reader?

If your sentences pass all six tests of successful sentence style, you may be confident that they are both technically correct and pleasing to the ear. No reader could ask for more.

Grammar

12

Choosing
the Correct Verb Form

Errors in grammar are like flies in soup. Most of the time, they don't affect meaning any more than flies affect flavour, but they are distracting and irritating. You must eliminate grammar errors from your writing if you want your readers to pay attention to what you say rather than to how you say it.

Good writers·pay careful attention to verbs. A verb is to a sentence what an engine is to a car; it is the source of power and a frequent cause of trouble.

The Principal Parts of Verbs

Every verb has four forms, called its **principal parts:**

1. The **base** form: used by itself or with *can, may, might, shall, will, could, should, would, must*
2. The **past tense** form: used by itself
3. The **present participle** (the **-ing**) form: used with *am, is, are; was, were; will be; have been*, etc.
4. The **past participle** form: used with *have, has, had; is, are; was, were*, etc.

Here are some examples:

Base	Past Tense	Present Participle	Past Participle
dance	danced	dancing	danced
talk	talked	talking	talked
play	played	playing	played
grab	grabbed	grabbing	grabbed

Errors in grammar are like flies in soup: distracting and irritating.

To use verbs correctly, you must be familiar with their principal parts. Knowing three facts will help you. First, you won't have trouble with the present participle, the *-ing* form. It is always made up of the base form of the verb + *ing*. Second, your dictionary will give you the principal parts of all **irregular** verbs. Look up the base form, and you'll find the past tense and the present and past participles given beside it, usually in parentheses. For example, if you look up "sing" in your dictionary, you will find *sang* (past tense), *sung* (past participle), and *singing* (present participle) listed immediately after the verb itself. If the past tense and past participle are not given, the verb is **regular.** So, third, you need to know how to form the past tense and the past participle of regular verbs: add *-ed* to the base form. The examples listed above — *dance, talk, play, grab* — are all regular verbs.

Unfortunately, many of the most common English verbs are irregular. Their past tenses and past participles are formed in unpredictable ways. The verbs in the list that follows are used so often that it is worth your time to memorize their principal parts. (We have not included the *-ing* form because, as we have noted above, it never causes any difficulty.)

The Principal Parts of Irregular Verbs

Base (Use with *can, may, might, shall, will, could, would, should, must*)	Past Tense	Past Participle (Use with *have, has, had; is, are; was, were*)
awake	awoke/awaked	awaked/awoken
be (am, is)	was/were	been
bear	bore	borne
beat	beat	beaten
become	became	become
begin	began	begun
bid (offer to pay)	bid	bid
bid (say, command)	bid/bade	bid/bidden
bite	bit	bitten
bleed	bled	bled
blow	blew	blown
break	broke	broken
bring	brought (*not* brang)	brought (*not* brung)
broadcast	broadcast	broadcast
build	built	built
burst	burst	burst
buy	bought	bought
catch	caught	caught
choose	chose	chosen
come	came	come
cost	cost	cost
cut	cut	cut
deal	dealt	dealt
dig	dug	dug
dive	dived/dove	dived
do	did (*not* done)	done
draw	drew	drawn
dream	dreamed/dreamt	dreamed/dreamt
drink	drank (*not* drunk)	drunk
eat	ate	eaten
fall	fell	fallen
feed	fed	fed

Base (Use with *can, may, might, shall, will, could, would, should, must*)	Past Tense	Past Participle (Use with *have, has, had; is, are; was, were*)
feel	felt	felt
fight	fought	fought
find	found	found
fling	flung	flung
fly	flew	flown
forget	forgot	forgotten/forgot
forgive	forgave	forgiven
freeze	froze	frozen
get	got	got/gotten
give	gave	given
go	went	gone (*not* went)
grow	grew	grown
hang (suspend)	hung	hung
hang (put to death)	hanged	hanged
have	had	had
hear	heard	heard
hide	hid	hidden
hit	hit	hit
hold	held	held
hurt	hurt	hurt
keep	kept	kept
know	knew	known
lay (to put or place)	laid	laid
lead	led	led
leave	left	left
lend	lent (*not* loaned)	lent (*not* loaned)
lie (to recline)	lay	lain (*not* layed)
light	lit/lighted	lit/lighted
lose	lost	lost
mean	meant	meant
meet	met	met
pay	paid	paid
raise (to lift up, increase, bring up)	raised	raised
ride	rode	ridden
ring	rang	rung

Base (Use with *can, may, might, shall, will, could, would, should, must*)	**Past Tense**	**Past Participle** (Use with *have, has, had; is, are; was, were*)
rise	rose	risen
run	ran	run
say	said	said
see	saw (*not* seen)	seen
sell	sold	sold
set (put or place)	set	set
shake	shook	shaken (*not* shook)
shine	shone	shone
sing	sang	sung
sink	sank	sunk
sit	sat	sat
sleep	slept	slept
slide	slid	slid
speak	spoke	spoken
speed	sped	sped
steal	stole	stolen
stick	stuck	stuck
strike (hit)	struck	struck
strike (affect)	struck	stricken
swear	swore	sworn
swim	swam	swum
swing	swung (*not* swang)	swung
take	took	taken
teach	taught	taught
tear	tore	torn
tell	told	told
think	thought	thought
throw	threw	thrown
wake	woke/waked	waked/woken
wear	wore	worn
weave	wove	woven
win	won	won
wind	wound	wound
wring	wrung	wrung
write	wrote	written

Exercise 12.1

Fill in each blank with the correct form (past tense or past participle) of the verb shown to the left of the sentence. Do not add or remove helping verbs. Answers begin on page 339.

1. bite   A rattlesnake _____ Joe on our last hike, so naturally all of us were worried about being _____ as we headed toward the trail.

2. eat   Alison had never _____ lobster until she had a lobster supper in Prince Edward Island, where she _____ three lobsters at one sitting.

3. forgive   Anthony's wife, Francesca, told him that she _____ him for forgetting their anniversary, but deep in his heart he knew he would never really be_____.

4. hide   My mom _____ chocolate bunnies and eggs throughout the house on Easter morning, and we spent the rest of the day trying to discover where they were _____.

5. write   I _____ a novel when I was in college, but I have not _____ anything since.

6. lie   The treasure still _____ at the bottom of an old mine shaft, where it had _____ for nearly 300 years.

7. tell   We could have _____ her the truth, but that wasn't very interesting, so we _____ her that we were Mounties.

8. shake   Tremors _____ the little town for days after it had been _____ by the earthquake.

9. lay   Biff _____ his weapons on the pile where the other bikers had _____ theirs.

10. strike   Sir Gawain _____ a mightly blow that would have killed an ordinary man, but the Green Knight, who had been _____ by many such blows, didn't even flinch.

GO TO WEB

EXERCISES 12.1, 12.2

Exercise 12.2

Find and correct the verb errors in the following sentences.

1. I would have came on time if I had knew you were serving dinner.

2. The dealer at Casino Niagara dealed me a lousy hand, but I winned anyway.

3. My aunt had already gave her daughter the family home; in her will, she also leaved her a car, several valuable paintings, and her jewellery.

4. The front doorbell rung twice; you could have cutted the tension with a knife.

5. Margie could have drank another bottle of beer if she hadn't eat the rest of the pizza.

6. Jared could never have got as far north as Edmonton if he hadn't meet a friendly truck driver in Lethbridge.

7. At the Camp Berwick reunion, we sung all the old camp songs, rose our mugs of cocoa to toast absent friends, and sweared eternal friendship by the campfire.

8. When I was four or five, my grandfather first told me the story of his journey from Nigeria to Canada, many details of which have sticked in my memory.

9. Near the end of term, it occurred to us that if only we had went to class and did the homework, we could probably have passed the course.

10. Capital punishment is no longer practise in Canada, but in some states of the U.S., you can be hung if you have broke certain laws.

GO TO WEB

EXERCISES 12.3, 12.4

Exercise 12.3

As a final test of your mastery of verb forms, correct the 25 errors in this exercise.

1. The news of the first prisoner's escape from Kingston had just been broadcasted when the second prisoner digged his way out from beneath the prison walls and run to the nearest bus station.

2. When her balloon bursted, the little girl throwed a temper tantrum, and laid down on the sidewalk, kicking and screaming.

3. Before the Mounties brang order to the West and the new settlements become civilized, lynch mobs regularly hanged wrongdoers without a trial.

4. If she had only knew about the secret tunnel, Isabel would not have flinged herself off the balcony and broke her leg.

5. I had a terrible evening. Every time I laid down, either the telephone or the doorbell rang.

6. Lawren Harris never losed the sense of wonder that rose his paintings above the level of the ordinary and shown us the awesomeness of the Canadian landscape.

7. The first time I seen him, Randy stealed my heart; the second time I seen him, he teared it in two.

8. When I got to the buoy, I knew that I had swam too far, so I catched hold of the rope with one hand and seeked help.

9. After they had finished breakfast, the team was still hungry. Unfortunately, they had already eat up their meal allowance for the whole day.

10. Mark was so excited that he run to the top of the hill, swung himself up into the tree, and wokened the whole neighbourhood with his joyful shouting.

13

Mastering Subject–Verb Agreement

One of the most common grammatical errors is failure to make the subject and the verb in a sentence agree with each other. Here is the rule for subject–verb agreement.

> Singular subjects take singular verbs.
> Plural subjects take plural verbs.

Singular and Plural

Here's an example of the singular and plural forms of a regular verb in the present tense:

	Singular	**Plural**
first person	I work	we work
second person	you work	you work
third person	*she (he, it, one, the student) works	*they (the students) work

From this example, you can figure out what **person** means. We have asterisked the third-person singular and plural forms of the verb because they are the only forms likely to cause you trouble. In the third person, the endings of verbs and their subjects do not match. Singular verbs end in *s* (*works*), but singular subjects do not (*student*). Plural subjects regularly end in *s* (*students*), but plural verbs do not (*work*). When you are using a regular verb in the third person, remember that either the subject or the verb ends in *s*, but not both.

Singular words concern one person or thing:

The <u>phone</u> <u>rings</u>. <u>Alun</u> <u>sleeps</u>.

Plural words (and multiple subjects) concern more than one person or thing:

The <u>phones</u> <u>ring</u>. The <u>boys</u> <u>sleep</u>. <u>Alun and Saieed</u> <u>snore</u>.

The rule governing subject–verb agreement will cause you no difficulty so long as you make sure that the word the verb agrees with is really the subject of the sentence. To see how problems can arise, look at this example:

One of the <u>dogs</u> are eating the garbage.

The writer of this sentence forgot that the subject of a sentence is never in a prepositional phrase. The verb needs to be changed to agree with the true subject, *One:*

<u>One</u> ~~of the dogs~~ <u>is eating</u> the garbage.

If you're careful about identifying the subject of your sentence, you'll have no difficulty with subject–verb agreement. To sharpen your subject-finding ability, review Chapter 6, "Cracking the Sentence Code." Then do the following exercises.

Exercise 13.1

Underline the subject in each sentence. Answers begin on page 340.

1. The ringing of the bell disturbed the lighthouse keeper's sleep.
2. Does anyone know how to carve a turkey?
3. According to my typing teacher, keyboarding has become the fourth critical life skill.
4. Since his holiday in France, many of Howard's clothes have become too tight.
5. Where in the world have you been for the last two days?
6. Sailing is an expensive sport to pursue, whether on Lake Ontario, Okanagan Lake, or Howe Sound.
7. Surprised by the party in her honour, Susan blushed and giggled.
8. Among the many menu choices are several delicious Cantonese dishes.
9. The results of our experiment were questioned by the scientists at the National Research Council.
10. Dreams of wealth, prestige, and fame motivate young entrepreneurs.

Rewrite each of the following sentences, using the alternative beginning shown. For example:

My <u>roommate</u> <u>hates</u> her organic chemistry course.
My <u>roommates</u> <u>hate</u> their organic chemistry course.

1. The river empties into Hudson's Bay.

   The rivers

2. A new Canadian appreciates meeting other people who share the same cultural background.

   New Canadians

3. My grandfather gives me peppermint candies whenever I visit him in the nursing home.

   My grandparents

4. The latest album from The Tragically Hip is selling quickly.

   The latest albums

5. The sailors miss Canadian bacon and maple syrup.

   The sailor

6. Bald eagles are rare birds.

   The bald eagle

7. They talk constantly during a movie.

   She

8. Each province sends a delegate to the conference.

   All

9. Our supervisor wants us to take a more positive approach to customer service.

Our supervisors

10. Neither of the latecomers was able to talk her teacher into letting her write the exam.

Both the latecomers

GO TO WEB

EXERCISES 13.1, 13.2

So far, so good. You can find the subject, even when it's hiding on the far side of the verb or buried under a load of prepositional phrases. You can match up singular subjects with singular verbs and plural subjects with plural verbs. Now let's take a look at a few of the complications that make subject–verb agreement such a disagreeable problem.

Six Special Cases

Some subjects are tricky. They look singular but are actually plural, or they look plural when they're really singular. There are six kinds of these slippery subjects, all of them common and all of them likely to trip up the unwary writer.

1. Multiple subjects joined by *or; either...or; neither...nor;* or *not ...but.*

Most multiple subjects we've dealt with so far have been joined by *and* and have required plural verbs, so agreement hasn't been a problem. But watch out when the two or more elements of a compound subject are joined by *or; either...or; neither...nor;* or *not...but.* In these cases, the verb agrees in number with the nearest subject. That is, if the subject closest to the verb is singular, the verb will be singular; if the subject closest to the verb is plural, the verb must be plural too.

Neither the <u>federal government</u> nor the <u>provinces</u> <u>seem</u> to care much about pollution.

Neither the <u>provinces</u> nor the <u>federal government</u> <u>seems</u> to care much about pollution.

Exercise 13.3

1. Neither Bradley nor Brandon ever (answer answers) the phone.
2. For a general arts program, either of the colleges you are interested in (is are) a good choice.
3. Neither threats nor bribery (influence influences) my decisions.
4. Anna claims that neither she nor her friends (recall recalls) the events of last night.
5. Neither the beaver nor the maple leaf adequately (represent represents) the Canadian spirit.
6. According to the camp rules, either two nurses or a life guard (supervise supervises) the beach at all times.
7. At the Canadian National Exhibition, not the auctions but the midway (interest interests) me most.
8. Either the tenant or the co-tenants (sign signs) the lease.
9. Not the four-star restaurants but the luxurious day spa (is are) responsible for the hotel's fine reputation.
10. Measles, mumps, or the flu seriously (endanger endangers) elderly patients.

2. Subjects that look multiple but really aren't.

Don't be fooled by phrases beginning with words such as *with, like, as well as, together with, in addition to,* and *including.* These prepositional phrases are NOT part of the subject of the sentence. Since they do not affect the verb, you can mentally cross them out.

My math teacher, ~~as well as my counsellor,~~ has advised me to change my major.

Two people were involved in the advising; nevertheless, the subject (math <u>teacher</u>) is singular, so the verb must be singular (<u>has advised</u>).

Hard cheeses, ~~in addition to milk,~~ are good sources of calcium.

If you mentally cross out the phrase "in addition to milk" you can easily see that the verb (<u>are</u>) must be plural to agree with the plural subject (<u>cheeses</u>).

Exercise 13.4

Circle the correct verb.

1. Anyone who thinks this course is easy (isn't aren't) working hard enough.
2. John Crosbie, like many Newfoundlanders, (is are) proud of his provincial identity.
3. A vacuum cleaner with hand tools (cost costs) twice as much as one without accessories.
4. The new gun control legislation, including regulations regarding firearm registration, (irritate irritates) many gun owners.
5. Leon's fiancée, in cooperation with his friends, (keep keeps) close track of his activities now that he's out of jail.
6. Anger, as well as sadness, (occur, occurs) during the grieving process.
7. Our itinerary, including a whirlwind tour of Casa Loma and the CN Tower, (promise promises) to be exhausting.
8. Together with several other indicators, the appearance of an unusual number of tornadoes this year (demonstrate demonstrates) the impact of global warming.
9. The folk songs of Stan Rogers, along with his radio opera, (form forms) a Canadian music legacy.
10. Naomi Klein's *Globe and Mail* columns, in addition to her book *No Logo*, (offer offers) thought-provoking criticisms of our consumer culture.

---

3. Words ending in *-one*, *-thing*, or *-body*.

When used as subjects, the words below are always singular. They require singular verbs.

anyone	anything	anybody
everyone	everything	everybody
no one	nothing	nobody
someone	something	somebody

The last part of the pronoun subject is the tip-off here: every*one*, any*thing*, no*body*. If you focus on the last syllable, you'll remember to use a singular verb with these subjects. Usually, these words cause trouble only when modifiers appear between them and their verbs. For example, you would never write "Everyone are here." The trouble starts when you sandwich a group of words in between the subject and the verb. You might, if you weren't careful, write this: "Everyone involved in implementing the company's new policies and procedures are here." The meaning is plural: several people are present. But the subject (every*one*) is singular, so the verb must be *is*.

Exercise 13.5

Circle the correct verb.

1. Once everyone (finish finishes) eating, the servers will bring coffee and tea.
2. Something about the way he moves (make makes) me uncomfortable.
3. Although Giselle is not tall, everybody (find finds) her attractive.
4. After the summer holidays, no one (visit visits) the provincial park.
5. I keep hearing the doorbell; (is are) there someone outside?.
6. In the ideal world, nothing awkward or embarrassing ever (happen happens) between friends.
7. After midnight, nobody (dare dares) lift the latch.
8. The RCMP constable plans to question anyone who (live lives) within 5 km of the crime scene.
9. I like to learn about new time management methods; I'll try anything that (save saves) time.
10. Nothing human (is are) so inevitable as error.

4. *Each (of), either (of), neither (of).*

Used as subjects, these words take singular verbs. (Remember, the subject is never in a prepositional phrase.)

Either <u>is</u> suitable for the job.

<u>Each</u> of us <u>wants</u> the last doughnut.

<u>Neither</u> of the lacrosse teams <u>has</u> a coach.

Exercise 13.6

Circle the correct verb.

1. Neither of us (want wants) to drive.
2. Each of the solutions (offer offers) unique advantages.
3. Either of these ties (match matches) your suit.
4. Each of the cities (is are) well equipped to host the hockey tournament.
5. During the round table discussions, each of the guests (speak speaks) at least twice.
6. According to the results of a viewer survey, neither Lloyd Robertson nor Peter Mansbridge (wear wears) attractive ties.
7. If either of the twins (wake up wakes up), please phone me at the theatre.
8. Neither of these nominees (has served have served) on an advisory committee.
9. Neither of our cars (run runs) on diesel fuel.
10. I know that every one of my relatives (influence influences) my behaviour in different ways.

5. Collective nouns.

A collective noun is a word naming a group. Some examples are *band, gang, orchestra, company, class, committee, team, crowd, public, family, audience, group,* and *majority.* When you are referring to the group acting as a unit, use a singular verb. When you are referring to the members of the group acting individually, use a plural verb.

The <u>committee</u> <u>meets</u> the first Tuesday of every month. (Here *committee* refers to the group acting as a whole.)

The <u>committee</u> <u>are</u> voting on the resolution. (The separate members of the committee are acting individually.)

Exercise 13.7

Circle the correct verb.

1. The public (love loves) any political scandal involving adultery, blackmail, or bribery.
2. The team (is are) looking forward to spending some time with their families.

3. The orchestra (is scheduled are scheduled) to play three more cities before the end of their tour.
4. When the board of governors (argue argues) among themselves, their raised voices are clearly audible in the hall.
5. After breakfast, the family (brush brushes) their teeth.
6. After brushing their teeth, the family (leave leaves) for work.
7. Either of the twins (sing sings) well enough to lead.
8. The soccer team (play plays) best on artificial turf.
9. In general, the Canadian public (prefer prefers) sports to theatre.
10. The town's first fire brigade (is are) commemorated in the local museum.

6. Units of money, time, mass, length, and distance.

These expressions require singular verbs.

Twelve dollars is too much to pay for a hamburger.

Three hours passes quickly on a cruise.

Three kilograms of chicken is enough for dinner.

Ten kilometres is the length of the Terry Fox Run.

Exercise 13.8

Circle the correct verb.

1. Sixty dollars (seem seems) an extravagant price for a bottle of wine.
2. Seven metres of cable (hold holds) the pole erect.
3. Twenty kilograms (is are) a lot of weight to lose, even on the grapefruit diet.
4. An hour at the front desk really (drag drags) when I work the night shift.
5. During a wrestling match, the audience (hurl hurls) insults at one another.
6. Two inches (equal equals) five centimetres.
7. According to my mother's recipe for Beef Wellington, 2 kg of beef (take takes) about an hour and a half to cook.
8. The pawnbroker insisted that fifteen dollars for the ring (was were) a bargain.

9. When you're waiting for a search plane, ten minutes (crawl crawls) by like two hours.
10. Thirty minutes of aerobic activity, combined with strength training exercises three times a week, (is are) the basis of a healthy lifestyle.

In Exercises 13.9 and 13.10, correct the errors in subject–verb agreement. Check your answers to each exercise before going on.

Exercise 13.9

1. No one who care about the environment will use plastic or Styrofoam cups.
2. After each of the couples have paid the fees, the mass wedding can begin.
3. As the mayor passed the crowd that were gathered in front of the bank, he raised his hand and waved.
4. There is no good reasons for rejecting this application.
5. The amount of federal government resources directed towards job creation are enormous.
6. The rust problem, not the broken water pump or the faulty brakes, were what made me decide to sell the car.
7. Did you interview everybody who live within 2 km of the tar ponds?
8. Val Grabove, together with two or three part-time instructors, are planning to offer a course in winter wilderness camping.
9. The scarcity of jobs in small communities cause widespread depression.
10. Seven years are a long time to spend in a jail cell.

Exercise 13.10

There are ten errors in this paragraph. Can you find and correct them?

Although most jobs now requires the use of computers, the digital revolution does not seem to be improving our overall quality of life. Since a desktop computer, complete with headphones for voice-activated functions, exist in every office, work should be becoming simpler. However, neither increased efficiency nor improved employee morale have resulted from computer use. Rather, each worker's tasks has become more complex. In the past, for example, an invoice or two purchase orders was necessary to complete a request for supplies. The process, including online confirmation, now require five separate documents. The obvious results of this complication is frustration and curses. Everybody, including the supervisors, are fed up with the extra workload. When our division implement a new computer system next month, I expect at least two of my coworkers to quit. Fifteen hours of training are needed to learn the new system, and that is more time than any of us have to waste.

Exercise 13.11

Correct the following passage, which contains ten errors in subject–verb agreement.

Canada's national luge team practise at the luge track in Calgary, Alberta. Luge, like bobsledding, are a relatively new sport for most Canadians. Because there is few places in the world where an athlete can train for the luge, the number of lugers in the world, let alone in our country, remain small. Membership in this elite group of athletes require nerves of titanium. Eighty kilometres per hour are the beginning speed on a luge track. Moreover, not the luge's speed, which can reach 150 kilometres per hour, but the layout of the track present the real breathtaking challenge of the sport. Anyone who experience vertigo should steer clear of the luge's twisting track. One of the curves in the Calgary track, called the "Kriesel," require lugers to endure G forces greater than 4Gs. Only serious daredevils, such as jet pilots or skydivers, qualifies for this demanding sport.

Exercise 13.12

Complete the sentences in the exercises below using present-tense verbs. After you complete each set, check the answer section to see whether your verbs should be singular or plural.

1. Anyone with red hair

2. Not the instructor but the students

3. A herd of cattle

4. Each of the bagpipers

5. Two hours

6. Nobody outside the gate

7. Neither the farmers nor the banker

8. The entire audience, including the star's parents,

9. A chorus of voices

10. Someone other than the author

GO TO WEB

EXERCISES 13.3, 13.4

Exercise 13.13

Write your own sentences, choosing your subjects as indicated and using present-tense verbs.

1. Use a unit of distance (e.g., thirty kilometres) as your subject.

2. Use a multiple subject.

3. Use *nobody* as your subject.

4. Use *anything* as your subject.

5. Use *either...or.*

6. Use a dollar value as a subject.

7. Use *neither...nor.*

8. Use *group* as a singular subject.

9. Use *group* as a plural subject.

10. Use *each of.*

GO TO WEB

EXERCISES 13.5, 13.6

The box below contains a summary of the rules governing subject–verb agreement. Review them carefully before you try the mastery test for this chapter.

Summary

1. Subjects and verbs must agree: both must be singular, or both must be plural.
2. Subjects joined by *and* are always plural.
3. When subjects are joined by *or; either...or; neither...nor;* or *not...but,* the verb agrees with the subject that is closest to it.
4. The subject is never in a prepositional phrase. Ignore phrases beginning with *as well as, including, in addition to, like, together with,* etc., when deciding whether to use a singular or plural verb.
5. Pronouns ending *in -one, -thing,* or *-body* are singular and require singular verbs.
6. Used as subjects, *each, either,* and *neither* require singular verbs.
7. Collective nouns are usually singular.
8. Units of money, time, mass, length, and distance are always singular.

Exercise 13.14

As a final check of your mastery of subject–verb agreement, correct the following sentences.

1. According to the survey, not environmental issues but child poverty are the priority of most Canadians.

2. Either Yan's mother or her brother iron her clothes.

3. Anyone allergic to shellfish tempt fate by sampling the seafood chowder.

4. Appearing on *Open Mike* tonight is Michael Burgess, the former star of *Les Misérables*, and Natalie McMaster, the Cape Breton fiddler.

5. If you default on this loan, neither the bank nor your other creditors owes you any back interest.

6. Each of the experts agree that the mysterious circles in the corn field resemble the rings of Saturn.

7. Oranges, lemons, and olive oil remind Carmen of her home on the Mediterranean Sea.

8. Even if one or two patients protest, everybody need to provide a blood sample.

9. A flock of Canada geese fly overhead most mornings.

10. Anne Michaels, along with Margaret Atwood and Carol Shields, have won international recognition for her books.

14

Keeping Your Tenses Consistent

Verbs are time markers. Changes in tense express changes in time: past, present, or future.

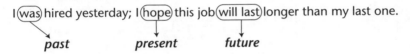

I ⟨was⟩ hired yesterday; I ⟨hope⟩ this job ⟨will last⟩ longer than my last one.

    past   *present*   *future*

Sometimes, as in the sentence above, it is necessary to use several different tenses in a single sentence to get the meaning across. But most of the time, whether you're writing a sentence or a paragraph, you use one tense throughout. Normally, you choose either the past or the present tense, depending on the nature of your topic. (Few paragraphs are written completely in the future tense.) Here is the rule to follow.

Don't change tense unless meaning requires it.

Readers like and expect consistency. If you begin a sentence with "I argued, protested, and even attempted an appeal to his masculine pride," the reader will tune in to the past tense verbs and expect any other verbs in the sentence to be in the past tense too. So, if you finish the sentence with "... but he looks at me with those big blue eyes and gets me to pay for dinner," your readers will be jolted abruptly out of one time frame into another. This sort of jolting is uncomfortable, and readers don't like it.

Shifting tenses is like shifting gears: it should be done smoothly and when necessary—never abruptly, out of carelessness, or on a whim. Avoid causing verbal whiplash; keep your tenses consistent.

Problem:	Minnie goes into the garage and tried to start the car.
Solution 1:	Minnie went into the garage and tried to start the car.
Solution 2:	Minnie goes into the garage and tries to start the car.

Problem:	Tony delayed until the last possible minute, but then he begins to write his paper. When he gets halfway through, he decided to change his topic.
Solution 1:	Tony delayed until the last possible minute, but then he began to write his paper. When he got halfway through, he decided to change his topic.
Solution 2:	Tony delays until the last possible minute, but then he begins to write his paper. When he gets halfway through, he decides to change his topic.

In the following exercises, most of the sentences contain unnecessary tense shifts. Use the first verb in each sentence as your time marker, and change the tense(s) of the other verb(s) to agree with it. Answers begin on page 342.

Exercise 14.1

1. Steve Nash plays for the Dallas Mavericks and was arguably Canada's best basketball player.

2. I used to listen to Peter Gzowski on CBC Radio before I go to my afternoon classes at the college.

3. James gets up at six o'clock and went to work in an office downtown.

4. I have been very unhappy since my cat died, but I still get up every morning and ate breakfast.

5. William went to Winnipeg for his vacation every summer and stays with his best friend, Omar.

6. I stayed up reading most of the night until I finally fell asleep.

7. George and Martha are best friends who loved to go hiking together in the mountains on warm, sunny days.

8. We were very excited when the Canadian men's hockey team wins the gold medal at the 2002 Olympic games in Salt Lake City.

9. Ben and Camille sat in their basement night after night until they completed their grammar exercises.

10. Nabil still likes to play cricket with his friends from Canada even though most of them didn't understand any of the rules.

Exercise 14.2

1. Jay went to the movies every night while his friends stay at home and study.

2. International studies consistently rank Canada as one of the best places in the world to have lived.

3. Jean knew his day was off to a bad start when he discovered the cat had thrown up in his shoe.

4. Many students the reporter interviewed liked to listen to country music, but few are aware of great singers and songwriters from Canada's past, such as Hank Snow and Gene MacLellan.

5. I knew I would be late for my meeting in Vancouver when a snowstorm delays my flight from Calgary.

6. Marcella visited her grandmother every week even though she has to travel more than two hours to reach the nursing home.

7. My friends and I think most Canadian politicians serving in parliament today were greedy and dishonest.

8. Kim couldn't remember where she had put her passport and had to search through all of her luggage to find it.

9. When the new neighbours refused to turn down the music at their party, my dad calls the police.

10. After the movie *Titanic* was released, thousands of tourists are coming to Halifax to visit a memorial to the victims of this famous maritime disaster.

Exercise 14.3

Using the italicized verb as your time marker, find and correct the 15 faulty shifts in tense in the paragraph that follows.

I sometimes think that life *was* much simpler forty or fifty years ago. For example, it seemed to me that food was a lot less complicated. There are simply not as many nutritional concerns for us to worry about every day. We just drank our milk and eat our vegetables; we don't bother with reading low-fat cookbooks and counting every calorie. Eating meat is not a political statement, and dessert was a treat to be enjoyed, not a substance you have to analyze. Also, we had known nothing about Mad Cow Disease, so we cooked our burgers medium-rare and were gobbling them without anxiety. Without worrying about pesticides, we bought plenty of farm-fresh produce when it is in season. Because genetically modified foods were developed much later, we thought that Frankenfood is the stuff of science fiction, not standard grocery fare. We never imagined that even basic foods, such as milk, will become controversial. Neither did we realize that scientists will one day have been growing new varieties of grain in test tubes. Certainly, we cannot have predicted the mammoth health food industry that would develop. I remember that, when I was a youngster, "granola" was an exotic food, wheat germ sounds like a contagious disease, and the word "organic" applies to a branch of chemistry.

GO TO WEB

EXERCISE 14.1

Exercise 14.4

Test your mastery of tense consistency by correcting the following sentences. Use the first verb in the sentence as your tense (time) marker.

1. The psychiatrist was convinced that the cause of most of her patients' problems is low self-esteem.

2. Before he goes to school every morning, Timothy delivered copies of the *Charlottetown Guardian* to everybody in his neighbourhood.

3. Mario was surprised to learn that the Montreal Canadiens is the last Canadian team to win the Stanley Cup.

4. When I wake up on Monday mornings, the first thing I have to do was put out the garbage.

5. How long a minute is depends on which side of the bathroom door you happened to be on.

6. The Queen attracts huge crowds of people every time she visited Canada.

7. Andrea lost the notes she was taking for her history paper when a virus wipes out her hard drive.

8. Whenever I have a cold, my mother will make me chicken noodle soup.

9. Many Americans do not know that Jim Carrey, Martin Short, Mike Myers, and a number of other successful comedians were from Canada.

10. I wonder why it is that when you dialed a wrong number, you never get a busy signal.

15

Choosing the Correct Pronoun Form

After verbs, pronouns are the class of words most likely to cause problems for writers. In this chapter and the two following, we will look at the three aspects of pronoun usage that can trip you up if you're not careful: pronoun **form**, **agreement**, and **consistency**. We will also consider the special problems of usage that can lead to sexist language.

English has eight different kinds of pronouns, but only three kinds are potentially troublesome for the writer:

personal pronouns	I, we, she, they, etc.
relative pronouns	who, which, that, etc.
indefinite pronouns	any, somebody, none, each, etc.

(You will find a complete list of these pronouns on page 317.)

The first thing you need to do is be sure you are using correct pronoun forms. Look at these examples of incorrect pronoun usage:

Her and me offered to pick up a video.
This conversation is just between you and I.

How do you know which form of a pronoun to use? The answer depends on the pronoun's place and function in your sentence.

There are two forms of personal pronouns. One is used for subjects, and one is used for objects. Pronoun errors occur when you confuse the two. In Chapter 6, you learned to identify the subject of a sentence. Keep that information in mind as you learn the following basic rule.

When the subject of a sentence is (or is referred to by) a pronoun, that pronoun must be in **subject form**; otherwise, use the **object form**.

Subject Pronouns

Singular	Plural
I	we
you	you
he, she, it, one	they

She and *I* decided to rent a video.
(The pronouns are the subject of the sentence.)

The most likely candidate for re-election is *she*.
(The pronoun refers to the subject of the sentence, "candidate.")

The only local contestants in the national competition were *they*.
(The pronoun refers to the subject of the sentence, "contestants.")

We discriminating food critics rarely award a restaurant five stars.
(The pronoun refers to the subject of the sentence, "critics.")

Object Pronouns

Singular	Plural
me	us
you	you
him, her, it, one	them

Between you and *me*, I think Biff is cheating again.
("Me" is not the subject of the sentence; it is one of the objects of the preposition "between.")

Clara invited *him* and *me* to the birthday party.
("Him" and "me"are not the subject of the verb "invited"; Clara is, so the pronouns must be in object form.)

The <u>islanders</u> <u>are</u> often wary of *us* mainlanders.
("Us" does not refer to the subject of the sentence, "islanders"; it refers to "mainlanders," the object of the preposition "of.")

Be especially careful with pronouns in multiple subjects or following prepositions. If you remember the following two rules, you'll be able to eliminate most potential errors in pronoun form.

1. A pronoun that is part of a multiple subject is *always* in subject form.
2. A pronoun that comes after a preposition is *always* in object form.

She and *I* <u>have</u> season's tickets.
(The pronouns are used as a multiple subject.)

We are counting on *you* and *him* to complete the project.
(The pronouns follow the preposition "on.")

I can't believe Chandra would break up with me after she and I got matching tattoos and navel rings.

Here's a practically foolproof way for native English speakers to tell which pronoun form is needed. (ESL speakers, unfortunately, must rely on memorizing the rules.) When the sentence contains a pair of pronouns, mentally check it with one pronoun at a time. Applying this technique to the first example above, you get "*She* has tickets" and "*I* have tickets," both of which sound right and are correct. In the second sentence, if you try the pronouns separately, you get "We are counting on *you*" and "We are counting on *him*." Again, you know by the sound that these are the correct forms. You would never say "*Her* had tickets," or "*Me* had tickets," or "We are counting on *he*." If you deal with paired pronouns one at a time, you are unlikely to choose the wrong form.

Exercise 15.1

Choose the correct pronouns from the words given in parentheses. Answers begin on page 344.

1. In the end, both of (we us) were disappointed.
2. As a result of her persistence, the team leader nominated (her she) for a special company award.
3. Years ago, (him he) and his uncle ran a hotel on the shore of Lake Superior.
4. Grandmother knit new angora sweaters for my cousin and (I me).
5. I can get along with Adam and Janna, but I can't work with (they them).
6. (We Us) skiers like to see a snowstorm arrive in the Rockies.
7. Jacob was afraid the instructor wouldn't believe (he him) when he said that neither of (we us) had checked our answers against the textbook.
8. When Francesca gets here, (she her) and (I me) are planning to go shopping at the West Edmonton Mall.
9. It is difficult to choose between (she her) and (he him).
10. If the managers approve the recommendation (we us) team leaders have made, (we us) and (they them) will exchange shifts.

Exercise 15.2

Correct the errors in pronoun form in the following sentences.

1. Him and George take the same photography class.

2. Neither Jody nor me managed to get to the bank before it closed.

3. For once, there was no one in front of Bob and I in the bookstore line-up.

4. Will Shirley and him visit the Arctic again next summer?

5. We want you and she to correct the errors the interns made on the spreadsheet.

6. Sheldon and me are going to be your trainers for the next month.

7. I think Franz and her would make a good team.

8. If the decision were up to you and I, we'd get the new office furniture.

9. Us and our partners agreed to expand, but only if it was them who raised the extra capital.

10. One thing is clear to we parents: those who say they sleep like a baby do not have one.

Choosing the correct pronoun form is more than just a matter of not wanting to appear ignorant or careless. Sometimes the form you use determines the meaning of your sentence. Consider these two sentences:

Susan treats her dog better than *I*.
Susan treats her dog better than *me*.

There's a world of difference between the meaning of the subject form—"Susan treats her dog better than *I* [do]"—and the object form—"Susan treats her dog better than [she treats] *me*."

When using a pronoun after *than, as well as,* or *as,* decide whether you mean to contrast the pronoun with the subject of the sentence. If you do, use the subject form of the pronoun. If not, use the object form.

Pierre would rather be with Samantha than I.
(*I* is contrasted with *Pierre*.)

Pierre would rather be with Samantha than me.
(*Me* is contrasted with *Samantha*.)

Exercise 15.3

Correct the following sentences where necessary.

1. Stan trusts his psychologist more than he trusts I.

2. Everyone except Jan and me gave *The Hanging Garden* glowing reviews.

3. All of we put more work into the class project than did Ursula or him.

4. Finally, I have found a lab partner who works as hard as me.

5. Because she grew up in Digby, Kyla enjoys scallops more than me.

6. Tristan thinks that, as the oldest in the family, he should use the family car more than me.

7. Although I generally trust friendly people, I dislike salespeople who smile as much as him.

8. The entrance to the secret garden was as high as him but not as wide as me.

9. Few Canadians know as much as him about the occult experiences of William Lyon Mackenzie King.

10. The real difference between Diana Krall and I is style, not skill.

Exercise 15.4

Revise the paragraphs below to correct the ten errors in pronoun form.

In my family, everyone is over two metres tall except I. This means that everyone, including my youngest brother, is taller than me. Both him and my younger sister play on the high school basketball team, while my older brother stars on his college team. As for I, I can hardly shoot the ball high enough to get it in the hoop, even when I stand on my tiptoes. Whether on or off the basketball court, us vertically challenged folk face many difficulties. The world, it seems, is made for my siblings, not I. Each time I struggle to reach a book on a high library shelf, or roll my shirtsleeves up to prevent them from dragging in my soup, I wish that I were as tall as them.

Recently, however, by exploring my family history, I learned that being overly tall has disadvantages. One of my family's nineteenth-century ancestors, Anna Swan, known as the Giantess of Nova Scotia, was so tall that her and her husband had to have their carriage, their furniture, and even their church pew specially made. Although she had hoped to become a teacher, Anna felt such a misfit at the Truro Normal School (teacher's college) that she decided to make her living as a "freak" in P.T. Barnum's shows. Here she met other extraordinary mortals like she—one of whom became her husband, the giant from Kentucky, Martin van Buren Bates. The two giants lived quietly in Seville, Ohio, where they were active and well-liked members of the community. Tragically, though, Anna's tall life was not a long one. Both Anna and her husband suffered from health problems, but the giant spouse who died first was her, at the early age of forty-two.

GO TO WEB

EXERCISES 15.1, 15.2

Exercise 15.5

Correct the faulty pronoun forms in the following sentences.

1. Lydia and me are going to donate the clothes we can't fit into to the local women's shelter.

2. As citizens, the Americans are more concerned about their individual freedoms than us Canadians.

3. Once my brother and me had experienced a prairie winter, we decided to move to Victoria.

4. Savanna would much rather drink coffee than me. Her, of all my friends, spends the most time at Starbucks.

5. Intelligence is not something anyone can give you or I. However, us students can and should learn to develop the intellectual gifts we possess.

6. Saving 10 percent of our gross annual income has been a priority for my wife and I ever since we were married.

7. Her and her sister have travelled to six continents, and each time they leave home they take more luggage with them.

8. After looking for six months, him and Grandma found a small bungalow in the east end of town, where they could plant a small garden and invite all of we grandchildren over to play.

9. "No one wants to see you succeed more than me," my mother remarked emphatically.

10. Our supervisor says she respects Basil and I equally, but she gives him more responsibility than I.

16

Mastering Pronoun–Antecedent Agreement

Now that you know how to choose the correct form of pronouns within a sentence, let's look at how to use pronouns consistently throughout a sentence and a paragraph.

Pronoun–Antecedent Agreement

The name of this pronoun problem may sound difficult, but the idea is simple. Pronouns are words that substitute for or refer to the name of a person, place, or thing mentioned elsewhere in your sentence or your paragraph. The word(s) that a pronoun substitutes for or refers to is called the **antecedent.**

This(game) is as close as(it)can be.

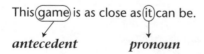

Usually, as in these two examples, the antecedent comes before the pronoun that refers to it. Here is the rule to remember.

A pronoun must agree with its antecedent in
- number (singular or plural)
- person (first, second, or third)
- gender (masculine, feminine, or neuter)

Most of the time, you follow this rule without even realizing that you know it. For example, you would never write

This game is as close as *they* can be.

Hannibal had *your* own way of doing things.

This game is as close as *she* can be.

You know these sentences are incorrect even if you don't know precisely why they are wrong.

There are three kinds of pronoun–antecedent agreement that you do need to learn about. They lead to errors that, unlike the examples above, are not obvious, and you need to know them so you can watch out for them. The rules you need to learn involve relative pronouns; indefinite pronouns ending in -*one*, -*thing*, or -*body*; and vague references.

1. Relative Pronouns

The first potential difficulty with pronoun–antecedent agreement is how to use relative pronouns—*who, whom, which,* and *that*—correctly. Relative pronouns must refer to someone or something already mentioned in the sentence. Here is the guideline to follow.

Who and *whom*, and *whoever* and *whomever* refer to people.
That and *which* refer to everything else.

The clown *who* was riding the bicycle carried a Canadian flag.

The department heads *who* were present rejected the president's proposal.

The moose *that* I met looked hostile.

Her report, *which* is due today, will address most of the concerns *that* the union has raised.

Whether you need *who* or *whom, whoever* or *whomever,* depends on the pronoun's place and function in your sentence. Apply the basic pronoun rule.

> If the pronoun is, or refers to, the subject of the sentence, use *who/whoever.* Otherwise, use *whom/whomever.*

Who decided we had to take English? (The pronoun "who" is the subject of the sentence.)

It was she *who* filled out the form that won us the trip to Moosonee. (The pronoun refers to the subject of the sentence, "she.")

The trip's promoters were willing to settle for *whomever* they could get. (The pronoun does not refer to the subject, "promoters"; it is the object of the preposition "for.")

Often you can solve this problem by rewriting the sentence so you don't need either *who* or *whom:*

Letitia filled out the form that won us the trip to Moosonee.

The trip's promoters were willing to settle for anyone they could get.

That is required more often than *which.* You should use *which* only in a clause that is separated from the rest of the sentence by commas.

The moose *that* I met looked hostile.

The moose, *which* was standing right in front of my car, looked hostile.

Exercise 16.1

Correct the following sentences where necessary. Answers begin on page 345.

1. Jim Cuddy is a singer-songwriter that truly depicts his soul in his music.

2. I would love to own any car which had the name Ferrari on it.

3. Are you sure that Colleen Jones is the reporter that became a curling champion?

4. My second wife was a woman that I met on a blind date.

5. The book report, that was due on Wednesday, has not yet been handed in.

6. Successful farmers understand the climate and know the crops which they are raising.

7. It was Trent McCleary that was severely injured in the Canadiens–Flyers game in Montreal in January 2000.

8. My aunt is the one that drove the car which ended up in the creek after the wedding.

9. I cannot stand people that are always late.

10. Students that try their best will succeed more often than students which never have to try.

2. Pronouns Ending in -one, -body, -thing

The second tricky aspect of pronoun–antecedent agreement involves these **indefinite pronouns**:

anyone	anybody	anything
everyone	everybody	everything
no one	nobody	nothing
someone	somebody	something
each (one)		

In Chapter 13, you learned that, when these words are used as subjects, they are singular and require singular verbs. So it makes sense that the pronouns that stand for or refer to them must also be singular.

Antecedents ending in *-one*, *-body*, and *-thing* are singular.
They must be referred to by singular pronouns: *he, she, it; his, her, its.*

Everyone deserves a break from *her* children now and then.

Everything has *its* place and should be in it.

Anyone new must register *his* name at the front desk.

Everybody on the boat could feel the salt spray sting *his* eyes.

But take another look at the last two sentences. Until about twenty years ago, the pronouns *he, him,* and *his* were used with singular antecedents and referred to both men and women. Today, however, many readers are sensitive to sex bias in writing and think that it is not appropriate to use the masculine pronoun when referring to both sexes. As a writer, you should be aware of this sensitivity. If you want to appeal to the broadest possible audience, you should avoid what some readers may consider to be sexist language.

In speech, it has become acceptable to use plural pronouns with *-one,* *-body,* and *-thing* antecedents. Although they are grammatically singular, they are often plural in meaning, and in conversation we tend to say

Anyone new must register their name at the front desk.

Everybody on the boat could feel the salt spray sting their eyes.

This usage is acceptable in speech, but it is not acceptable in standard written English. Writers sometimes make errors in pronoun–antecedent agreement because they are trying to write without indicating whether the person referred to is male or female. "Anyone new must register *their* name" is incorrect, as we have seen; however, it does avoid making "anyone" male. The writer could replace the plural *their* with the singular and non-sexist *his or her*—"Anyone new must register *his* or her *name*"—but *his or her* sounds clumsy if it is used frequently.

There are two better ways to solve the problem.

1. Revise the sentence to leave the pronoun out.

Anyone new must register at the front desk.

The eyes of everybody on the boat were stinging from the salt spray.

Such creative avoidance of sex-specific language or incorrect constructions can be an interesting intellectual challenge. The results sometimes sound a little artificial, however. The second solution is easier to accomplish.

2. Revise the sentence to make both the antecedent and the pronoun plural.

All newcomers must register *their* names at the front desk.

All the passengers on the boat could feel the salt spray sting *their* eyes.

Here are a couple of examples for you to study:

Problem: Everybody has been given his assignment.
Revision 1: Everybody has been given an assignment.
Revision 2: All of the students have been given their assignments.

Problem: Everyone is optimistic about the future when he is fifteen.
Revision 1: Everyone is optimistic about the future at fifteen.
Revision 2: All fifteen-year-olds are optimistic about their future.

Tip: If you are writing on a word processor, you can use the search function to ensure agreement between pronouns and their antecedents. Search your paper for every occurrence of *their* and *they*, and check each one to be sure its antecedent is not a pronoun ending in *-one*, *-thing*, or *-body*.

Exercise 16.2

Identify the most appropriate word(s) from the choices given in parentheses. Check your answers carefully before continuing.

1. All of the girls in the class began to argue; everyone wanted to speak (her, their) own mind.
2. I wish someone would invite me to (his, their, a) party this weekend so that I am not bored to death.
3. The prime minister expects everyone in Canada to do (his, her, his or her, their) share in keeping our country clean.

4. Any woman (that, who) buys groceries more than three times a week must have something wrong with (her, their) appetite.

5. Each of the songs that Leonard Cohen writes has (its, their, his) own merits.

6. Nothing bad could be said about Linus; neither could (they, it) be said about Lynne.

7. No one in the church lifted (its, his, a) head while the minister said the prayers.

8. Each of us is expected to donate (his, her, their, his or her, a) part of the proceeds to the charity of our choice.

9. Anyone would love to have (his, her, his or her, a) first edition of Aritha Van Herk's book *No Fixed Address*.

10. The anonymous caller refused to leave (their, his, her, a) name or a message.

Exercise 16.3

Correct the errors in the following sentences, being careful to avoid awkward repetition and sexist language. Then compare your answers with our suggestions.

1. It's not every day that someone sacrifices their sleep to serve you breakfast in bed.

2. Do you think anyone will send copies of their photos to me?

3. Nobody loves his neighbours as much as the Joneses love the Guptas.

4. Cooking is a great activity for anyone who wants to show off his creativity as well as his project management skills.

5. Everyone who has been to Winnipeg Beach Provincial Park tells their friends it's one of the most beautiful places to spend the summer.

6. Everyone must get in their own seat before class begins.

7. Each dancer must consult their partner in choosing the music and costumes for their competition next fall.

8. Every child rushes towards their adulthood; once they grow up, they wish they had their childhood back.

9. Anyone who eats peanut butter and pickle sandwiches should have their head examined.

10. Everyone must attend the party or their membership in the club will be cancelled.

---

3. Vague Reference

Avoiding the third potential difficulty with pronoun–antecedent agreement requires common sense and an ability to put yourself in your reader's place. If you look at your writing from your reader's point of view, it is unlikely that you will break the following rule.

A pronoun must refer clearly to the correct antecedent.

The mistake that occurs when you fail to follow this rule is called **vague reference.**

Kenny phoned Phil because he knew he needed to borrow his car.

Who needed to borrow whose car? Here's another:

Sabina thought that Mary should have been more careful with her album when she lent it to her because she was a good friend of her husband.

Who owns the album? Who has the husband?

In sentences like these, you can only guess the meaning because you don't know who is being referred to by the pronouns. The antecedents are not clear. You can make such sentences less confusing either by using proper names (Kenny, Phil, Sabina, Mary) more frequently or by changing the sentences around. These solutions aren't difficult; they just take a little time and some imagination. Try them on our examples.

Another type of vague reference occurs when there is no antecedent in the sentence for the pronoun to refer to.

I admire CF-118 pilots and would like to do it myself. (Do what?)

Snowboarding is her favourite winter sport, so it's odd that she doesn't own one. (One what?)

How would you revise these sentences?

Make sure that every pronoun has a clear antecedent and that every pronoun agrees with its antecedent. Both must be singular, or both must be plural. Once you have mastered this principle, you'll have no trouble with pronoun–antecedent agreement.

Exercise 16.4

Correct the following sentences where necessary. There are several ways to fix these sentences. In some cases, the antecedent is missing, and you need to supply one. In other cases, the antecedent is so vague that the meaning of the sentence can be interpreted in more than one way, and you need to rewrite the sentence to make it clear.

1. Each time the newborn grabbed her mother's hand, she smiled.

2. Donald gave his dad his ring yesterday.

3. Figure skating is my least favourite sport although I've owned a pair for several years.

4. As a child, Wanda was a gifted musician, which she practised at least four hours every day.

Every time David looked at the dog, he barked.

5. I did not see the girls' dance recital which was due to my absence.

6. What did Susan say to her mother before she hung up the phone?

7. At our church, they ensure everyone is looked after.

8. That Charles would be Joe's neighbour never occurred to him.

9. Upset, I slammed my drink on the table and broke it.

10. When Jane and Tory met, she thought she was a bit odd.

The following exercises contain all three kinds of pronoun–antecedent agreement errors. Correct each sentence any way you choose, remembering that your answers may differ from the answers we've provided and still be correct. Our suggested answers begin on page 346.

Exercise 16.5

1. The culprit must be someone that is left-handed.

2. Each of the televisions had their pros and cons, but the Sony was the one for me.

3. Katrina is the only person I know who can play the piano while they juggle.

4. Mona can't figure out why Margaret hasn't called her since her birthday.

5. A diplomat is someone that can tell you to go to hell in a way that makes you feel grateful to be on your way.

6. Cycling is Mohammed's favourite pastime, but he had to sell three of them to get some cash.

7. Each committee chair knows exactly what their duties are for next year.

8. Watching TV requires little mental or physical effort, and we all need more of this.

9. Everyone should live every day to its fullest and reach for their dreams; that is how they will find true happiness.

10. Last year my brother taught me how to ski, but I have yet to buy any of my own.

GO TO WEB

EXERCISES 16.1, 16.2, 16.3, 16.4

Exercise 16.6

1. Before they take any medication, a pregnant woman should consult their physician.
2. Anyone that has finished one hundred math problems in three minutes can't possibly have all the correct answers.
3. I have gone hunting four times, and I have never shot one.
4. When Mrs. Tomak saw Ayat and Mary yesterday she thought she must have been mistaken about her trip to her parents' home in Egypt.
5. Lack of exercise will cause anyone to lose their tone and flexibility.
6. I am sure every teacher will be there even though they aren't required to be at the hockey games.
7. Opportunities are everywhere for anyone, as long as they know where to look.
8. When Ben and Tom returned from the tour of the CBC building, he said he would think of pursuing a career in journalism.
9. Every acting student must pick their favourite play or movie as one of this year's projects.
10. A woman who marries a man that has been married before is doing their best to be ecologically responsible. Since there are more women than men, it makes sense to recycle.

Correct the problems in the following paragraphs, which contain 15 errors. Part of the challenge in this exercise is to make the paragraph not only grammatically correct but also free of sexist language.

Anyone that visits Toronto notices the CN Tower as a prominent feature of the skyline. As one approaches the city from the air, they can see it pointing upwards like a silver needle from the shore of Lake Ontario. A visitor can see the famous structure from many vantage points downtown. As one emerges from the St. George subway station, he can see it clearly past the Bata Shoe Museum, even though it is still a twenty-minute walk away. Everyone that walks down University Avenue or Spadina Avenue has a clear view of the Tower, and every tourist that strolls along the harbourfront can't help but notice it.

The CN Tower stands as a symbol of Toronto's industrial and economic importance, but anyone that travels to the city should know that Toronto is also home to much natural beauty: there are many lush ravines and tranquil green spaces. For picnickers, there are beautiful city parks where one can have their choice of peaceful picnic spots. For families with small children, there are plenty of great playgrounds to visit. For cyclists, there are numerous bike trails for one to try. Moreover, anyone that enjoys waterside walks can visit the Don River, Grenadier Pond, or the boardwalk along Lake Ontario.

Everyone that visits Toronto should spend some time in High Park, my favourite green space in the city. The park is most beautiful in May, when the ornamental fruit trees are in bloom. One can walk along the park paths and delight in the billows of pink blossoms. Even someone that has grown up in the Niagara region or the Okanagan Valley would have to agree that the sight is spectacular. In addition to its fruit trees, High Park also offers the visitor their choice of several other attractions, including a large playground, a duck pond, and a tiny train which takes children on a ride around the park. No one should miss the park's summer theatre festival, which features plays by Shakespeare performed in a natural amphi-theatre. Go early, though, to get a seat, since everybody in the city throngs to the park for their free entertainment.

Before you try the final exercise for this chapter, it may be helpful for you to review the rules for pronoun–antecedent agreement.

Summary

- Every pronoun must agree with its antecedent (a word or word group that appears earlier in the sentence or paragraph); both must be singular, or both must be plural.
- Use *who/whoever* and *whom/whomever* to refer to people; use *that* and *which* to refer to animals, objects, and ideas.
- Antecedents ending in *-one*, *-thing*, and *-body* are singular and must be referred to by singular pronouns: *he, she, it; his, her, its.*
- A pronoun must clearly refer to a specific antecedent.

Check your mastery of pronoun–antecedent agreement by correcting the errors in the following sentences.

1. Is Sarah the girl that stole the wallet from Judith's purse?

2. Everyone should be aware of what is going on in their province, both politically and economically.

3. Henry's dog is the one who was run over by the tractor and lived to bark about it later.

4. When a man talks about a woman, they always complain about how long it takes them to get dressed.

5. Lucy told Laura that she had a surprise for her; then she asked her for a loan.

6. You know you're living in a new age when a pre-schooler knows more about computers than their parents do.

7. Drinking too much can be hazardous to your health, your safety and to those around you; be sure not to have too many.

8. When Noah goes to the library, he always checks out one on sailing.

9. Each of the boys claims that their favourite activity is playing cops and robbers, while each of the girls claims that their favourite pastime is playing with the boys.

10. The average man has six items—toothbrush, toothpaste, razor, shaving cream, soap and towel—in their bathroom. The average woman, on the other hand, stores a hundred or more items in their bathroom, most of which no man would be able to identify.

17

Maintaining Person Agreement

So far, we have focussed on using pronouns correctly and clearly within a sentence. Now let's turn to the problem of **person agreement**, which means using pronouns consistently throughout a sentence or a paragraph. There are three categories of person that we use when we write or speak:

	Singular	**Plural**
first person	I; me	we; us
second person	you	you
third person	she, he, it, one; her, him *and all pronouns ending in* -one, -thing, -body	they; them

Here is the rule for person agreement.

Do not mix "persons" unless meaning requires it.

In other words, be consistent. If you begin a sentence using a second-person pronoun, you must use second person all the way through. Look at this sentence:

If *you* wish to succeed, *one* must work hard.

This is the most common error—mixing second-person *you* with third-person *one.*

Here's another example:

One can live happily in Vancouver if *you* have a sturdy umbrella.

We can correct this error by using the second person throughout:

You can live happily in Vancouver if *you* have a sturdy umbrella.

We can also correct it by using the third person throughout:

One can live happily in Vancouver if *one* has a sturdy umbrella.

or

One can live happily in Vancouver if *he or she* has a sturdy umbrella.

These last three sentences raise two points of style that you should consider.

1. Don't overuse *one*. Although all three revised sentences are correct, the impression they make on the reader is different. The first sentence, in the second person, sounds the most informal and natural — like something you would say. It's a bit casual for general writing purposes. The second sentence, which uses *one* twice, sounds the most formal — even a little stilted. The third sentence falls between the other two in formality and is the one you'd be most likely to use in writing for school or business. It's grammatically correct and non-sexist, but it raises another potential problem.

2. Don't overuse *he or she*. If this construction occurs frequently, the reader cannot help shifting focus from what you're saying to how you're saying it. The best writing is transparent — that is, it doesn't call attention to itself. If your reader becomes distracted by your style, your meaning gets lost. Consider this sentence:

A salesperson can improve himself or herself by practising his or her public speaking skills whenever he or she can.

Awkward, isn't it? Imagine being the unfortunate reader who has to struggle through a whole paragraph filled with this clumsy construction!

The solutions to this problem are the same as those for making pronouns ending in *-one, -body,* or *-thing* agree with their antecedents. You can either change the whole sentence to the plural —

Salespersons can improve themselves by practising their public speaking skills whenever they can.

— or you can rewrite the sentence without using pronouns:

Salespersons can improve by practising public speaking skills whenever possible.

Exercise 17.1

Choose the correct word(s) from the parentheses. Answers begin on page 348.

1. You really shouldn't eat with your mouth open if (one wants, you want, he or she wants) to show good manners.
2. To prevent razor burn, (one, you) should always moisten your skin before shaving.
3. You can't really understand everything if (you don't, one doesn't, they don't) read, study, and review all material.
4. We guarantee that any man will be happy with the results if (you, he, one) uses our hair care products daily.
5. If you exercise regularly, (one will, he will, you will) soon improve both your physical and your mental health.
6. When we sped over the bridge, (one, we, you) didn't see the police car waiting on the other side.
7. One can learn another language if (they study, you study, he or she studies) diligently.
8. If you want to avoid accidents, (one, you, they) should take a defensive driving course.
9. You can't do well in customer service unless (one has, you have) good communication skills.
10. I don't understand why anyone would try so hard to impress (your, her, their) in-laws.

Exercise 17.2

In the following paragraph, choose the correct pronoun from those given in parentheses.

Students who manage full-time careers while (they're, one is) in college may do better at (your, their, one's) academic work than those who do nothing but study. Because (he, they, you) have a steady job, students who work full-time benefit from a stable lifestyle and may actually be more dedicated to (their, your, his) classes. (One, They, We) may be better able to concentrate, partly because of the ability to apply some of (their, his, one's) work skills, such as the ability to manage projects, to (one's, his, their) studies. The challenge of balancing job responsibilities with academic commitments motivates (one, them, him) to do (his, one's, their) best at both work and at school. College students with full-time jobs also tend to appreciate (his, one's, their) education more than the students who do not work during (their, one's, his) college years. They can see the direct relevance of (their, one's, his) class work to the tasks (one faces, he faces, they face) in the workplace. Working students make many sacrifices to attend college, so they know they must perform well to prove to (himself, themselves, one-self) that (their, his, one's) education is worth all the hard work (one does, he does, they do).

Exercise 17.3

Correct the following sentences where necessary. For those sentences containing language that might be considered sexist, try correcting them twice: first, to ensure person agreement; second, to avoid gender bias. Turn to pages 348–49 to compare your answers with our suggestions.

1. It's hard for Canadians to accept that we will always live in the shadow of America.

2. Baking a cake is not difficult for one to do as long as you have the right ingredients, a functioning oven, and confidence.

3. One would be a hypocrite if you preached against fashion *faux pas* and then showed up at a classical music performance wearing an orange skirt with a green and purple blouse.

4. The emotional turmoil that results from breast cancer can affect a woman's physical health as well as their psychological well-being.

5. Beer is good for one, even better for you than red wine.

6. If one puts on a smile and a confident attitude, then you might win the partner of your dreams.

7. One should talk to someone about what's bothering them, so they can get help if necessary.

8. After graduation night, the partying and lack of sleep made it hard for one to keep themselves awake.

9. One cannot be convicted of a crime until they have had a fair trial.

10. It's difficult for someone to cope without their loved one when your heart has been broken.

GO TO WEB

EXERCISES 17.1, 17.2

Exercise 17.4

Rewrite the following paragraphs, changing the 25 third-person pronouns to second-person pronouns and correcting any verb errors that result from your revisions.

How can one prevent frostbite? Frostbite usually affects areas that are exposed to the cold, such as one's cheeks, nose, ears, and chin. One's extremities (one's hands and feet) are also at higher risk than the rest of one's body. In order to avoid freezing one's skin, one must prepare oneself before venturing outdoors in winter weather. For best insulation, one should dress in loose, warm layers of clothing. A hat is essential since much of one's body heat escapes from the top of one's head. Another important way to prevent frostbite is to avoid getting oneself wet.

If, in spite of one's precautions, one develops frostbite, one must take care to prevent permanent skin damage. One should thaw the affected skin slowly by wrapping it in warm clothes or soaking it in warm water. If one has ever had frostbite, one knows that thawing the skin is a painful process. One does not try to speed up thawing by applying direct heat, since one can cause blisters that way. One should never rub ice or snow on frozen skin, no matter what one's grandmother says. When one's skin is pink, and one feels normal sensation return to the area, the skin has been successfully thawed. One should then wrap the affected area and seek medical attention as soon as possible.

Exercise 17.5

Find and correct the inconsistencies in pronoun person in the following paragraph, which contains ten potential errors. Revise the paragraph twice: once in the second person and once in the third person. Which version do you prefer?

Mike Weir said, "Sometimes the hardest thing to do in golf is wait." We have to wait on the tee, wait in the fairway, and wait—ever so patiently—for our success. Because we spend so much time waiting, we are often tempted to give up. However, Weir is a good example of someone who trained himself to wait patiently for success. He won the Ontario Junior Championship in 1988. As a golf fan, I agree that his road to international fame has been lengthy. We can use Weir as a role-model by striving to match his patience, endurance, and confidence. Weir proved that patience pays off when he won the Masters in 2003 and became the first Canadian man to win a major tournament. If we have that same attitude, then surely we can make it as successful golfers, too. If we are young and have a positive attitude, then we can make it from the local to the national junior golf tournaments, all the way to the PGA. We just have to do one thing: wait.

GO TO WEB

EXERCISES 17.3, 17.4

Exercise 17.6

As a final test of your mastery of person consistency, correct the errors in the following sentences.

1. I enjoy living with air conditioning in my home because you don't have to take off your clothes to be cool.

2. A sure way to lose all one's friends is to eat all the popcorn yourself.

3. One doesn't have to listen to one's heart to hear the voices of love speaking to you.

4. People always want what you don't have and have what you don't need.

5. When we walked into the room, the applause was enough to make you blush.

6. When one is dying her hair, be sure to start at the roots and work your way to the ends.

7. Traditional Newfoundland music might not immediately appeal to the urban kids of downtown Vancouver, but you can learn to appreciate it.

8. Anyone who dives head first into quicksand should be aware of how insane they are.

9. Hockey and ringette are both fast-paced ice sports in which players use a stick to pass, carry, and shoot your puck or ring to score goals.

10. I can hardly believe I've finished this exercise. Sometimes one gets so tired of grammar that you want to give up.

Exercise 17.7

Think of a significant experience you've had since coming to college. (If you don't like "significant," try embarrassing, enlightening, or disturbing.) Write an account of this experience, telling your story in the third person: that is, instead of using *I*, use *he* or *she*. When you have finished your paper, reread it carefully. Check your sentence structure. Check your spelling. Check the agreement of your subjects and verbs and of your pronouns and antecedents. Finally, check that you have maintained consistency of verb tense and pronoun person in each paragraph of your paper.

UNIT 4

Punctuation

18

The Comma

The comma is the most frequently used—and misused—punctuation mark in English. Leaving out a necessary comma can distort the meaning of your sentence. Including unnecessary commas can distract the reader and give your sentences a jerky quality. Perhaps nothing is so sure a sign of a competent writer as the correct use of commas, so it is very important that you master them. This chapter presents four comma rules that will give you a good indication of when you should use a comma. If you apply these four rules faithfully, your reader will never be confused by missing or misplaced commas in your writing. And if, as occasionally happens, the sentence you are writing is not covered by one of our four rules, remember the first commandment of comma usage: when in doubt, leave it out.

Four Comma Rules

Here are the four essential rules that cover most instances in which you need to use a comma.

1. Use commas to separate items in a series of three or more.

The required subjects in this program are math, physics, and English.

My grandfather worked as a miner, a waiter, and a carpenter.

Tom went to the movies, Jan and Yasmin went to play pool, and I went to bed.

The comma before the *and* at the end of the list is optional; use it or leave it out, but be consistent.

Exercise 18.1

Insert commas where necessary in the following sentences, and then check your answers on page 350.

1. The five largest cities in Canada were once Montreal Toronto Quebec Ottawa and Hamilton.
2. Red and white are the colours of the Canadian flag.
3. I want my wedding to be unusual, but I can't decide whether the bridesmaids should wear black brown or olive dresses.
4. Heather is a well-rounded student; she does well in mathematics English history and science.
5. Mr. Doberman came to the dance wearing a short-sleeved green shirt and chinos.
6. My favourite bands are The Tragically Hip Blue Rodeo and the Matthew Good Band.
7. Brushing my teeth combing my hair and putting in my contacts are automatically part of my morning routine.
8. My favourite animals are llamas chimpanzees and zebras.
9. Do you think crop circles are of the work of aliens humans or gods?
10. I enjoy listening to country music rap and jazz.

2. Use commas to set off any word or phrase that is not ESSENTIAL to the main idea of the sentence.

To find out whether a word, phrase, or clause is essential, try crossing it out. If the main idea remains unchanged and the sentence still makes sense, the crossed-out expression is *non-essential* and should be set off by commas. Study the following four examples.

Writing a good letter of application isn't difficult, ~~if you're careful~~.

The phrase "if you're careful" is not essential to the main idea of the sentence, so it's separated from the rest of the sentence by a comma.

Writing a letter of application ~~that is clear and concise~~ is a challenge.

If you take out "that is clear and concise," you change the meaning of the sentence. Not all letters of application are a challenge to write: only clear and concise ones. Writing vague and wordy letters is easy; anyone can do it. The words "that is clear and concise" are therefore essential to the meaning of the sentence, so they are not set off by commas.

~~In the morning~~, I like to drink my coffee and read *The Globe and Mail*.

The phrase "in the morning" is not essential to the main idea; it just gives us additional information about the writer of the sentence. Leaving it out does not change the meaning, so it is set off by a comma.

When non-essential or supplementary information occurs in the middle of the sentence, rather than at the beginning or the end, be sure to put commas both before and after it.

My aunt and uncle, ~~who moved to Sicily in 1992~~, return home to Yarmouth each July to celebrate Canada Day with us.

The phrase "who moved to Sicily in 1992" is a supplementary detail. It is not essential to the meaning of the sentence, so it is set off by commas.

Exercise 18.2

Insert commas where necessary in the following sentences. Check your answers before going on.

1. Sandra a recovering alcoholic has been sober for twelve years.
2. Coach Quarles my favourite teacher taught us the value of determination.
3. Practicing the piano is an excellent way to release tension while engaging the mind in a creative process.
4. *The Enchanted Echo* published in 1944 was Al Purdy's first collection of poetry.
5. The medical examiner a man of his word promised the family he would respect the widow's privacy.
6. Dr. Kozey the town's newest dentist just moved here from Gimli.
7. Despite his lead roles in *Double Jeopardy* and *Thirteen Days* Bruce Greenwood has not achieved the fame that Harrison Ford has.
8. Anyone who has seen a hockey game knows there is more to the sport than meets the fist.
9. Do you know Anne Murray the former physical education teacher from Nova Scotia?
10. My father's favourite song believe it or not is "Snowbird."

3. Put a comma between independent clauses when they are joined by these transitional words:

for	but	so
and	or	
nor	yet	

(You can remember these words easily if you notice that their first letters spell "fanboys.")

I hope I do well in the interview, for I really want this job.

Kevin is a better actor, but Bruce gets more parts.

I rang the doorbell, and my neighbour suddenly appeared in his bathrobe.

Ted plans to visit China next year, so he is taking a class in conversational Mandarin.

Be sure that the sentence you are punctuating contains two independent clauses rather than one clause with a single subject and a multiple verb.

We loved the book but hated the movie.
(We is the subject, and there are two verbs, *loved* and *hated*. Do not put a comma between two or more verbs that share a single subject.)

We both loved the book, but Kim hated the movie.
(This sentence contains two independent clauses — *We loved* and *Kim hated* — joined by *but*. The comma is required here.)

Exercise 18.3

Insert commas where they are needed in the following sentences. Check your answers when you're done.

1. We can't see our children nor can we hear them.
2. Please pay attention for the lesson today will be on the exam.
3. No one who has seen him play doubts that he is destined to be a superstar.
4. This is my first full-time job so I don't want to mess it up.
5. Dave and Angus are moving to Inuvik and Mel is moving to Corner Brook.
6. We have a choice: we can stand on our hands or walk on our knees.

7. I would love to pay off my student loans, but I have barely enough money for rent.
8. The deer ran across the road and I just missed it.
9. Either you are Denver's wife or she has a twin.
10. Michelle doesn't see Chloe very often yet the two of them are always in touch.

4. Put a comma after a word or group of words that comes before an independent clause.

Jan, please take notes for us.

On her way to the Juno Awards, Shania was mobbed by autograph seekers.

Approaching her thirtieth birthday, Rita compensated by buying a sports car and finding a younger boyfriend.

If Kraft Dinner is their idea of lunch, we'd better bring our own sandwiches.

Exercise 18.4

Insert commas where they are needed in the following sentences. Check your answers when you have finished all ten.

1. Daddy why is the sky blue?
2. Walking slowly across the beam I made it to the other side without looking at the water below.
3. Shania Twain finally made her break in Nashville.
4. Until I received a raise I didn't think I was appreciated at work.
5. No matter how long I practice I can never seem to play that song very well.
6. Touched by the toast the bride fought back her tears.
7. When our boss talks about improving productivity she is never talking about herself.
8. When the first leaves fall from the trees I prepare myself for another school year filled with new faces, old memories, and new challenges.

9. Although Jed is originally from Medicine Hat he calls Regina his home.
10. Where the little one-room schoolhouse had stood for 100 years a Canadian Tire now stands.

The rest of the exercises in this chapter require you to apply all four comma rules. Before you begin, write out the four rules on a sheet of paper and keep it in front of you as you work through the excercises. Refer to the four rules frequently as you punctuate the sentences that follow. After you've finished each exercise, check your answers and make sure you understand any mistakes you've made.

Exercise 18.5

1. Hot sunny and muggy days are what the weather reporter predicts for this week.
2. Inside the children are laughing at their principal.
3. Despite the news of his disappearance Faye remained confident her son's life was not in danger.
4. As their wedding anniversary approached the couple began to look at travel brochures.
5. I loved John Irving's novel *A Prayer for Owen Meany* but I did not enjoy *Simon Birch*.
6. One of my favourite bands Blue Rodeo played in Halifax in February.
7. After class today I plan to deliver applications to CTV CBC and the BBC.
8. You can't believe everything you read everything you hear or everything you see.
9. Surprisingly David Foster has produced as many albums as Quincy Jones.
10. Foster has produced albums for such well-known artists as Chicago Celine Dion The Corrs and Michael Jackson.

Exercise 18.6

In this exercise, after you have punctuated each sentence, identify the rule(s) you applied. For example:

On Tuesday our marks will be posted.
On Tuesday, our marks will be posted. **(rule 4)**

1. Acadians the French-speaking settlers from Nova Scotia and New Brunswick became known in Louisiana as Cajuns.
2. After being diagnosed with Hepatitis C Pamela Anderson started to speak out about the need for health research.
3. Maya you aren't colouring inside the lines!
4. We won the first game but we lost the second and third.
5. Trevor laughs like a chicken walks like a duck and sings like a turkey.
6. If you know what you are doing driving a vehicle with a manual transmission isn't difficult.
7. The Apple Blossom Festival which takes place every May brings in thousands of tourists.
8. If you enjoy running through the woods swimming in the lake and cycling through the mountains you might consider competing in a triathlon.
9. On Wednesday evening the budget committee will meet to elect a new chair for the next fiscal year.
10. When my family moved to Victoria from Labrador City I felt as if I had moved from one country to another.

GO TO WEB

EXERCISES 18.1, 18.2

Exercise 18.7

Insert the 15 commas that are missing in this paragraph.

Ringette first played in 1963 is a Canadian game that started in North Bay, Ontario. Designed with girls in mind ringette is similar to ice hockey. Players use a straight stick rather than one with a curved blade to manipulate a rubber ring and score goals. In the beginning most ringette teams were in Ontario and Quebec. By the 1970s however the sport had established itself in all regions of Canada. Today ringette is a popular pastime with girls and women but it also appeals to boys and men. There are over 50,000 ringette players in Canada and this number continues to grow. The ringette community now boasts 9,000 coaches 2,866 trained referees and many thousands of volunteers. The volunteers run ringette organizations from British Columbia to Newfoundland taking care of countless administrative details including registration and fund-raising.

GO TO WEB

EXERCISE 18.3

Exercise 18.8

This paragraph contains 15 comma errors that are often found in student writing. Your task is to remove all unnecessary commas and insert commas where they belong, according to the four comma rules. (Be careful! Some of the commas in these sentences are correctly placed.)

Since Confederation Quebec has produced many remarkable federal leaders including two of our most famous prime ministers Sir Wilfrid Laurier and Pierre Trudeau. According to a nineteenth-century rumour *la belle province* then known as Lower Canada may also have produced an American president. Chester Arthur was running, for president, in 1881 when the Democrats paid a lawyer Arthur Hinman to investigate his past. Hinman alleged, that Arthur was born in Dunham, Quebec, and moved to Fairfield, Vermont his official birthplace as an infant. Hinman's theories have since been discredited but they created a controversy during Arthur's presidency, which lasted from 1881 to 1885. In 1884, Hinman created a temporary scandal when he printed his claims in a pamphlet titled "How a British Subject, Became President of the United States."

Exercise 18.9

Insert the missing 20 commas where they are needed in the following sentences.

1. On the day of your surgery be sure to show up one hour in advance for blood work and x-rays.

2. If she can help just one person by telling her story the loss of privacy will be worthwhile.

3. Music's impact is deeper than anything else I've experienced for it affects me on a physical emotional and spiritual level.

4. I don't agree with your opinion but I respect your right to express it.

5. I like to sit on the back porch listening to the crickets watching the fireflies and inhaling the scent of spruce needles.

6. When the nurse calls your name identify yourself right away. Don't let her wander about the waiting room wondering where you are.

7. Starting a small business once the dream of only a few adventurous souls has become a realistic option for many young people.

8. Unfortunately most of the food was left and we were forced to eat it ourselves.

9. The males of the tribe were going on a trip to a holy mountain and I watched as they rode off into the sunset. I wondered if I would ever see them again or if this had been our last good-bye.

10. Studies show that drinking milk in the quantities recommended by Canada's Food Guide lowers the risk of death from all causes including heart disease stroke and cancer.

19

The
Semicolon

The colon and the semicolon are often confused and used as if they were interchangeable. They serve very different functions, however, and their correct use can dramatically improve a reader's understanding of your writing. Here is one function of the semicolon.

A semicolon can replace a period; in other words, it can appear between two independent clauses.

You should use the semicolon when the two clauses (sentences) you are joining are closely connected in meaning or when there is a cause-and-effect relationship between them.

> I'm too tired; I can't stay awake any longer.

> There's a good movie on tonight; it's Michael Moore's *Bowling for Columbine*.

A period could have been used instead of the semicolon in either of these sentences, but the close connection between the clauses prompted the writer to use a semicolon.

Certain connecting or transitional words are sometimes put between independent clauses to show a cause-effect relationship or the continuation of an idea. Words or phrases used in this way are usually preceded by a semicolon and followed by a comma.

; also,	; furthermore,	; nevertheless,
; as a result,	; however,	; on the other hand,
; besides,	; in addition,	; otherwise,
; consequently,	; in fact,	; then,
; finally,	; instead,	; therefore,
; for example,	; moreover,	; thus,

Spencer studied all night; as a result, he fell asleep in the middle of the exam.

There are only two of us; however, we're both pretty big.

Our neighbours have put in a new pool; as a result, we've become best friends.

In other words, *a semicolon + a transitional word/phrase + a comma* = a link strong enough to come between two related independent clauses.

Note, however, that when the highlighted words and phrases are used as non-essential expressions rather than as connecting words, they are separated from the rest of the sentence by commas (comma rule 2, page 184).

However hard I try, I just can't seem to master particle physics.

Ten years from now, however, I'm sure I'll have no difficulty with the subject.

To make a COMPLEX LIST easier to read and understand, put semicolons between the items instead of commas.

A complex list is one in which at least one component part already contains commas. Here's an example:

We need to pack several items: matches to start a fire; an axe or hatchet to cut wood; cooking utensils and eating implements; and, of course, food.

In Exercises 19.1 and 19.2, put a check mark (✔) next to the sentences that are correctly punctuated. Consult the answers on page 353 before continuing.

Exercise 19.1

1. _____ We arrived at the wedding a little late; in fact, we missed the first prayer and the vows.

2. _____ The weather was beautiful; perfect for the wedding.

3. _____ The groom untied his bowtie; he felt a bit claustrophobic.

4. _____ The bride stumbled in the aisle; when the heel of her shoe broke.

5 _____ The minister sneezed during the bride and groom's kiss; of course, he apologized.

6. _____ I wanted to attend the reception at the Saint Mary's Boat Club, however, my fear of boats prevailed, and I did not go.

7. _____ The bride and groom bought many things at the last minute: candles for the reception tables, flowers and candelabra for the ceremony, ribbon, fabric, and satin hearts for the decorations, and, finally, a lacy garter for the bride.

8. _____ The minister encouraged the couple to recite traditional vows, instead, they wrote their own.

9. _____ At first, the couple thought they would be married in the bride's hometown of Sydney; later, they decided it would be more convenient to be wed in Halifax, where they both live.

10. _____ The flower girls wore white, the bridesmaids wore yellow.

Exercise 19.2

1. _____ We should get in bed early tonight; for we have to be up by 6:00 a.m.

2. _____ Zach missed the David Usher concert; however, he knew he couldn't really afford to take the time off work.

3. _____ Cigarette prices are outrageous, still my parents continue to smoke.

4. _____ David Suzuki visited my school last week; I found his life story to be very interesting.

5. _____ Due to the widespread drought; forest fires have been a serious problem this summer.

6. _____ If you need any help renovating your home; Ty would be glad to help.

7. _____ Nikita bought a dress and make-up, Chelsea bought a purse and a wallet, Kara bought a watch, a school bag, and a pair of shoes, but Jess bought a car.

8. _____ Many people can juggle three balls; Mr. Peddle can juggle seven.

9. _____ I wanted an exciting adventure; so we went to the Calgary Stampede.

10. _____ Carlos wants to be a doctor; consequently, he is practicing an illegible signature.

Some people are skilled in many fields;
Kumari, for example, is both a good
plumber and a great cook.

Exercise 19.3

Correct the faulty sentences in Exercise 19.1.

Exercise 19.4

Correct the faulty sentences in Exercise 19.2.

Exercise 19.5

Insert commas and semicolons where necessary in these sentences. Be careful: some of the punctuation we've included is incorrect. Then check your answers carefully.

1. When I was four years old my parents told me I was adopted ever since then I have wondered who my biological parents are.
2. My brother has two children I have seven children my younger sister has only one child and my older sister, who is not married, has none.
3. Michelle who is from Chicoutimi and Niko who is from Bathurst speak French at home but at work they speak mainly English.
4. Brant couldn't afford a diamond ring for Anne-Marie, therefore he bought her a cubic zirconia.
5. When I take a long time at a task I am slow when my boss takes a long time he is thorough.
6. When James graduated from Sheridan College he went to California to work in an animation studio as a result his family lost touch with him.
7. There will be plenty of time for you to watch television later but right now I need you to clean the bathroom.
8. *Anne of Green Gables* by L.M. Montgomery is the story of a red-haired orphan from Prince Edward Island. First published in 1908 it is one of the best-selling Canadian books of all time.
9. I collect autographs of famous people, for example I have signatures from Kurt Browning Mike Myers and Catriona Le May Doan.
10. The comforter is blue and yellow plaid we chose the curtains and wall colour to complement it.

GO TO WEB

EXERCISES 19.1, 19.2

Exercise 19.6

Correct the punctuation in these sentences by inserting commas and semi-colons where necessary.

1. Marwan and Dahlia did not want a big wedding ceremony so they eloped to Las Vegas instead.

2. Art Linkletter is 90 years old however he doesn't look a day over 70.

3. When Mary Jane and Mary Anne go out together in public people always confuse them after all they are identical twins.

4. I wondered why Sparky was limping unfortunately he had a splinter in his paw.

5. At the beginning of the school year, I am always faced with the same problems: buying new school supplies registering for my courses buying new clothes and making new friends.

6. The idea of a voyage to the moon was once science fiction now there is talk of sending a spacecraft to Pluto.

7. We have continually adjusted the budget by decreasing expenditures and increasing revenue, this careful monitoring has produced higher net income.

8. Running the red light at 100 km/h, Ian crashed into a truck, fortunately no one was hurt.

9. Please leave the books on the counter I'll sort through them later.

10. There is much debate over who actually invented the baseball glove nevertheless Canadians are convinced that the true inventor is Art Irwin, from Toronto.

Exercise 19.7

Correct these sentences where necessary.

1. I have read about the seven wonders of the world I think the CN Tower should be included.

2. Alex Trebek hosts *Jeopardy!* on television I wish I could be a contestant on that show.

3. The twins took a train trip to Alberta, they were exhausted by the end of the long ride.

4. My mother is going back to school, she has already bought her books and a backpack.

5. I can't believe Satchel called me yesterday, I thought he was planting trees in British Columbia.

6. Timothy Eaton established a chain of Canadian department stores he started a mail-order business in 1884.

7. Angus McAskill, the Cape Breton giant, was not unusually large at birth as an adult, however, he measured a startling 2.36 metres tall.

8. The toboggan is a sled designed by Aboriginal peoples for work not pleasure today it is most commonly used by children.

9. There are many famous Bobbys in hockey: Bobby Hull was famous for his slapshot Bobby Orr for speed and Bobby Clarke for his tough attitude.

10. Klondike ice-cream bars are named for the place where gold was first discovered during the Yukon Gold Rush, the lucky explorers who started the rush to the Klondike were George Carmac Skookum Jim and Tagish Charley.

Exercise 19.8

All the punctuation marks that appear in the following paragraph are correct; however, 15 punctuation marks are missing. Correct the paragraph by inserting commas and semicolons where they are needed.

In Winnipeg's Assiniboine Zoo you can see a statue of the original bear cub who inspired the children's stories about Winnie-the-Pooh Piglet and the rest of the animals from the Hundred Acre Woods. Some people think that Winnie-the-Pooh was created by Walt Disney actually he was the brain-child of British author A.A. Milne. During the First World War Milne and his young son, Christopher, used to visit a bear cub named Winnie at the London zoo. The bear itself was a visitor a Canadian soldier Captain Harry Colebourn had adopted the cub as a pet in Ontario in 1914 and brought it with him overseas. Because he hailed from Winnipeg Colebourn gave the cub the name of his hometown. When he was called to the front he left the cub with the London zoo. Thanks to Captain Colebourn's bequest to the zoo generations of children have grown up reading about the adventures of the fictional bear, Winnie-the-Pooh watching the Disney cartoons and movies about his adventures wearing his image on shirts, hats, socks, and sleepwear and dressing up in his likeness for costume parties and Hallowe'en night.

GO TO WEB

EXERCISE 19.3

Exercise 19.9

Have you mastered the semicolon? Try this exercise and find out. Insert semi-colons, commas, and change commas to semicolons as necessary in the following sentences. Twenty corrections are needed in this exercise.

1. Don't try to be irreplaceable. If you can't be replaced you can't be promoted.

2. Spring is almost here we must begin putting together our résumés for summer jobs.

3. If it weren't for our great pitching we would be in last place, our hitting is pathetic, our fielding is laughable, and our base stealing is nonexistent.

4. The class began on time, however it quickly became obvious that no one had done the assigned reading.

5. I'm sure you understand that I would like nothing better than for you to pass this course, however there may be a small fee involved.

6. It isn't pollution that is harming our environment, it is the impurities in the air and water that are doing it.

7. The class was not happy with the instructor's evaluations of their papers in fact some students decided immediately to appeal their grades.

8. Clothes it is said make the man. It must be true for naked people have little or no influence on society.

9. On my last trip to the French Riviera my Porsche broke down I lost money in the casinos and the models I was supposed to meet there never showed up. In short the trip was a disaster.

10. For some reason, my parents are not as enthusiastic as I am about my plan to live at home until I have saved enough money for the apartment of my dreams, in fact they are downright hostile.

20

The Colon

The **colon** functions as an introducer. When a statement is followed by a list or by one or more examples, the colon between the statement and what follows alerts the reader to what is coming.

> We have two choices: to study or to fail.

> There are two main requirements for success: hard work and good communication skills.

> Consider the alternative to moving: commuting four hours a day.

The statement that precedes the colon must be a complete sentence (independent clause). Therefore, a colon can never come immediately after *is* or *are*. Here's an example of what *not* to write.

> Three things I am violently allergic to are: cats, ragweed, and country music.

This is incorrect because the statement before the colon is not a complete sentence.

The colon, then, follows a complete statement and introduces a list or example(s) that defines or amplifies something in the statement. The information after the colon often answers the question "what?" or "who?"

> I am violently allergic to three things: (*what?*) cats, ragweed, and country music.

The farmer decided to try a new crop: (*what?*) ginseng.

The evil queen gazed into the mirror to admire the reflection of the fairest woman of them all: (*who?*) herself.

And finally, the colon is used after a complete sentence introducing a quotation.

Stephen Leacock did not think very highly of his readers' tastes in literature: "There are only two subjects that appeal nowadays to the general public: murder and sex; and, for people of culture, sex-murder."

The uses of the colon can be summed up as follows.

> The colon follows an independent clause and introduces one of three things: an example, a list, or a quotation.

Exercise 20.1

Put a check mark (✔) next to the sentences that are correctly punctuated, and then turn to page 355 to check your answers.

1. _____ The new federal law is: harsh and unfair.

2. _____ I take my approach to dieting from Marie Antoinette: "Let them eat cake."

3. _____ There are three documents that every Air Canada passenger requires: a plane ticket, a passport, and a boarding pass.

4. _____ Two reasons for the bankruptcy are: overspending and bad investments.

5. _____ Consider this example, John Turner.

6. _____ Don't forget to invite: Sarah, John, and Yvor.

7. _____ Carmen scooped her favourite flavours of ice cream into the bowl: strawberry, chocolate fudge, and banana ripple.

8. _____ Several factors contributed to the project's success, including: Jan's computer skills and Gary's rapid editing.

9. _____ One tool more was needed the screwdriver.

10. _____ As a result of that nerve-wracking interview with CBC radio, I learned something important about myself: I don't speak coherently under pressure.

GO TO WEB

EXERCISES 20.1, 20.2

Exercise 20.2

Insert colons in the following sentences where necessary, and then check your answers. If you find you've made any mistakes, review the explanation, and be sure you understand why your answers were wrong.

1. The list of ingredients in Bonnie Stern's new stir-fry recipe includes such exotic spices as saffron and five-spice powder.

2. Although the famous athlete had won many prizes, he was proudest of one particular achievement the Citizen of the Year award, from his home town in Saskatchewan.

3. The contents of my grandfather's desk drawer included the following items a bag of barley sugar candy, a stapler, three pencils, and a pocket watch.

4. As we drove through the Rockies, our cousin from Austria harped on one topic the spectacular beauty of the Alps.

5. Two items remain on the agenda the bake sale and the bottle drive.

6. Petula calls herself an omnivore, but there is one food she will not eat haggis.

7. I was surprised to discover that Katie is related to one of Canada's most famous painters A.J. Casson.

8. The premier gave a catchy slogan to his budget-cutting measures The Common-Sense Revolution.

9. Clearly, there was only one thing to do open the mysterious package.

10. After several days adrift at sea, the sailors were glad to see the rescue helicopter.

Exercise 20.3

Correct the incorrectly punctuated sentences in Exercise 20.1.

GO TO WEB

EXERCISES 20.3, 20.4

Exercise 20.4

As a test of your ability to use colons, correct the errors in the following sentences.

1. Lyle's new clarinet teacher says that: his perfect pitch is remarkable.

2. In Flaherty's case, the motive for learning to play the guitar was clear; to attract young women.

3. Guy and Gus, the neighbour's teenaged twins, are identical in appearance except for one feature Guy's purple, spiked hair.

4. Having spent two summers in Fort McMurray, I maintain that: it is the friendliest town I have ever visited.

5. Famous environmental activist, David Suzuki, made an insightful comment about modern consumer culture; "We want Earth to speed up; our forests don't grow fast enough for us."

6. Because the airline has lost my luggage more than once, I always pack three indispensable items in my carry-on luggage; a toothbrush, a clean pair of underwear, and a box of MacKintosh toffee.

7. One of the most important pieces of advice my Oma gave me was: to get at least eight hours of sleep a night.

8. For each and every action, there is: an equal and opposite criticism.

9. Portia is smitten with her new boyfriend and believes he is: better looking than Jason Priestly and funnier than Matthew Perry.

10. There are several features of rural life that appeal to me, such as: clean air, closeness to nature, and low housing costs.

21

Quotation Marks

Quotation marks (" ") are used to set off direct speech or dialogue, short passages of quoted material, and some titles. They are a signal to the reader that the words in quotation marks are not yours but someone else's. Quotation marks come in pairs; there must be a set to show where the dialogue, quotation, or title begins and a set to show where it ends. You must be absolutely sure that whatever you put between them is stated *exactly* as it is in the source you are using. The only other thing you need to know about quotation marks is how to punctuate what comes between them.

Dialogue

When you quote direct speech, include normal sentence punctuation. If the speaker's name or a comment about the speaker is included in your own sentence, set it off with commas. A comma or the end punctuation mark comes *inside* the final set of quotation marks.

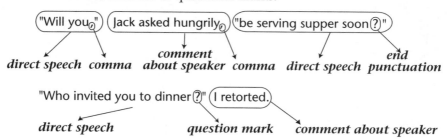

Be careful to put quotation marks only around direct speech (someone's exact words). Don't use quotation marks with indirect speech (a paraphrase of someone's words).

Jack asked hungrily whether I would be serving supper soon.
(These are not Jack's exact words, nor is the sentence a question.)

A quotation *within* a quotation is punctuated by single quotation marks:

According to John Robert Colombo, "the most widely quoted Canadian aphorism of all time is Marshall McLuhan's 'The medium is the message.'"

Quoted Material

When you quote a **short** passage (three lines of print or less), you can work it into your own sentence. Use a comma to introduce a quotation of one or more sentences, and include normal sentence punctuation within the quotation marks.

Speaking to the Canadian League of Poets, Maude Barlow declared, "If you want to know who is going to change this country, go home and look in the mirror."

"As you grow old," wrote Richard Needham, "you lose your interest in sex, your friends drift away, your children ignore you. There are other advantages, of course, but these would seem to me the outstanding ones."

Describing her childhood, author Carol Shields has said, "It was all very good, but it wasn't enough."

If your own introductory words form a complete sentence, use a colon to introduce the quotation:

Author Carol Shields expresses only one regret about her childhood: "It was all very good, but it wasn't enough."

If the passage you are quoting is a word or two, a phrase, or anything less than a complete sentence, do not use a comma or a colon to introduce it.

It was not until 1929 that Canadian women were legally recognized as "persons."

When Lester B. Pearson received the Nobel Peace Prize in 1957, the presentation speech recognized his "powerful initiative, strength, and perseverance."

This year's winner of the Wacky Warning Label Contest is, "Never iron clothes while they are being worn."

All the lines of a *long* quoted passage (more than three lines of print) should be indented ten spaces from the left margin. Long quotations are not enclosed in quotation marks. The block indentation indicates to the reader that the words set off in this way are not yours but some other writer's. (Turn to Chapter 26 to find examples of the treatment of long quotations.)

College writing normally requires that you indicate the source of any material you quote. The easiest way to do this is to give the author's surname, if it's not already included in your sentence, and the page reference in parentheses at the end of the quotation.

For example:

In the eighteenth century, a lifelong bachelor observed, "Marriage has many pains, but celibacy has no pleasures" (Johnson 214).

According to Dr. Samuel Johnson, "Marriage has many pains, but celibacy has no pleasures" (214).

These source identifications are called parenthetical citations.

Some instructors prefer footnotes or endnotes to parenthetical citations. Find out what format your instructor requires and follow it. In any library or bookstore, you will find a variety of style guides and handbooks that explain different styles of documentation. Your instructor will be happy to recommend one.

Titles

Unless you are using a word processor that prints *italics,* titles of books or other entire works should be <u>underlined</u>. Titles of parts of those books or works should be put in quotation marks. Thus, titles of books, magazines, pamphlets, newspapers, plays, films, and albums should be italicized or underlined. Titles of single articles, essays, stories, poems, or songs should be placed in quotation marks.

Below, you will find an example of a bibliography (a list of works consulted or cited in a research paper) showing how titles of different kinds of publications are punctuated.

Essay in an anthology	Atwood, Margaret. "Pornography." *Canadian Content.* Ed. Sarah Norton and Nell Waldman. 4th ed. Toronto: Harcourt, 2000. 347–53.
Speech reprinted in a book	Brown, Rosemary. "Overcoming Sexism and Racism — How?" *Racism in Canada.* Ed. Ormond McKague. Saskatoon: Fifth House, 1991. 163–77.
Song lyric reprinted in an anthology	Cohen, Leonard. "Suzanne Takes You Down." *An Anthology of Canadian Literature in English.* Ed. Donna Bennett and Russell Brown. 2 vols. Toronto: Oxford, 1983. 2:350.
Book review in a periodical	Conway, J.F. "The Good, the Bad, the Ugly." *The Literary Review of Canada* Apr. 1995:17–19.
Article in a newspaper	Delacourt, Susan. "Losing Interest." *Globe and Mail* 1 Apr. 1995: D1.
Encyclopedia entry	"Flag Debate." *The Canadian Encyclopedia.* 2nd ed. Edmonton: Hurtig, 1988. 2:789.
Novel	Findley, Timothy. *Headhunter.* Toronto: HarperCollins, 1993.
Article in a magazine	McMurdy, Deirdre. "Drugstore Cowboy." *Maclean's* 2 Dec. 1991: 74.
Chapter in a book	Norton, Sarah, and Brian Green. "Cracking the Sentence Code." *The Bare Essentials, Form A.* 5th ed. Toronto: Harcourt, 2001. 55–69.

In the following exercises, place quotation marks where they are needed and insert any necessary punctuation before and after each quotation. The answers for this chapter begin on page 356.

Exercise 21.1

1. The steak and eggs are delicious said Ian.

2. Ahmad said that he'd like to take Susan to dinner.

3. Frustrated with his reading assignment, Ben asked his instructor Is Margaret Atwood really one of Canada's best authors?

4. The *World Guide to Beer* describes Labatt's Blue as another sweetish pale lager.

5. Mt. Royal College has a good public relations program said Nancy.

6. In his poem A Road Not Taken, Robert Frost explains how he chose his particular path in life: I took the one less traveled by/ And that has made all the difference.

7. The children asked the teacher who had painted the mural on the classroom wall.

8. The front-page headline of today's Daily News is Shooting Foiled.

9. I'm not sure if my favourite song is Somewhere Over the Rainbow or Follow the Yellow Brick Road.

10. Bert asked Jim Why were you late for work today?

GO TO WEB

EXERCISES 21.1, 21.2

Exercise 21.2

1. After fourteen years in Nova Scotia said Dan I am finally applying for Canadian citizenship.

2. Michelle asked whether Tim Horton's was open 24 hours a day.

3. Everyone should know the procedures for protecting oneself in a household fire: stop, drop, and roll.

4. Why in the world asked Yosef would you gamble away $5,000?

5. Children are encouraged to ask their parents for genealogical information for the family tree project.

6. The monument to Samuel de Champlain quotes from his journal: As for me, I labour always to prepare a way for those willing to follow.

7. Did Led Zeppelin sing the old Hank Snow song, I'm Moving On?

8. I wish I were as wealthy as you, said Ashley, wondering why her debt load was so high.

9. After recording his voice on a wax cylinder for an Edison phonograph, Peter Jennings said This is something you get to do only once in your life.

10. I will never forget two of my mother's sayings Never ask yourself a question and Never give yourself an answer if you do.

GO TO WEB

EXERCISES 21.3, 21.4

Exercise 21.3

This exercise is designed to test your understanding of how to punctuate dialogue, quotations, and titles in your writing. When and where do you use quotation marks? Italics (or underlining)? Which punctuation marks precede and follow a quotation?

1. If you enjoyed The Pelican Brief, you will surely like The Firm.

2. Holy Hotcakes! exclaimed Robin after watching Batman eat a huge breakfast.

3. An annual article in the magazine Atlantic Progress is Best Companies to Work For in Atlantic Canada.

4. One of the most romantic classic novels is Wuthering Heights by Emily Brontë.

5. When a reporter asked Pierre Trudeau how far he was willing to go to crush the FLQ crisis, Trudeau said Just watch me!

6. On my computer screen saver, I have these lines from In Flanders Fields by John McCrae: In Flanders fields the poppies blow/ Between the crosses, row on row.

7. John Ralston Saul has emphatically stated The French language in Canada is stronger than ever and, in fact, is getting stronger every day.

8. David Usher's most intense song might be My Way Out from his solo album Morning Orbit.

9. Samantha doesn't care too much for curling, but she says there is one activity she is very familiar with: "Curling my hair!"

10. Charlotte Whitton, once the mayor of Ottawa, summarized for many women the frustrations of the fight for equality To be considered half as good as a man, a woman has to be twice as smart. But then she added Fortunately, it's not difficult.

22

Question Marks, Exclamation Marks, and Punctuation Review

The Question Mark

Everyone knows that a **question mark** follows an interrogative, or asking, sentence, but we all sometimes forget to include it. Let this chapter serve as a reminder not to forget!

Put a question mark at the end of every interrogative sentence.

The question mark gives your readers an important clue to the meaning of your sentence. "There's more?" (interrogative) means something quite different from "There's more!"(exclamatory), and both are different from "There's more."(declarative). When you speak, your tone of voice conveys the meaning you intend; when you write, your punctuation tells your reader what you mean.

The only time you don't end a question with a question mark is when the question is part of a statement.

Question	Statement
Are you going?	I asked whether you were going.
Do you know the answer?	I wonder if you know the answer.
Is there enough evidence to convict him?	The jury deliberated whether there was enough evidence to convict him.

Exercise 22.1

Supply the correct end punctuation for these sentences, and then check your answers on page 357.

1. Rosa inquired whether the Chateau Frontenac would charge her for an additional night's stay
2. Does it make any difference to you if we bring our Duck Tolling Retriever with us when we visit
3. I often wonder if there is life on other planets
4. Should you decide to purchase this dishwasher, I will give you a free box of detergent as a bonus
5. How can anyone possibly eat an entire lobster without making a mess
6. Please tell me whether I can get my money back if I return these shoes before Saturday
7. When the Blue Jays make it to the finals again, do you think Trisha will finally agree to watch a baseball game with us
8. Whatever happened to the University of Winnipeg jacket Dad bought in 1972
9. The pressing question that remains is whether the new premier will change the carpet in the legislature buildings
10. Did you know that Manitoba's Golden Boy, the province's symbol of hope and prosperity, is over 5 m tall

GO TO WEB

EXERCISES 22.1, 22.2

The Exclamation Mark

Consider the difference in tone between these two sentences:

There's a man behind you.
There's a man behind you!

In the first sentence, information is being supplied, perhaps about the line of people waiting their turn at a grocery store checkout counter. The second sentence might be a shouted warning about a mugger.

Use an **exclamation mark** as end punctuation only in sentences requiring extreme emphasis or dramatic effect.

Note that the exclamation mark will have "punch" or dramatic effect only if you use it sparingly. If you use an exclamation mark after every other sentence, how will your readers know when you really mean to indicate excitement? Overuse of exclamation marks is a technique used by comic book writers to try to heighten the impact of their characters' words. Ironically, the effect is to neutralize the impact. You will seldom find exclamation marks in academic or business writing.

Practically any sentence could have an exclamation mark after it, but remember that the punctuation changes the meaning of the sentence. Read the following sentences with and without an exclamation mark, and picture the situation that would call for each reading.

She's gone   Speak softly
The window was open   Move quickly

Exercise 22.2

Supply appropriate end punctuation in these sentences.

1. Please pour me a drink That salsa is hot
2. I'm shocked   After nine years of dating, Blair finally proposed to Camilla
3. "More, More " screamed the crowd at the Barenaked Ladies concert
4. Leave this house at once I never want to see you again
5. The War of 1812 called forth feats of extraordinary bravery
6. You've torn a hole in my shirt
7. "Help I'm drowning " came a cry from the lake
8. I was astonished by the latest figures describing child poverty in Canada They indicate that one out of five children lives in desperately poor circumstances
9. Don't look back It's gaining on us
10. I can't endure this torture any longer I'm leaving

Exercise 22.3

Supply appropriate punctuation for the 15 sentences in the following paragraph. No answers are given for this exercise.

(1) I used to wonder why my great-grandfather never talked about his youth, even when we youngsters plied him with questions (2) Then, to my surprise, I discovered that he was ashamed of his past as a circus clown (3) How could anyone be embarrassed about such a fascinating career (4) It has been my life-long ambition to become comedian, like Matthew Perry or Jim Carrey, so what more prestigious pedigree could I claim (5) Grandpapa, however, doesn't see his past from my perspective (6) Because his father was a lawyer and his two brothers were doctors, he always felt his choice of career was second-rate (7) "How could a circus buffoon hold his head up around such serious professionals " he asks (8) I try to tell Grandpapa that he was a kind of doctor, too (9) After all, don't people say that laughter is the best form of medicine (10) Researchers have conducted studies to confirm this truth (11) I question whether there is any higher calling than helping people laugh (12) Laughter not only breaks down social barriers, it

also releases powerful brain chemicals called endorphins (13) Endorphins create such an overwhelming feeling of relaxation and well-being that they can actually ease pain (14) Comedy functions as such effective natural medicine that you could say clowns and comedians serve as naturopathic doctors (15) Is there, then, any more noble way to spend one's career than clowning around

GO TO WEB

EXERCISES 22.3, 22.4, 22.5, 22.6

Punctuation Review

The following exercises will test your knowledge of all the punctuation you have studied in Unit 4. All of the sentences below contain errors: punctuation is either misused or missing. Work through these exercises slowly and carefully, checking your answers to each set before going on to the next. If you make a mistake, go back to the chapter dealing with that punctuation mark and review the explanation and examples.

Exercise 22.4

1. Wait for us we cried as their boat headed toward the rapids unfortunately we were too late to take the plunge.

2. Every day on the guided wilderness hike includes a new adventure, such as: canoeing rock climbing and eagle watching.

3. I didn't know if I would be able to meet Wendy at Green Gables so after much discussion we decided to meet at the ice cream parlour in downtown Cavendish.

4. Our accounting instructor was surprised to learn that most of us had never before heard of debits or credits, in fact many of us had never even balanced a chequebook.

5. The visiting Texan wondered why Canadians were so slow to boast about their many accomplishments?

6. Don't forget to take your gloves my mother advised.

7. Even though the audience at The Pantages Theatre was shouting Bravo the actor had no choice, but to follow the two police officers off the stage and into the paddy wagon.

8. According to the recipe this cake requires two eggs, however I'm sure we could substitute one egg and two egg whites.

9. Sharon Pollock's play Blood Relations creates two possible portraits of the accused murderer Lizzie Borden; a dutiful nineteenth-century daughter and an outraged feminist rebel.

10. Tell me a little about yourself; the interviewer asked. What makes you think you can handle this job.

GO TO WEB

EXERCISES 22.7, 22.8

Exercise 22.5

Insert the 25 punctuation marks that are missing from this paragraph.

Although we usually work well together Chantal and I had a hard time deciding on a figure to carve for this year's Winterlude ice-carving competition. At first we both favoured a Walt Disney design such as Mickey Mouse Pluto or Winnie-the-Pooh. We soon realized however that there was a crucial flaw common to all these ideas none of them involved a Canadian theme.

We flipped through popular magazines we quizzed our friends and we even searched the Internet to try to find a Canadian alternative but we had no luck. Everywhere we looked we seemed to be surrounded by American images.

Chantal finally had an idea. Why don't we carve an ice statue of Louis Riel she said. He's a Canadian hero.

That's too complicated I protested. What about a Canadian beaver "That's too boring," was Chantal's response.

We argued back and forth about the design for days we were both so annoyed that we were almost ready to withdraw from the competition. In the end, we settled on a compromise that reflected humorously on our own frustration a tableau featuring a baffled-looking beaver surrounded by a jeering gang of Disney characters.

Exercise 22.6

Correct the 20 misused or missing punctuation marks in this paragraph.

My cousins from Alberta Jeff and Janet decided to spend their summer vacation touring British Columbia. They wanted to experience the full flavour of local hospitality so they chose to stay in a bed and breakfast in each town they visited. To their surprise they soon discovered that staying in a quaint bed and breakfast can involve some unexpected adventures!

In Victoria Jeff and Janet slept on a hundred-year-old bed that was so saggy it gave them both terrible backaches no matter how much they tossed and turned they could not find a comfortable position. In Whistler they discovered an additional guest in the turn-of-the-century converted stable loft they had rented a green-eyed Siamese cat that was accustomed to sleeping at the foot of the bed. In Kelowna they were startled awake at 8 a.m. by their exuberant host who delivered them an unannounced breakfast in bed!

After hearing about my cousins' experiences, I wonder why anyone would opt to stay in a bed and breakfast? Because I am someone who values privacy, I can't imagine a more nerve-wracking way to spend my vacation. I guess Jeff and Janet have a more flexible sense of humour than I do, they took all these unexpected incidents in stride. When I asked them whether they regretted their choice of accommodation they told me that "all their future travel plans would include bed and breakfasts." We've never had so much fun they declared enthusiastically.

Exercise 22.7

This is the last test of your punctuation skills. Supply any missing punctuation and correct any punctuation errors in the following sentences.

1. When a national contest invited Canadians to come up with an alternative to the expression as American as apple pie the winning entry was as Canadian as possible under the circumstances.

2. Lorie Kane and Mike Weir are two golfers who are putting Canada on the map in world-class golf tournaments and we should all be proud of them.

3. When the young freelance journalist placed his first article in Maclean's he insisted to everyone he knew You must read my masterpiece.

4. In 1850 Henry David Thoreau spent a week in Canada but was not much impressed by his experience I fear that I have not got much to say about Canada, not having seen much, what I got by going to Canada was a cold.

5. William Shatner who played Captain Kirk on *Star Trek* is now over seventy years old but few people would question that he was more than fifty?

6. Your son's favourite movie Franklin the Green Knight plays regularly on CBC television so why don't you make a recording of it.

7. As far as Albert is concerned a livable city must have three important things an NHL hockey team a CFL football team and a Swiss Chalet with delivery service.

8. What is the Canadian equivalent to Patrick Henry's famous pronouncement during the American War of Independence Give me liberty or give me death

9. Thank you Estelle for all your help with the bake sale Laura mumbled her mouth full of chocolate chip cookies.

10. After much consideration my uncle decided to stop subscribing to The Globe and Mail instead he decided to order three new papers The National Post The Vancouver Sun and The St. John's Telegram.

Exercise 22.8

Write a paper of approximately two pages describing and reflecting upon a significant event in your life. When you've finished, review your paper carefully, checking spelling, sentence structure, and grammar. Pay particular attention to punctuation. Be sure you have put a question mark at the end of every interrogative sentence and used exclamation marks only when necessary, for emphasis. Check your placement of commas, semicolons, and colons. If you quote, either in dialogue or from a source, check the position of your quotation marks and the punctuation that precedes and follows each quotation. Here are some topics you might consider:

1. A move from one town or city to another
2. The birth of a sibling or a child
3. Your first date
4. A sports achievement
5. A memorable vacation
6. A meeting with a famous person
7. Your first term at college
8. The death of a relative
9. A serious mistake from which you learned a valuable lesson
10. A moment of spiritual revelation

UNIT 5

Organizing Your Writing

23

Finding Something to Write About

Everybody knows that content is important in writing. Not so many writers seem to know that form is just as important. In fact, you can't really separate the two: *what you say is how you say it.* Writing a paper (or an essay, or a report, or a letter, or anything else) is like doing a chemistry experiment: you need the right amount of the right ingredients put together in the right proportions and in the right order. There are five steps to follow.

1. Choose a satisfactory subject
2. Select the main points of your subject
3. Write a thesis statement
        or
   Write an outline
4. Write the paragraphs
5. Revise the paper

If you follow these steps faithfully, in order, we guarantee that you will write clear, organized papers.

Note that, when you get to step 3, you have a choice. You can choose to organize your paper by means of a thesis statement or by means of an outline. The thesis statement approach works well for short papers—those no longer than about 500 words. An outline is necessary for longer papers and is often useful for organizing shorter papers. Ideally, you should learn to use both methods of organizing your writing; in fact, your teacher may require that you do so.

Steps 1, 2, and 3 make up the planning stage of the writing process. Be warned: done properly, these three steps will take you at least as long as steps 4 and 5, which involve the actual writing. The longer you spend on the preliminary steps, the less time your writing will take, and the better your paper will be.

Choose a Satisfactory Subject

Unless you are assigned a specific subject by a teacher or supervisor, choosing your subject can be the most difficult part of writing a paper. Apply the following guidelines carefully, because no amount of instruction can help you to write a good paper on something you don't know anything about or on something that is inappropriate for your audience or purpose. Your subject should satisfy the **4-S test**.

A satisfactory subject is SIGNIFICANT, SINGLE, SPECIFIC, and SUPPORTABLE.

1. Your subject should be **significant.** Write about something that your reader needs to know or might want to know. Consider your audience and choose a subject that will be significant to that audience. This doesn't mean that you can't ever be humorous, but, unless you're another Stephen Leacock, an essay on "How I Deposit Money in My Bank" will probably be of little significance to your reader. The subject you choose must be worthy of the time and attention you expect your reader to give to your paper.

2. Your subject should be **single.** Don't try to do too much in your paper. A thorough discussion of one topic is much more satisfying to read than a skimpy, superficial treatment of several topics. A subject such as "The challenge of government funding cutbacks to colleges and universities" includes too much to deal with satisfactorily in one paper. Limit yourself to a single topic, such as "How private sector donations are helping our college meet the challenge of funding cutbacks."

3. Your subject should be **specific.** This requirement is closely tied to the "single" requirement. Given a choice between a general topic and a specific one, you should choose the latter. In a short paper, you can't hope to say anything new or significant about a large topic: "Employment opportunities in Canada," for example. But you could write an interesting, detailed discussion on a more specific topic, such as "Employment opportunities in Nova Scotia's hospitality industry." You can narrow a broad subject by applying one or more **limiting factors** to it. Try thinking of your subject in terms of a specific *kind*, or

time, or *place*, or *number*, or *person* associated with it. To come up with the hospitality topic, for example, we limited the subject of employment opportunities in Canada in terms of both place and kind.

4. Your subject must be **supportable.** You must know something about the subject (preferably, more than your reader does), or you must be able to find out about it. Your discussion of your subject will be clear and convincing only if you can include examples, facts, quotations, descriptions, anecdotes, and other details. Supporting evidence can be taken from your own experience or from the experience of other people. In other words, your topic may require you to do some research.

Exercise 23.1

Imagine that you have been asked to write a 500-word paper and given this list of subjects to choose from. Test each subject against the guidelines we've given and identify what's wrong with it. When you're finished, check your answers on page 359.

1. The grocery industry
2. Our universe
3. Changing a printer cartridge
4. The pros and cons of self-directed mutual funds
5. My nephew's first birthday party
6. Acadian culture in Nova Scotia, New Brunswick, and Prince Edward Island
7. Capital punishment is wrong
8. Problems with Canada's new gun control laws
9. How to teach yourself the flute or the clarinet
10. Fundamentals of quantum physics

Exercise 23.2

Consider the following subjects in terms of the 4-S guidelines. Some are possibilities for satisfactory papers of 300 to 500 words but fail to satisfy one or more of the guidelines. Others are hopeless. Revise the "possible" subjects to make them significant, single, specific, and supportable.

1. Some insects are helpful to farmers
2. The best way to curl your hair
3. The Canadian Shield
4. The role of the Métis in Canadian history
5. How to prevent damage to your computer
6. Avoiding national debt

7. Obstacles facing lumber companies
8. Internet piracy
9. Great women senators
10. Pollution is a serious problem

Exercise 23.3

List five subjects that you might choose to write about. Be sure each subject is *significant*, *single*, *specific*, and *supportable*.

Select the Main Points of Your Subject

Now that you have an appropriate subject for your paper, give some thought to the approach you're going to take to develop it. There are many possible ways of thinking and writing about a subject. In a short paper, you can deal effectively with only a few aspects of your topic. How do you decide which aspects of your subject to discuss, which **main points** to make and explain? One way is to make a list of everything you can think of that you might want to say about the subject. Some preliminary research may help too. You may discover some points about the subject that you hadn't thought of.

Another way—especially useful if you find you're stuck for ideas—is to ask yourself questions about your subject. Run your subject through this list of questions and see which one "fits" it best. (The symbol S stands for your subject.)

1. How do you make or do S? (What are the main steps to follow in accomplishing S?)
2. How does S work?
3. What are the main parts or components of S?
4. What are the main functions of S?
5. What are the important features or characteristics of S?
6. What are the main kinds or types of S?
7. What are some significant examples of S?
8. What are the causes of S?
9. What are the effects or consequences of S?
10. What are the main similarities and/or differences between S and _____ ?
11. What are the main advantages (or disadvantages) of S?
12. What are the reasons for (or against) S?

These questions suggest some of the various ways of looking at or thinking about a subject. Most subjects will yield answers to more than one of these questions. You should focus on the question that produces the answers that are closest to what you want to say about your subject. These answers are the main points that you will discuss in your paper.

Here's how the procedure works. Assume you've been forced to accept as your subject "Writing good business letters." Don't despair. Run down the list of questions until you find one you can answer intelligently. The process might go something like this:

1. How do you write a business letter?
   No answer comes to mind. Scratch that question.

2. How does a business letter work?
   Silly question; it doesn't make sense.

3. What are the main parts of a business letter?
   Well, there are the inside address, the body, the salutation, and the complimentary close, but you don't know enough about them to write anything intelligent or original on them.

4. What are the main functions of the business letter?
   You can think of three: to request information, to place an order, and to complain about some product or service. This has possibilities, but you find these aspects of your subject too dull to write a paper on, so you continue.

5. What are the important characteristics of a good business letter?
   At last! Here's one you can answer satisfactorily. You know that a business letter should be clear, brief and to the point, and courteous. Assuming that you know or can find out some pertinent and interesting information about these characteristics, you're all set. Clarity, conciseness, and courtesy are the points you will discuss in your paper. (Before you go any further, though, it's a good idea to apply the remaining questions in the box to your subject, just to be sure there isn't another question that yields answers you like even better.)

Selecting the main points to write about isn't a difficult process, but it is time-consuming. Don't rush. Take the necessary time. This is a crucial stage in the writing process.

Here are a few sample subjects, together with some main points that were discovered by applying the list of questions highlighted on page 228. Study the chart below until you're sure you understand how to find suitable main points for any subject.

Subject	Selected Question	Main Points
A good teacher	5. What are the important characteristics of a good teacher?	• subject knowledge • ability to communicate this knowledge • respect for students
Choosing a college	12. What are the reasons for choosing a particular college?	• tuition costs • program offerings • availability of distance education options
Urban life	11. What are the main advantages of urban life?	• accessibility of various forms of entertainment • minimum commuting time to the workplace • ethnically diverse neighbourhoods
Heart disease	8. What are the causes of heart disease?	• lack of exercise • stress • poor diet
A fulfilling job	1. How do you find a fulfilling job?	• take inventory of your personal strengths and interests • interview people working in different fields • choose the field that best suits your abilities and your personality • network with people working in your chosen field

Subject	Selected Question	Main Points
The accounting profession	6. What are the main kinds of accountants?	• Chartered Accountant • Registered Industrial Accountant • Certified General Accountant

As a general rule, you should try to identify between *two* and *five* main ideas for your subject. If you have only one main idea, you have a subject suitable for a paragraph, not an essay. If you have more than five, you have too much material for a short paper. Select the most important aspects of the subject, or take another look at it to see how you can focus it more specifically.

Exercise 23.4

In this exercise, select a question from the highlighted list on page 228 and generate good main points for each subject.

Subject	Selected Question	Main Points
1. My home town		• • • •
2. My chosen career		• • • •
3. A family ritual		• • • •

Subject	Selected Question	Main Points
4. Travelling alone		•
		•
		•
		•
5. Canadian foods		•
		•
		•
		•

Exercise 23.5

For each of the five subjects you chose in Exercise 23.3, list two to five main points. If suitable main points do not immediately come to mind, apply to your subject the 12 questions highlighted on page 228, one at a time, until you find the one that fits best. The answers to that question are your main points.

TESTING YOUR MAIN POINTS

Now take a close look at the main points you've chosen in Exercise 23.5. It may be necessary to revise some of them before going any further. Are some points really too minor to bother with? Do any of the points overlap in meaning? Are there any points that are not directly related to the subject?

Main points must be SIGNIFICANT, DISTINCT, and RELEVANT.

To be completely satisfactory, the main points you have chosen to write about must all be **significant:** worth writing a paragraph or more on. You shouldn't have any trivial ideas mixed in with the important ones.

Each of the main points you've chosen must also be **distinct.** That is, each must be different from all the others. There must be no overlap in meaning. Check to be sure you haven't given two different labels to what is really one aspect of the subject.

Finally, each main point must be **relevant**; it must be clearly **related** to the subject. It must be an aspect of the subject you are writing about, not some other subject. For example, if you're writing about the advantages of a subject, cross out any disadvantages that may have appeared on your list.

Exercise 23.6

Here is a list of subjects, each of which is followed by some possible main points. Circle the unsatisfactory point(s) in each group.

1. Reasons for quitting smoking
   - financial savings
   - threat of lung cancer
   - threat of heart disease
   - high cost of cigarettes

2. How to train a dog
   - establish authority
   - give commands clearly
   - leash and clicker
   - give rewards promptly

3. The disadvantages of computer-assisted distance education
   - lack of contact with instructor
   - additional expenses for computer, modem, and Internet connection
   - lack of contact with peers
   - lack of motivation due to isolation
   - unreliability of technology

4. Characteristics of depression
   - fatigue
   - weight gain or loss
   - loss of sex drive
   - insomnia
   - feelings of sadness
   - low self-esteem
   - depression in adolescents

5. Responsibilities of the office administrator
   - answer telephone
   - maintain supervisor's personal agenda

- take a half-hour lunch break
- monitor internal and external correspondence
- prepare budgets
- schedule meetings

6. Controversial technologies

- cloning
- stem cell collection
- electronic fingerprinting
- cold fusion
- risk of radiation

7. The main energy sources used in Canada

- coal
- natural gas
- water
- nuclear power
- wood
- hydroelectric power
- oil

8. Consequences of the destruction of the World Trade Centre on 11 September 2001

- tightening of airport security
- rise in insurance rates
- decrease in tourism
- economic downturn
- increased defence spending

GO TO WEB

EXERCISE 23.1

Exercise 23.7

Study the main points you chose in Exercise 23.5 on page 232. Cross out any that are not *significant*, *distinct*, or *relevant* to the subject. If necessary, add new main points so that you end up with at least three main points for each subject.

ORGANIZING YOUR MAIN POINTS

Now that you've decided on three or four main points to discuss, you need to decide in what order you wish to present them in your paper. Choose the order that is most appropriate for your particular subject.

There are four basic ways to arrange main points in an essay: CHRONOLOGICAL, CLIMACTIC, LOGICALLY LINKED, and RANDOM order.

1. **Chronological order** means in order of time sequence, from first to last. Here's an example:

   Subject

   The development of a relationship

   Main Points

   - attraction
   - meeting
   - discovery
   - intimacy
   - disillusionment

2. **Climactic order** means presenting your strongest or most important point last. Generally, you would discuss your second-strongest point first and the others in between, like this:

   Subject

   Reasons for eating organic food

   Main Points

   - avoid contact with toxic substances
   - reduce risk of some cancers
   - support local growers
   - promote a healthy environment

3. **Logically linked** order means that the main points are connected in such a way that one point must be explained before the next can be understood. Consider this example:

   Subject

   Main causes of obsesity in children

   Main Points

   - too much television
   - too many high-fat snacks
   - not enough exercise

The logical link here is this: because chilldren watch too much television, they consume too many high-fat, packaged snacks while they are sitting in front of the screen. Consequently, they need more exercise to burn up the additional calories, but they don't get it. Thus, childhood obesity results. The first two points must be explained before the reader can fully under-stand the third.

4. **Random order** means the points can be satisfactorily explained in any order. A random arrangement of points is possible only if the main points are *equally significant* and *not chronologically or causally linked*, as in this example:

Subject	Main Points
Reasons for shopping online	• save money • save time • locate hard-to-find items

Exercise 23.8

Below we have identified eight subjects, together with several main points that could be used to develop them. For each subject, number the points so that they are arranged in the order suggested.

Subject	Order	Main Points
1. How to send an e-mail message	chronological	_____ start e-mail program _____ enter name of recipient and subject of message in spaces provided _____ click on "New Document" icon to start a new message _____ click on "Send" icon to send message _____ type body of message
2. Differences between amateur and professional figure skating	climactic	_____ amateur skaters focus on the skating judges; professional skaters focus on the audience _____ amateur skaters are not paid; professional skaters are paid

Subject	Order	Main Points
		_____ amateur skaters must include mandatory elements in their programs; professional skaters have more artistic licence
3. How to prepare for a job interview	chronological	_____ visit the company's Web site _____ dress carefully _____ prepare answers to standard interview questions _____ ask a friend to role play the interview with you
4. How the Olympic Games benefit Canadians	logical	_____ they provide role models of active, goal-oriented achievers _____ they enhance the profile of amateur sport in Canada _____ they encourage young people to pursue their dreams
5. Negative effects of pesticides	logical	_____ pesticides cause deformity and death in birds _____ pesticides kill the bugs that birds eat _____ pesticides release toxic chemicals into the air and ground
6. Why affirmative action policies are necessary	chronological	_____ they place members of visible minorities in positions of power _____ they foster the development of a more egalitarian society

Subject	Order	Main Points
		_____ they create powerful role models for future generations of visible minority groups
7. Why affirmative action policies should be discontinued	climactic	_____ there is no evidence that they help improve social attitudes toward members of visible minorities _____ they create an unrealistic distribution of power and rewards _____ they create unfair hiring practices
8. Why Canadian nurses emigrate to the United States	climactic	_____ salaries are higher in the U.S. _____ jobs are more plentiful in the U.S. _____ working conditions are more pleasant in the U.S.

Exercise 23.9

Using your list of subjects and main points from Exercise 23.7, arrange the main points for each subject in the most appropriate order. (*Note:* Keep your answer sheet. You will need it in some of the exercises that follow.)

In this chapter, you've learned how to choose a satisfactory subject and how to select and arrange the main points of that subject—the first two steps in the five-step process we outlined at the beginning of the chapter. Now it's time to decide whether you'll develop your paper by the thesis statement method or by the outline method. We think the former generally works best for short papers and the latter for long papers, but this distinction isn't hard and fast. Your wisest choice is to learn both ways to structure a paper. You will often get the best results if you use them together.

24

Writing the Thesis Statement

In Chapter 23, you chose a topic and selected some aspects of it to discuss. Now you're ready for the third step in developing a paper. If you're writing a short paper, we recommend that you use the method presented in this chapter. If you're writing a longer paper or if your teacher prefers the outline method, you may prefer to turn now to Chapter 25, "Writing the Outline."

The key to a clearly organized paper is a **thesis statement**—a statement near the beginning of your paper that announces its subject and scope. The thesis statement helps both you and your readers because it plans your paper for you, and it tells your readers exactly what they are going to read about. In fiction, telling readers in advance what they are going to find would never do. But for practical, everyday kinds of writing, advance notice works well. Term papers, technical reports, research papers, office memoranda, and business letters are no place for suspense or surprises. In these kinds of writing, you're more likely to get and keep your readers' attention if you indicate the subject and scope of your paper at the outset. The thesis statement acts like a table of contents, giving a clear indication of what follows. It's a kind of map of the territory covered in your paper: it keeps your reader (and you) on the right track.

A thesis statement is a sentence that clearly and concisely indicates the SUBJECT of your paper, the MAIN POINTS you will discuss, and the ORDER in which you will discuss them.

To write a thesis statement, you join your **subject** to your **main points**, which you have arranged in order. To join the two parts of a thesis statement, you use a **link**. Your link can be a word or a phrase such as *are*, *include, consist of, because,* or *since,* or it can be a colon.[1] Here is the simple formula for constructing a thesis statement.

S consists of 1, 2, 3 ... n.

subject + link + main points

Here's an example:

Three characteristics of a good business letter (are) conciseness, clarity, and courtesy.

       subject   *link*   *main points*

Exercise 24.1

In each of the following thesis statements, underline the subject with a wavy line, circle the link, and underline the main points with a straight line. Answers begin on page 362.

1. Although each region of the country has its own local symbol, the universal Canadian symbols are the maple leaf, the beaver, and the moose.

2. According to the Conference Board of Canada, among the skills most desired by today's employers are the ability to listen carefully, speak clearly, and write effectively.

3. Many people with chronic indigestion may actually be suffering from one of three ailments: lactose intolerance, complex carbohydrate intolerance, or irritable bowel syndrome.

4. In order to find prosperity in the twenty-first century, Canada must abandon its dependence on a resource-based economy, cultivate a spirit of entrepreneurship, and encourage immigration.

5. International travel has expanded my horizons in several ways: it has exposed me to the ways of other cultures, it has taught me foreign languages, and it has made history a living experience for me.

---

[1] Remember that a colon can be used only after an independent clause. See Chapter 20 if you need a review.

6. Learning a musical instrument benefits a child in several important ways, including the development of self-discipline, listening skills, and hand-eye coordination.

7. Because they lack a strategic plan, personnel, or funding, many young companies falter in the early growth stage.

8. The elderly, children, and asthmatics form the main population groups that suffer from air pollution.

9. Youth organizations that encourage leadership in young people include Scouts, Junior Achievement, and Boys and Girls clubs.

10. Margaret Laurence's *Stone Angel*, Margaret Atwood's *Robber Bride*, and Michael Ondaatje's *In the Skin of a Lion* are three of the most critically-acclaimed Canadian novels.

When you combine your subject with your main points to form a thesis statement, there is an important rule to remember.

The main points should be **grammatically parallel.**

This rule means that, if main point 1 is a word, then main points 2 and 3 and so on must be words too. If main point 1 is a phrase, then the rest must be phrases. If your first main point is a dependent clause, then the rest must be dependent clauses. Study the model thesis statements you analyzed in Exercise 24.1. In every example, the main points are in grammatically parallel form. For each of those thesis statements, decide whether words, phrases, or clauses were used. If you think your understanding of parallelism is a bit wobbly, review Chapter 10 before doing the following exercises.

Exercise 24.2

This exercise will test your grasp of the parallelism principle. In each question below, one main point is not parallel to the others. Circle the faulty main point and rewrite it to make it grammatically parallel.

1. The reunion episode of *The Beachcombers* was
   a. touching
   b. made me laugh
   c. suspenseful
   d. tragic

2. Young creatures of any species appeal to us because they are
   a. small
   b. vulnerable
   c. respond to affection
   d. cuddly

3. Dan's favourite uncle is
   a. tall
   b. wealthy
   c. good-natured
   d. gives away a lot of money to charity

4. A successful investigative journalist requires
   a. relentless curiosity
   b. able to write rapidly
   c. stamina to work long hours
   d. keen interviewing skills

5. Gina lost 12 pounds by
   a. exercising daily
   b. smaller portions
   c. increasing her water intake
   d. giving up ice cream

6. Antoinette uses the World Wide Web to
   a. access her bank accounts
   b. order her groceries
   c. online bingo
   d. buy her work uniforms

7. To be an effective manager, you must
   a. maintain open lines of communication
   b. allow free exchange of ideas
   c. encourage input from subordinates
   d. creating opportunities for advancement

8. In order to encourage an entrepreneurial spirit in school children, we need to
   a. make entrepreneurship part of the curriculum
   b. experiential learning should be encouraged
   c. allow children to make mistakes and learn from them
   d. profile the achievements of successful Canadian entrepreneurs

Exercise 24.3

Put a check mark (✔) before the sentences that are grammatically parallel. When you have completed the exercise, check your answers on page 363.

1. _____ Frequent causes of failure in college are lack of responsibility, lack of discipline, and not knowing basic skills.

2. _____ Organization, expression, and revision are the three keys to good writing.

3. _____ As a person ages, time moves more quickly, the body moves more slowly, and you have to get artificial teeth.

4. _____ I can't decide whether to take a certificate program in computing, accounting, or learn to be a dental assistant.

5. _____ A first-class baseball team must have a superb pitching staff, a top-notch hitting line-up, and a speedy outfield.

6. _____ Daycare, parental leave, and having work equity are not just women's issues.

7. _____ Although both Canada and the United States are affluent societies, Canadians seem to be more obsessed than their American cousins with life insurance, pension plans, and savings.

8. _____ There are two important questions about the high-technology field: will it remain a fast-track industry and Canada's role in it.

9. _____ No matter how hard I search, I cannot seem to find the hospitality, generosity, or people working together as a community that I remember from my youth in Newfoundland.

10. _____ Organizational behaviourists teach that managers assume three different corporate roles: they are *disseminators* when communicating their goals; when they lead working groups, they are *negotiators*; and they are *figureheads* when they represent the company to outside agencies.

Exercise 24.4

Now revise the incorrect sentences in Exercise 24.3.

GO TO WEB

EXERCISES 24.1, 24.2

Exercise 24.5

Revise the following draft thesis statements. Be sure that the main points of each statement are significant, distinct, relevant, and grammatically parallel. Some sentences contain more than one kind of error. Make corrections as needed; then compare your revisions with our suggested answers on page 363.

1. Under the "Skills" section of his résumé, George highlighted his abilities as a writer, a bilingual communicator, a listener, and a speaker.

2. Pierre Trudeau will always be remembered as one of Canada's most influential prime ministers because he was intelligent, progressive, provocative, and who can forget the pirouette he did behind Queen Elizabeth's back.

3. We hope that the new provincial Minister of Health will establish wellness clinics, fund nurse practitioners, legislate midwifery, and also change the Ministry logo.

4. His dedication to physical fitness is so extreme that he exercises for three hours a day, follows a strict diet he obtained from a Tibetan monk, and rides on a stationery bicycle while he dictates his correspondence.

5. Even though it is a dead language, Latin is worth learning because you learn the history of the English language, improves one's ability to recognize problems with English grammar, and there are a lot of funny Latin jokes.

GO TO WEB

EXERCISE 24.3

Exercise 24.6

Find the subjects and main points you produced for Exercise 23.9 in Chapter 23. Combine each subject with its main points to make a thesis statement. Be sure the main points are expressed in parallel form.

We said at the beginning of this chapter that a thesis statement outlines your paper for you. Before we turn to the actual writing of the paper, it will be useful for you to have a general idea of what the finished product will look like.

In a short paper, each main point can be explained in a single paragraph. The main points of your subject become the **topics** of the paragraphs, as shown below in the model format for a paper with three main points.

paragraph 1: contains your introduction and thesis statement

Title
_____
_____
_____
_____
S consists of 1, 2, and 3.

paragraph 2: explains your first main point

Topic sentence introducing main point 1.
_____
_____
_____
_____
_____
_____
_____ .

paragraph 3: explains your second main point

Topic sentence introducing main point 2.
_____
_____
_____
_____
_____ .

paragraph 4: explains your third main point

Topic sentence introducing main point 3.
_____
_____
_____
_____
_____
_____ .

paragraph 5: states your conclusion

_____
_____
_____
_____ .

Notice the proportions of the paragraphs in the model format. This format is for a paper whose main points are approximately equal in significance, so the body paragraphs are approximately equal in length. (In a paper in which your last main point is more important than the other points, however, the paragraph that explains it will probably be longer than the other paragraphs.)

Notice, too, that the introductory and concluding paragraphs are much shorter than the ones that explain the main points. Your introduction should not ramble on, and your conclusion should not trail off. Get to your main points as quickly as you can, and end with a bang, not a whimper.

Exercise 24.7

An example of a paper that follows the model format exactly is Nancy Marshall's "Consequences in Parenting" which appears in Appendix A. Read it through; then go back and underline the thesis statement and the topic sentences.

25

Writing the Outline

For longer compositions — business and technical reports, research papers, and the like — an outline is often necessary. A good outline maps out your paper from beginning to end. It shows you before you begin to write what you have to say about each of your main points. Outlining spares you the agony of discovering too late that you have too much information about one point and little or nothing to say about another.

Once you've chosen a satisfactory subject and main points to discuss, the next step is to expand what you have into an organized plan for your finished paper. To do this, you may need to do some more thinking or reading to gather additional information and supporting details. (For ideas about what kinds of information you might use, see "Developing Your Paragraphs" in Chapter 26.) After you've assembled all the information you think you'll need, prepare the outline.

First, write down your main points in the order you've decided is best for your presentation. Leave lots of space under each main point. Using Roman numerals (I, II, III, and so on), number your main points. Now, under each main point, indent and list the examples, facts, quotations, or other supporting information you're going to use to explain it. Again, leave lots of space. Check to be sure these items are arranged in an order that will be clear to your reader.[1] Label your supporting points *A, B, C,* and so on.

If some of these supporting points need to be explained or developed, indent again and list the second level of supporting points, numbering them *1, 2, 3,* and so on. Third-level supporting details, if there are any, should be

---

[1] The four kinds of order explained in Chapter 23 apply to the arrangement of ideas within a paragraph as well as to the arrangement of main points in a paper.

indented under the points to which they relate and labelled *a, b, c,* and so on. Add the introduction and the conclusion, and you're done. Your outline might look something like the following one.

Introduction
    Attention-getter
    Thesis statement/statement of subject

I. First main point
   A. Item that develops first main point
   B. Item that develops first main point
      1. Supporting material that develops item B
      2. Supporting material that develops item B

II. Second main point
   A. Item that develops second main point
   B. Item that develops second main point
   C. Item that develops second main point

III. Third main point
   A. Item that develops third main point
      1. Supporting material that develops item A
        a. Detail
        b. Detail
      2. Supporting material that develops item A
   B. Item that develops third main point

Conclusion
    Summary
    Memorable statement

Questions about how to arrange your information under each main point and how much time to spend on a particular point should be cleared up at the outline stage. If, for example, you find you have six subheadings under main point I and only one under main point II, you need to do some rethinking to balance your paper. Main points should be supported by approximately equal amounts of information.

Preparing a satisfactory outline takes time. Be prepared to spend time adding, deleting, and rearranging your ideas and supporting details until you're completely satisfied with the arrangement and proportions of your outline.

If you have access to a word-processing program with an outline feature, be sure to try it out! These programs can be very helpful to an inexperienced writer faced with a writing assignment and little knowledge of how to organize it.

After you have written and revised your outline, all you have to do to draft your paper is to make the main points into paragraph divisions, rework the supporting points into sentences, and add an introduction and a conclusion. Chapter 26 explains how.

To show you the relationship between an outline and the final product, we've recreated the outline that Martin Luther King, Jr. might have used in writing "The Dimensions of a Complete Life" (see pages 309–13):

The Dimensions of a Complete Life
Introduction
    Attention-getter: John's vision of the new Jerusalem and its meaning
    Statement of subject: the three dimensions of a complete life: length,
                            breadth, and height
I.   The length of life
    A. definition: the dimension of life in which one is concerned with self
    B. the need to love oneself properly
        1. Joshua Liebman's explanation in *Peace of Mind*
        2. responsibility of each person to discover his "calling"
            a. example of streetsweeper
            b. Douglas Mallock's verse
    C. the danger of getting "bogged down" in the length of life
II. The breadth of life
    A. definition: the dimension of life in which one is concerned about
        others
    B. the need to be concerned about all humanity
        1. the parable of the Good Samaritan
        2. the significance of the parable in our time
            a. racial groups often interested only in their own status
            b. nations often concerned only about their own well-being
        3. the interdependence of all individuals and nations
            a. poverty affects us all
            b. disease affects us all
            c. John Donne, "No man is an island..."
III. The height of life
    A. the danger of neglecting this dimension
    B. the difficulty of maintaining religious beliefs in our modern world
    C. the need to remember that "great things" are invisible
        1. law of gravitation

2. mind of an architect
3. human personality
4. God
   D. the power of belief in God
Conclusion
   Summary: relationship between the three dimensions of life and the
               Commandments
   Memorable statement: prayer that all people may share in John's
                        vision

Once you've mapped out your plan in an outline, the task of writing the essay is much easier. You can see where you're going and how to get there. Remember, the more time you spend on planning, the less time you will spend on writing—and the better your paper will be.

Exercise 25.1

Read "The Dimensions of a Complete Life" on pages 309–13 in Appendix A. Find the paragraphs that correspond to the various headings and subheadings in our outline of the piece. Label the paragraphs and sentences to show where they fit into the outline: I, A, B, 1, 2, and so on.

Exercise 25.2

Read Brian Green's "In Defence of Video Games" in Appendix A and write an outline for it. When you've finished, turn to pages 364–65 to compare your outline with ours.

Exercise 25.3

Turn to the subjects and main points you developed for Exercise 23.9 in Chapter 23 and create an outline for a paper on one of those subjects.

26

Writing the Paragraphs

You are now at step four in the writing process. With either a thesis state-ment or an outline before you, you are ready to turn your main points into paragraphs. Does that sound like a magician's trick? It isn't. The only skills involved are knowing what a paragraph looks like and how to put one together.

A paragraph looks like this:

Three or more sentences that specifically support or explain the topic go in here.

A sentence that introduces the **topic** (or main idea) of the paragraph goes here.
_____
_____
_____
_____
_____
_____
A sentence that concludes your explanation of the topic goes here.

Sometimes a main point can be explained satisfactorily in a single para-graph. If the main point is complicated and requires lots of support, several paragraphs are needed. Nevertheless, whether it is explaining a main point of a paper or an item supporting a main point, every paragraph contains two things: a **topic sentence** (usually the first sentence in the paragraph) and several sentences that develop the topic.

Beginning with a sentence that clearly states your main idea is a good way to start a paragraph. The sentences that follow support or expand on the topic. The key to making the paragraph *unified* (an important quality of

English paragraphs) is to make sure that each of your supporting sentences relates directly to the main idea introduced in the topic sentence.

Exercise 26.1

Turn to Appendix A and read Francine Letourneau's "Determining Personality Type: The Welland Method." Study the third, fourth, and fifth paragraphs and find in each the three basic components of a paragraph: the topic sentence, the supporting sentences, and the conclusion. Compare your answer with ours on pages 365–66.

Developing Your Paragraphs

How do you put a paragraph together? First, write your topic sentence, telling your reader what topic (main point or idea) you're going to discuss in the paragraph. Next, develop your topic. An adequately developed paragraph gives enough supporting information to make the topic completely clear to the reader. An average paragraph runs between 75 and 200 words (except for introductions and conclusions, which are shorter), so you will need lots of supporting information for each point.

Unless you are writing from a detailed outline and have all the supporting material you need listed in front of you, you need to do some more thinking at this point. Put yourself in your reader's place. What does your reader need to know in order to understand your point clearly? If you ask yourself the six questions listed below, you'll be able to decide what **kinds of development** to use to support a particular topic sentence. The kind of development you use is up to you. Decide on the basis of your topic and what the reader needs to know about it.

1. Is a **definition** necessary?

If you're using a term that may be unfamiliar to your reader, you should define it. Use your own words in the definition. Your reader needs to know what *you* mean by the term—and, besides, quoting from the dictionary is a boring way to develop a paragraph. Below, Francine Letourneau describes "Wheelers," a particular kind of personality type.

"Wheelers" responded to the bridge siren the way thoroughbreds respond to the starting gate. Unable to shift focus . . . when their journey was interrupted, Wheelers would dash through side streets at high speeds, trying to get to the next canal bridge before it went up. Sometimes they would make it and cross in triumph, racing back the way they had come (only on the other side of the canal) to resume their interrupted trip. It didn't seem to matter to them that this detour often took longer than waiting for a ship to pass, or that [other drivers] were streaming across the bridge by the time Wheelers arrived on the other side. A truly tragic sight was the Wheeler who dashed upstream or down, only to arrive at the next bridge seconds after its siren had sounded. Committed Wheelers would speed on to the third bridge, while the less fanatic would either wait where they were or return in defeat to the first bridge—which, by the time they arrived, would again be functioning. Disorganized and inefficient, Wheelers nonetheless were energetic, enthusiastic, and optimistic. They were often thin and nervous.

Letourneau, Francine. "Determining Personality Type: The Welland Method." Reprinted by permission of the author.

You should include a definition, too, if you're using a familiar term in a specific or unusual way. In the following paragraph, Martin Luther King, Jr. defines what he means by "the length of life."

Now let us notice first the length of life. I have said that this is the dimension of life in which the individual is concerned with developing his inner powers. It is that dimension of life in which the individual pursues personal ends and ambitions. This is perhaps the selfish dimension of life, and there is such a thing as moral and rational self-interest. If one is not concerned about himself, he cannot be totally concerned about other selves.

King, Martin Luther, Jr. "The Dimensions of a Complete Life." *The Measure of a Man.* Philadelphia: Christian Education Press, 1959.

Exercise 26.2

Write a paragraph in which you define one of the following terms:

patriotism	multiculturalism	courtesy
friendship	generosity	a soul mate
education	karma	a good parent

2. Would **examples** help to clarify the point?

Providing a number of examples is probably the most common method of developing a topic. Readers become confused, even suspicious, when they read unsupported generalizations or statements of opinion. One of the most effective ways of communicating your idea is by offering clear, relevant examples. Brian Green uses this technique throughout his essay "In Defence of Video Games." For example,

> Video games are not the mindless diversion television is. They demand skill, strategy, hand-eye co-ordination, and precision. Imagine combining the hands of a surgeon with the reflexes of a goalie and the mind of a chess grand master, and you'll begin to get a picture of the top game players. Most of the skills required seem to be genetically determined, but even the slowest and clumsiest of us could benefit from developing and augmenting whatever level of skill we have. On my favourite game I have twice achieved a score of 9,000. The fourteen-year-old daughter of a colleague consistently racks up scores of 200,000 on the same game. I would not hesitate to put my life in her hands in any situation requiring manual dexterity, quick reflexes, and steady nerves.

Green, Brian. "In Defence of Video Games." Reprinted by permission of the author.

Sometimes one example developed in detail is enough to allow the reader to understand what you mean. In the following paragraph, King uses a famous story from the Bible as an example of showing proper concern for others.

> You remember one day a man came to Jesus and he raised some significant questions. Finally he got around to the question, "Who is my neighbour?" This could easily have been a very abstract question left in mid-air. But Jesus immediately pulled that question out of mid-air and placed it on a dangerous curve between Jerusalem and Jericho. He talked about a certain man who fell among thieves. Three men passed, two of them on the other side. And finally another man came and helped the injured man on the ground. He is known to us as the Good Samaritan. Jesus says in substance that this is a great man. He was great because he could project the "I" into the "thou."

King, Martin Luther, Jr. "The Dimensions of a Complete Life." *The Measure of a Man.* Philadelphia: Christian Education Press, 1959.

Exercise 26.3

Write a six- to ten-sentence paragraph based on one of the topic sentences below, using examples to develop it.

Leisure time for the average Canadian worker is decreasing.
Why bother to learn a second language?
Nutrition has a significant impact on mental health.
Life begins at thirty (*or* twenty *or* forty, etc.).

3. Is a **series of steps** or **stages** involved?

Sometimes the most effective way to develop the main idea of your paragraph is by explaining how to do it — that is, by relating the process or series of steps involved. Make sure you break the process down into its component parts and explain the steps logically and precisely. The paragraph that follows explains, step by step, the process of pouring a perfect glass of beer.

> Holding the glass in your left hand and the bottle in your right, tilt the mouth of the glass 30 degrees to the right, toward the bottle. Hold the bottle so that its mouth just touches the rim of the glass, then tilt the bottom up and out, away from the glass, allowing the beer to flow slowly down the inside wall of the glass. Continue to raise the bottom of the bottle so that the flow of beer is slow and steady. Emptying the contents of the bottle into the glass should take about ten seconds. As the beer accumulating in the glass nears the rim, begin to tilt the glass upright, while maintaining an even flow from the bottle. The aim is to empty the bottle into the glass at a rate that will leave a head of foam approximately one to one-and-a-half inches tall on top of the beer in the glass.

Exercise 26.4

Write a paragraph developed as a series of steps telling your reader how to make or do something you are good at. (Choose a significant rather than a trivial topic.)

4. Would **specific details** be useful?

Providing your reader with concrete, specific, descriptive details can be an effective way of developing your main point. In some paragraphs, numerical facts or statistics can be used to support your point effectively — just be sure your facts are correct and your statistics up-to-date! In the following paragraph, underline the specific details that Susan Luey uses to develop this paragraph:

> You must prepare carefully for the event if you hope to avert disaster later in the process. To begin with, remove everyone except you and your pet from the war zone. This precaution is necessary both to ensure safety and to prevent recriminations later on when the cat tries to enlist sympathy from weak-willed family members (see "aftermath," below). Next, assemble your protective apparel. You will need impact-resistant ski goggles that can be tightly fitted over the face, and a helmet with ear flaps. A football helmet will do but is cumbersome. Professionals prefer the leather flying helmets favoured by old-time pilots; these not only provide adequate protection but also allow for manoeuvrability. A knee-length leather or heavy canvas waterproof coat, sturdy hip waders, and elbow-length gauntlets complete the ensemble. Fill a squirt gun or squeeze bottle with shampoo, stuff an old towel under your coat, and you are ready for combat.

Luey, Susan. "Here Kitty, Kitty." Reprinted by permission of the author.

Exercise 26.5

Write a six- to ten-sentence paragraph describing one of the following topics. Try to include details that involve several of the physical senses: sight, hearing, touch, smell, and taste. Be sure to begin with a clearly identifiable topic sentence.

Your favourite possession
A cherished pet
A natural (or physical) setting that is special to you
A place that makes you feel uncomfortable
A restaurant (or store, service provider, class, etc.) you will never go back to

5. Would a **comparison** or **contrast** help to clarify your point?

A **comparison** points out similarities between objects, people, or ideas; it shows how two different things are alike. A **contrast** points out dissimilarities between things; it shows how two objects, people, or ideas are different. A **comparison and contrast** identifies both similarities and differences. In the paragraph below, Sue Sutton explains the commonly debated differences between "tourists" and travellers."

The distinction between "tourists" and "travellers". . . goes like this. Tourists wear inappropriate clothes (either too bright, too expensive and fashionable, or laughably colonial, "safari" style), have too much money and spend it in the wrong places, don't care about the culture in which they travel, and don't stay long enough to understand or help. Travellers, on the other hand, are more benign, tactfully grubby, and have found a deeper connection with the culture in which they are moving.

Sutton, Sue. "Of Tourists, Travellers, and True Travellers." *Globe and Mail* 22 March 1995: A22.

In the following paragraph, notice how Martin Luther King, Jr. explains a difficult, abstract topic, "the dimensions of life," by comparing it to something with which the reader is familiar.

These are the three dimensions of life, and without the three being correlated, working harmoniously together, life is incomplete. Life is something of a great triangle. At one angle stands the individual person; at the other angle stand other persons; and at the top stands the Supreme, Infinite Person, God. These three must meet in every individual if that life is to be complete.

King, Martin Luther, Jr. "The Dimensions of a Complete Life." *The Measure of a Man.* Philadelphia: Christian Education Press, 1959.

Exercise 26.6

Write a paragraph comparing or contrasting two celebrities. Begin your paragraph with a topic sentence.

---

6. Would a **quotation** or **paraphrase** be appropriate?

Occasionally, you will find that someone else—an expert in a particular field, a well-known author, or a respected public figure—has said what you want to say better than you could ever hope to say it. In these cases, quotations—as long as they are kept short and not used too frequently—are useful in developing your topic. Notice how Martin Luther King, Jr. uses a famous quotation to sum up the point of this paragraph.

As long as there is poverty in the world I can never be rich, even if I have a billion dollars. As long as diseases are rampant and millions of people in this world cannot expect to live more than twenty-eight or thirty years, I can never be totally healthy even if I just got a good check-up at Mayo Clinic. I can never be what I ought to be until you are what you ought to be. This is the way our world is made. No individual or nation can stand out boasting of being independent. We are interdependent. So John Donne placed it in graphic terms when he affirmed, "No man is an island entire of itself. Every man is a piece of the continent, a part of the main." Then he goes on to say, "Any man's death diminishes me because I am involved in mankind, and therefore never send to know for whom the bell tolls; it tolls for thee."

King, Martin Luther, Jr. "The Dimensions of a Complete Life." *The Measure of a Man.* Philadelphia: Christian Education Press, 1959.

A **paraphrase** is a summary in your own words of someone else's idea. Remember to indicate whose idea you are paraphrasing, the way King does in the following paragraph.

Some years ago a learned rabbi, the late Joshua Liebman, wrote a book entitled *Peace of Mind.* He has a chapter in the book entitled "Love Thyself Properly." In this chapter he says in substance that it is impossible to love other selves adequately unless you love your own self properly. Many people have been plunged into the abyss of emotional fatalism because they did not love themselves properly. So every individual has a responsibility to be concerned about himself enough to discover what he is made for. After he discovers his calling he should set out to do it with all of the strength and power of his being....

King, Martin Luther, Jr. "The Dimensions of a Complete Life." *The Measure of a Man.* Philadelphia: Christian Education Press, 1959.

 College writing normally requires that you indicate the source of any material you quote. The easiest way to do this is to give the author's surname and the page reference in parentheses at the end of your quotation; for example, (Green 299–300). At the end of your paper, include a Works Cited page, which is a list, in alphabetical order by authors' surnames, of all the books, articles, and other sources from which you have quoted in your paper. See page 209 for an example of the format to use. Follow the instructions given in whatever style guide your instructor recommends, or consult Joseph Gibaldi, *MLA Handbook for Writers of Research Papers,* 6th ed. (New York: Modern Language Association, 2003. http://www.mla.org).

When you plan the paragraphs of your essay, remember that you will often need to use more than one method of development to explain your points. The six methods outlined above can be used in any combination. Choose whichever kinds of development will be most helpful to your reader.

Exercise 26.7

Identify the kinds of development used in the following paragraphs (more than one kind may be present in each). Then turn to page 366 to check your answers.

1. "Here Kitty, Kitty," paragraph 7

2. "In Defence of Video Games," paragraph 3

3. "The Dimensions of a Complete Life," paragraph 3

4. "The Dimensions of a Complete Life," paragraph 7

5. "The Dimensions of a Complete Life," paragraph 16

6. "Of Tourists, Travellers, and True Travellers," paragraph 3

7. "Determining Personality Type: The Welland Method," paragraph 3

8. "The Dimensions of a Complete Life," paragraph 13

9. "Consequences in Parenting," paragraph 2

10. "Of Tourists, Travellers, and True Travellers," paragraph 1

Exercise 26.8

Choose one of the following topic sentences or make up one of your own. Write a paragraph of 100 to 150 words, using at least two different methods of paragraph development.

1. _____ is a city worth visiting.
2. People choose pets that are like themselves.
3. Family conflict due to the generation gap is unavoidable.
4. Vacation time actually makes workers more productive.
5. Rudeness has become a social epidemic.

Writing Introductions and Conclusions

Two paragraphs in your paper are not developed in the way we've just out-lined: the introduction and the conclusion. All too often, these paragraphs are dull or clumsy and detract from a paper's effectiveness. But they needn't. Here's how to write good ones.

The introduction is worth special attention because that's where your reader either sits up and takes notice of your paper or sighs and pitches it into the wastebasket. Occasionally, for a short paper, you can begin simply with your thesis statement or statement of subject. More usually, though, an **attention-getter** comes before the thesis statement. An attention-getter is a sentence or two designed to get the reader interested in what you have to say.

There are several kinds of attention-getter to choose from.

1. A little-known or striking fact (see "Consequences in Parenting," paragraph 1)
2. An interesting incident or anecdote related to your subject (see "Of Tourists, Travellers, and True Travellers," paragraph 1)
3. An opinion that you intend to challenge (see "In Defence of Video Games," paragraph 1)
4. A brief outline of the historical context of your subject (see "Determining Personality Type: The Welland Method," paragraph 1)
5. A statement of the significance of your subject (see "Here Kitty, Kitty," paragraph 1)
6. A definition of your subject—in your own words

Add your thesis statement to the attention-getter and your introduction is complete.

The closing paragraph, too, usually has two parts: a **summary** of the main points of your paper (phrased differently, please—not a word-for-word repetition of your thesis statement or your topic sentences) and a **memorable statement.** Your memorable statement may take several forms.

1. Challenge the reader to get involved (see "In Defence of Video Games," paragraph 5; "Of Tourists, Travellers, and True Travellers," paragraph 7)
2. Propose a suggestion for change (see "Consequences in Parenting," paragraph 5)
3. Refer back to the content of your opening paragraph (see "The Dimensions of a Complete Life, paragraph 20; "Determining Personality Type: The Welland Method," paragraph 6)
4. Present a relevant or thought-provoking statement, question, or quotation (see "Here, Kitty, Kitty," paragraph 8)
5. Highlight the value or significance of your subject.

Exercise 26.9

Using as many of the different kinds as you can, write an attention-getter and a memorable statement for five of the following topics.

1. Canada is (not) the best place in the world to live.
2. People who smoke, consume alcohol, or are overweight should (not) be forced to pay for their health care.
3. Running your own business is (not) the best way to guarantee career fulfillment.
4. Curling should (not) be an Olympic sport.
5. Today's women have (not) achieved equality with men.
6. I love (hate) country music.
7. Consumer culture is (not) the biggest threat to today's teenagers.
8. The most valuable thing parents can give their children is (not) their time.
9. It is (not) as necessary to reduce and reuse as it is to recycle.
10. Stress-related sickness is (not) increasing because of new technologies in the workplace.

Keeping Your Reader with You

As you write your paragraphs, keep in mind that you want to make it as easy as possible for your reader to follow you through your paper. Clear **transitions** and an appropriate **tone** can make the difference between a paper that con-fuses or annoys readers and one that enlightens and pleases them.

TRANSITIONS

Transitions are those words or phrases that show the relationship between one point and the next, helping a paragraph or a paper to read smoothly. Like turn signals on a car, they tell the person following you where you're going. Here are some common transitions you can use to keep your reader on track.

1. *To show a time relation:* first, second, third, next, before, during, after, now, then, finally, last
2. *To add an idea or example:* in addition, also, another, furthermore, similarly, for example, for instance
3. *To show contrast:* although, but, however, instead, nevertheless, on the other hand, in contrast, on the contrary
4. *To show a cause–effect relation:* as a result, consequently, because, since, therefore, thus

Here is a paragraph that has adequate development but no transitions:

There are several good reasons why you should not smoke. Smoking is harmful to your lungs and heart. It is annoying and dangerous to those around you who do not smoke. Smoking is an unattractive and dirty habit. It is difficult to quit. Most worthwhile things in life are hard to achieve.

Not very easy to read, is it? Readers are jerked from point to point until, battered and bruised, they reach the end. This kind of writing is unfair to readers. It makes them do too much of the work. The ideas may all be there, but the readers have to figure out for themselves how they fit together. After a couple of paragraphs like this one, even a patient reader can become annoyed.

Now read the same paragraph with the transitions added:

There are several good reasons why you should not smoke. *Among them, three stand out as the most persuasive. First,* smoking is harmful to your lungs and heart. *Second,* it is *both* annoying and dangerous to those around you who do not smoke. *In addition to these compelling facts,* smoking is an unattractive and dirty habit. *Furthermore, once you begin,* it is difficult to quit; *but then,* most worthwhile things in life are hard to achieve.

In the revised paragraph, readers are gently guided from one point to the next. By the time they reach the conclusion, they know not only what ideas the writer had in mind but also how they fit together. Transitions make the reader's job easier and more rewarding.

TONE

One final point. As you write the paragraphs of your paper, try to be conscious of your **tone.** Tone is simply good manners on paper. The words you use, the examples, quotations, and other supporting materials you choose to help explain your main points—they all contribute to your tone. When you are trying to explain something to someone, particularly if it's something you feel strongly about, you may be tempted to be highly emotional in your discussion. If you allow yourself to get emotional, chances are you won't be convincing. What will be communicated is the strength of your feelings, not the depth of your understanding or the validity of your opinion. To be clear and credible, you need to restrain your enthusiasm or anger and present your points in a calm, reasonable way.

Here are a few suggestions to help you find and maintain the right tone. Never insult your reader, even unintentionally. Avoid phrases such as "any idiot can see," "no sane person could believe," and "it is obvious that. . . ." What is obvious to you isn't necessarily obvious to someone who has a limited understanding of your subject or who disagrees with your opinion. Don't talk down to your readers as though they were children or hopelessly ignorant. Don't use sarcasm, profanity, or slang.

And don't apologize for your interpretation of your subject. Have confidence in yourself. You've thought long and hard about your subject, you've found good supporting material to help explain it, and you believe in its significance. Present your subject in a positive manner. If you hang back, using phrases such as "I may be wrong, but . . ." or "I tend to feel that . . .", your reader won't be inclined to give your points the consideration they deserve. Keep your reader in mind as you write, and your writing will be both clear and convincing.

Exercise 26.10

Rewrite the following paragraph, adding transitions where necessary and correcting any lapses in tone. Compare your revision to ours on page 366.

I never knew my great-grandparents, but my generation has a lot in common with theirs. They grew up in the 1930s, during the Great

Depression, when jobs were scarce. I may be wrong, but I think the job market today is in desperate shape! My great-grandfather had to hitch a train ride from a dried-up farm in Saskatchewan all the way to Cape Breton to find a job as a miner. He was my age. He worked the night shift in the mine for peanuts. No job security, no sick pay, and no pension. My cousins from Cape Breton are so broke that they're moving to Alberta to look for work in the oil fields. The work there is hard, but the wages are a damn sight better than the Employment Insurance they've been drawing in Sydney. I'm thinking of following them next year, if I ever finish this diploma program. I might start my own business here in Antigonish, if I can raise enough capital. It looks to me like my peers and I will probably have to do without the social safety net, including public health care and the Canada Pension Plan, that our parents and grandparents could count on. Any fool can see that members of Generation Y will have to pay their bills without much government help, so the sooner I start making my own fortune the better.

Exercise 26.11

Do either A or B.

A. Using one of the thesis statements you prepared in Chapter 24, Exercise 24.6, write a paper of approximately 400 words.
B. Using the outline you prepared in Chapter 25, Exercise 25.3, write a paper of 500 to 600 words.

27

Revising Your Paper

No one can write in a single draft an essay that is perfectly organized and developed, let alone one that is free of errors in sentence structure, grammar, spelling, and punctuation. The purpose of the first draft is to get down on paper something you can work with until you're satisfied it will meet your reader's needs and expectations. Planning and drafting should take up about half the time you devote to writing a paper. The rest should be devoted to revision.

Revision is the process of refining your writing until it says what you want it to say in a way that enables your readers to understand your message and to receive it favourably. These two goals, clear understanding and favourable reception, constitute good communication. You can accomplish these goals only if you keep your readers in mind as you revise. Because it reflects the contents of the writer's mind, a first draft often seems all right to the writer. But in order to transfer an idea as clearly as possible from the mind of the writer to the mind of the reader, revision is necessary. The idea needs to be honed and refined until it is as clear to your reader as it is to you. By revising from your reader's point of view, you can avoid misunderstandings before they happen.

What Is Revision?

Revision means "re-seeing." It does *not* mean recopying. The aim of revision is to improve your writing's organization, accuracy, and style. Revising is a three-stage process. Each step requires that you read through your entire essay, painful though this may be. The goal of your first reading is to ensure that your reader's information needs are met. In your second reading, you focus on structure. Your third reading concentrates on correctness. Here are the steps to follow in revising a paper.

1. Improve the whole paper by revising its content and organization.
2. Refine paragraph and sentence structure, and correct any errors in grammar.
3. Edit and proofread to catch errors in word choice, spelling, and punctuation.

Inexperienced writers often skip the first two stages and concentrate on the third, thinking they will save time. This is a mistake. In fact, they waste time —both theirs and their readers'—because the result is writing that doesn't communicate clearly and won't make a positive impression.

The best way to begin revising is to do nothing to the first version of your paper for several days. Let as much time as possible pass between completing your first draft and rereading it. Ten minutes, or even half a day, is not enough. The danger in rereading too soon is that you're likely to "read" what you *think* you've written—what exists only in your head, not on the paper. But if, like many writers, you haven't allowed enough time for this cooling-off period, don't despair. There are two other things you can do to help you get some distance from your draft. If your first draft is handwritten, type it out. Reading your essay in a different form helps you to "re-see" its content. Alternatively, read your paper aloud and try to hear it from the point of view of your reader. Listen to how your explanation unfolds, and mark every place you find something unclear, irrelevant, inadequately developed, or out of order.

Step 1
Revise Content and Organization

As you read your paper aloud, keep in mind the three possible kinds of changes you can make at this stage:

1. You can **rearrange** information. This is the kind of revision that is most often needed but least often done. Consider the order in which you've arranged your paragraphs. From your reader's point of view, is this the most effective order in which to present your ideas? If you are not already using a word-processing program, now is the time to begin. With a good word processor, moving blocks of text around is as easy as dealing a deck of cards.

2. You can **add** information. Adding new main ideas or more development is often necessary to make your message interesting and convincing as well as clear. It's a good idea to ask a friend to read your draft and identify what needs to be expanded or clarified. (Be sure to return the favour. You can learn a great deal by critiquing other people's writing.)
3. You can **delete** information. Now is the time to cut out anything that is repetitious, insignificant, or irrelevant to your subject and reader.

Use the checklist that follows to guide you as you review your paper's form and content.

CONTENT AND ORGANIZATION CHECKLIST

ACCURACY

Is everything you have said accurate?
- Is your information consistent with your own experience and observations or with what you have discovered through research?
- Are all your facts and evidence up-to-date?

COMPLETENESS

Have you included enough main ideas and development to explain your subject and convince your reader? Remember that "enough" means from the reader's point of view, not the writer's.

SUBJECT

Is your subject
- significant? Does it avoid the trivial or the obvious?
- single? Does it avoid double or combined subjects?
- specific? Is it focussed and precise?
- supportable? Have you provided enough evidence to make your meaning clear?

MAIN POINTS

Are your main points
- significant? Have you deleted any unimportant ones?
- distinct? Are they all different from one another, or is there an overlap in content?
- relevant? Do all points relate directly to your subject?
- arranged in the most appropriate order? Again, "appropriate" means from the reader's perspective. Choose chronological, climactic, logical, or random order, depending on which is most likely to help the reader make sense of your information.

INTRODUCTION

Does your introduction
- catch the reader's attention and make him or her want to read on?
- contain a clearly identifiable thesis statement?
- identify the main points that your paper will explain?

CONCLUSION

Does your conclusion
- contain a summary or reinforcement of your main points, rephrased to avoid word-for-word repetition?
- contain a statement that effectively clinches your argument and leaves the reader with something to think about?

TONE

Is your tone consistent, reasonable, courteous, and confident throughout your essay?

When you have carefully considered these questions, it's time to move on to the second stage of the revision process.

Step 2
Revise Paragraphs and Sentences

Here, too, you should allow time — at least a couple of days — between your first revision and your second. Enough time must elapse to allow you to approach your paper as if you were seeing it for the first time. Once again, read your draft aloud, and use this list of questions to help you improve it.

PARAGRAPH AND SENTENCE CHECKLIST

PARAGRAPHS

Does each paragraph
- begin with a clear, identifiable topic sentence?
- develop one — and only one — main idea?
- present one or more kinds of development appropriate to the main idea?
- contain clear and effective transitions to signal the relationship between sentences? Between paragraphs?

SENTENCES

Sentence Structure

1. Is each sentence clear and complete?
   - Are there any fragments or run-ons?
   - Are there any misplaced or dangling modifiers?
   - Are all lists (whether words, phrases, or clauses) expressed in parallel form?
2. Are your sentences varied in length? Could some be combined to improve the clarity and impact of your message?

Grammar

1. Have you used verbs correctly?
   - Are all verbs in the correct form?
   - Do all verbs agree with their subjects?
   - Are all verbs in the correct tense?
   - Are there any confusing shifts in verb tense within a paragraph?
2. Have you used pronouns correctly?
   - Are all pronouns in the correct form?
   - Do all pronouns agree with their antecedents?
   - Have any vague pronoun references been eliminated?

When you're sure you've answered these questions satisfactorily, turn to the third and last stage of the revision process.

Step 3
Edit and Proofread

By now you're probably so tired of refining your paper that you may be tempted to skip **editing**—correcting errors in word choice, spelling, and punctuation—and **proofreading**—correcting errors in typing or writing that appear in the last draft. But these final tasks are essential if you want your paper to make a positive impression.

Misspellings, faulty punctuation, and messiness don't always create misunderstandings, but they do cause the reader to form a lower opinion of you and your work. Careful editing and proofreading are necessary if you want your writing to be favourably received.

Most word-processing programs include a grammar checker and a spell checker. It is worthwhile running your writing through these programs at the editing stage. The newer programs have some useful features. For

ALLWAYS PROOFREAD CARFULLY BEFORE HADNING IN YOU'RE PAPER.

example, they will question (but not correct) your use of apostrophes; they will sometimes catch errors in subject–verb agreement; and they will catch obvious misspellings and typos.

But don't make the mistake of assuming these programs will do all your editing for you. Many errors slip past a computer's database, no matter how comprehensive the salesperson told you it is. Only you or a knowledgeable and patient friend can find and correct all errors.

If spelling is a particular problem for you, you should first run your paper through a spell checker. After that, you're on your own. Read your paper backward word by word, from the end to the beginning. Reading backward forces you to look at each word by itself and helps you to spot those that look suspicious. Whenever you're in doubt about the spelling of a word, look it up! If you find this task too tedious to bear, ask a good speller to read through your paper for you and identify any errors. (Then take this person out for dinner. If you get an A, add a movie.)

Here are the questions to ask yourself when you are editing.

EDITING CHECKLIST
WORDS

Usage
Have you used words accurately, to "mean" rather than "impress"?
- Have you eliminated any clichés, jargon terms, and slang expressions?
- Have you cut out any unnecessary words?
- Have you corrected any "abusages"?

Spelling
Are all words spelled correctly?
- Have you double-checked any sound-alikes or look-alikes?
- Have you used capital letters where they are needed?
- Have you used apostrophes correctly for possessives and omitted them from plurals?

PUNCTUATION

1. **Within Sentences**
   - Have you eliminated any unnecessary commas and included commas where needed? (Refer to the four comma rules as you consider this question.)
   - Have you used colons and semicolons where appropriate?
   - Are quotations appropriately marked?

2. **Beginnings and Endings**
   - Does each sentence begin with a capital letter?
   - Do all questions—and only questions—end with a question mark?
   - Are all quotation marks correctly placed?

TIPS FOR EFFECTIVE PROOFREADING

By the time you have finished editing, you will have gone over your paper so many times you may have practically memorized it. When you are very familiar with a piece of writing, it's hard to spot the small mistakes that may have crept in as you produced your final copy. Here are some tips to help you find those tiny, elusive errors.

1. Read through your essay line by line, using a ruler to guide you.
2. If you've been keeping a list of your most frequent errors in this course, scan your essay for the mistakes you are most likely to make.
3. Using the "Quick Revision Guide" on the inside front cover of this book, make a final check of all aspects of your paper.

Your "last" draft may need further revision after your proofreading review. If so, take the time to rewrite the paper so that the version you hand in is clean and easy to read. If a word processor is available to you, use it. Computers make editing and proofreading almost painless, since errors are so easy to correct.

At long last, you're ready to submit your paper. If you've followed the three steps to revision conscientiously, you can hand it in with confidence that it says what you want it to say, both about your subject and about you. One last word of advice:

DON'T FORGET TO KEEP A COPY FOR YOUR FILES!

Exercise 27.1

Revise the paragraph below by applying the questions on the three checklists given in this chapter. Then compare your answer with ours, which appears on page 367.

What attracts Canadians to the country life. Could it be the slower pace and closer ties to neighbours. A recent survey conducted by Angus Reid for the royal bank of Canada suggests that country residents are more attached to there communities then urban residents. The survey concluded that on average irregardless of where they live or what their ages, Canadians stay in one community for 25 years surprisingly. In response to the survey, urban residents said that there was a twenty-eight percent chance they would move to a small town or country setting, however, only thirteen percent of rural respondents report any chance of moving to the city. One of the survey's most interesting findings was that there was no significant difference in their attitude to where they lived between older and younger

Canadians. Which appears to contradict the myth that young people cant

wait to leave small communities for the bright lights of the big city or that

their parents are counting the days until they can flee the urban hustle for

the country calm.

GO TO WEB

EXERCISE 27.1

Exercise 27.2

Turn to the draft paper you wrote for Exercise 26.11 in Chapter 26. Revise the
paper by applying to it the three steps of the revision process.

UNIT 6

Beyond the Bare Essentials

Introduction

We have now covered all the essentials for clear, correct, well-organized writing. In this short unit, we will go beyond those essentials to some stylistic matters you may encounter when practising what you've learned so far. We'll consider levels of language; how to avoid clichés, jargon, and slang; the problem of wordiness; and what we call *abusages*—misused words and phrases that creep into writing and reveal ignorance of the language.

Many of the errors we discuss in this unit are not grammatical errors, but they do interfere with your ability to communicate effectively. Readers may not understand what you're talking about if you use jargon or slang. They may think poorly of you if your level of language is inappropriate or if you use clichés or abusages. Your message will be communicated only if your writing is clear and correct—that is, if it satisfies the bare essentials. Your message will be more easily understood and more favourably received if your writing is appropriate to your subject and your readers—that is, if you care enough to go beyond the bare essentials.

The chapters in this unit contain information that will help you to create a positive impression when you write. Now that you're writing longer papers and having less trouble with the essentials, you are ready to practise the skills presented in this unit as you draft and revise your work. Your reward will be writing that is not only technically correct but also stylistically appropriate.

28

The Levels of Language

All communication involves three factors: a sender, a message, and a receiver. This book is designed to help the sender — the person who has something to say (or who has to say something) — to communicate effectively. What the sender has to say is, of course, the message. Messages should always be adjusted to suit the receiver — the reader. The adjustment is the responsibility of the writer. There is no point in sending a message, whether it's a love letter or a command, in Spanish if the reader understands only English. Similarly, there is little to be gained from sending a message in colloquial English, the sort of language you would use when speaking with close friends, when the receiver is a prospective employer whom you have just met.

Spoken English has several **levels of language.** They range from almost unintelligible mumblings, through colloquial slang and professional jargon, up to the formal English used in the law courts, in the speech from the throne, and on other formal occasions. The same range exists in written English: from graffiti up to the formal report.

The key to finding the appropriate level for your message is to consider not only your subject but also your audience. Sometimes compromises are necessary, such as when you send one message to a wide variety of receivers. In general, you aim at the highest level of receiver and trust that the others will understand. For this reason, wedding invitations, even those sent to the groom's best buddies, are usually stylized and formal.

No one has to tell you what level of language to use when you communicate with your friends or with your family. These levels have been established and practised over many years. In other situations, however, it's not so clear what level is appropriate. At such times, you must consider the expectations of your audience. If your sociology teacher wants you to write papers in a formal, academic style, and you want to get a good grade, you will write at a formal level. Similarly, because employers generally favour formal letters of application over casual ones, to get an interview you will have to write your letter of application using a higher level of language than you would use in an e-mail to a friend.

The levels of English usage are not clearly distinct from one another. They often overlap. To help you distinguish among them so that you can choose the style most appropriate to your message and to your reader, we have outlined the basic characteristics of informal, general, and formal English in the table that follows.

	Informal	**General**	**Formal**
Vocabulary	Casual, everyday; usually concrete; some slang, colloquial expressions, and contractions	The language of educated persons; non-specialized; balance of abstract and concrete; readily understood	Often abstract, technical, specialized; no contractions or colloquialisms
Sentence and paragraph structure	Short, simple sentences; some sentence fragments; short paragraphs	Complete sentences of varying length; paragraphs vary in length, but often short	All sentences complete; sentences usually long, complex; paragraphs fully developed, often at length
Tone	Conversational, casual; sounds like ordinary speech	Varies to suit message and purpose of writer	Impersonal, serious; often instructional
Typical uses	Personal letters; some fiction; some newspapers; much advertising	Most of what we read: newspapers, magazines, novels, business correspondence	Legal documents; some textbooks; academic writing; scientific reports

No one level is "better" than any other. Each has its place and function, depending on the communication situation. Your message, audience, and purpose in writing are the factors that determine which level of usage is most appropriate.

Exercise 28.1

Write two separate paragraphs explaining why you deserve a student bursary of $1,500 to help cover next year's tuition. Address one paragraph to the Dean of Student Affairs and one to your best friend. Adapt your level of language so that it is appropriate to each situation.

Exercise 28.2

1. Locate three articles on a topic of your choice. The articles should all address the same topic, but each one should demonstrate one of the three levels of language: informal, general, and formal. For instance, if your topic is Internet piracy, you might find the following pieces of writing:
   - an informal article in an e-zine (an online magazine)
   - a general article in a news magazine (such as *Macleans* or *Time*)
   - a formal article in an academic journal or a magazine aimed at a well-educated audience (such as *Atlantic Monthly* or *Harper's*).

2. For each of the articles, list the characteristics of the typical person for whom it is intended. In your description, include demographic data (age, level of education, socio-economic status), interests, activities, and anything else that you can speculate on.

29

Cutting Out Clichés, Jargon, and Slang

Clichés

A **cliché** is an expression that was created long ago and has been used and overused ever since. Cliché-filled writing is boring and often meaningless. Spoken English is full of clichés. In the rush to express an idea, we often take the easy way and use ready-made expressions to put our thoughts into words. There is less excuse to write in clichés. Writers have time to think through what they want to say. They also have the opportunity to revise and edit what they have said. Consider this example of thoughtless writing:

> The day was boiling hot—so hot you could fry an egg on the sidewalk— but Terry looked calm, cool, and collected.

"Boiling hot day," "so hot you could fry an egg," and "calm, cool, and collected" are clichés. Readers know more or less what these expressions mean, but they have been used so often they no longer communicate vividly. It's almost impossible to get rid of *all* clichés in your writing, but you can be aware of them and try to use them as seldom as possible.

If you are a native speaker of English, it is easy to recognize clichés. When you can read the first word or two of a phrase and fill in the rest automatically, you know the phrase is a cliché. For example, *all work and no _____* ; *better late than _____* ; *easier said than _____* ; *it goes without _____* . The endings are so predictable that readers can skip over them. And they do. Such phrases give readers the impression that there is nothing new in your writing. It's all been said before.

The solution to a cliché problem involves time and thought. Don't write automatically. Think carefully about what you want to say; then say it in your own words, not everyone else's.

Hit the books.

As you read through the following sentences, notice how hard it is to form a mental picture of what the sentences are saying and how hard it is to remember what you've read — even when you've just finished reading it.

Exercise 29.1

Rewrite these sentences, expressing the ideas in your own words.

1. Wayne Gretzky was a real national treasure. When it came to playing hockey, nobody could hold a candle to him.

2. As a general rule of thumb, when things are not going well, your best bet is to grit your teeth and let life run its course.

3. When you have more projects on the go than you can shake a stick at, it is wise to put some of them on the back burner.

4. Jane always kept her eyes peeled for bargains and bought most of her clothes dirt cheap at Value Village.

5. Because Fernando had not laid eyes on Juanita in ages, he was feeling down in the dumps.

6. When Maria came home from work dog tired, she made no bones about the fact that she expected her husband to wait on her hand and foot.

7. Celine Dion's music is not my cup of tea, but her new CD is selling like hotcakes and her fans are in seventh heaven.

8. The union leader pulled no punches when he told the workers that the company's management team had them over a barrel and was not willing to give an inch.

9. Life is often no bed of roses, but the long and the short of it is that you will never be happy unless you sometimes just let the chips fall where they may.

10. He was as smart as a whip but spent most of his life walking on eggs because he was afraid to rock the boat.

Broadcasting is one of the major sources of clichés. It's a rare newscast that doesn't include the expression "informed sources," "claimed the life," "tragic accident," or "last but not least." Listening carefully for such overworked phrases on radio and television will make you more aware of them in your own writing. When you're aware of them, you can choose not to use them.

List ten clichés that you hear frequently from teachers, friends, and parents.

List ten clichés that you hear on tonight's news and sports broadcast.

Jargon

Jargon is language that is incomprehensible to the reader. There are two kinds. One kind of jargon is the specialized vocabulary used in the sciences, arts, trades, and professions. Sometimes technical words and phrases ("shop talk") enter the language we use outside our jobs. The sports world, for example, has a highly developed jargon: "third and six," "at the post," "uppercut," "on deck." Many of these expressions have found their way into everyday conversation in contexts that have nothing to do with sports. The jargon of some professions is so highly specialized and technical that it amounts almost to a private language. Those in the profession are familiar with it and use it to communicate. Those not in the profession are "outsiders" to whom it is unintelligible.

The existence of technical jargon is not the problem. The abuse of jargon is the problem. It limits your audience to those who share your professional vocabulary. To the rest of the world, your writing will be difficult to understand or even meaningless. You can't expect to communicate in your English essays with sentences such as this: "The interviewer responded with a logical uppercut that caught Senator Sleaze right between the eyes and laid him out for the count." This may be a colourful way to describe an interview with a corrupt politician, but it will be effective only with readers who are boxing fans.

The second kind of jargon is sometimes called **gobbledygook.** This is pompous, pretentious language that *imitates* a specialized vocabulary. It features long, complex sentences and chains of abstract, multisyllable words that are intended to impress the reader. The result is sound without meaning, as the following example, a definition of "available computing," illustrates:

> The use of redundant components in conjunction with appropriate failover and restart mechanisms in both hardware and software to permit event notification of failure conditions coupled with application and/or database checkpointing and rollback/recover algorithms, thus establishing reasonable assurance within predicted norms that a combination

of redundancies will allow a confidence factor to exist and that mean time to repair shall be a small enough variable in conjunction with simultaneous mean time between failure of the aforementioned redundant components that the overall system availability will be significantly above normal performance.

Do you know what this means? Do you care? There are three problems with this kind of writing. First, it does not communicate. Second, it leaves readers with the sense that the writer is trying to hide meaning rather than communicate it. Third, it causes readers to lose respect for the writer.

The cure for jargon is simple: be considerate of your readers. If you want your readers to understand and respect you, write in a simple, straightforward style.

Exercise 29.4

Write as many examples of technical jargon as you can think of for each of the following occupations. If you do this exercise in a group, you'll quickly see just how many examples there are.

1. computer programming: bug, NNTP, beta release...

2. journalism: story, scoop, lead...

3. military: AWOL, pull rank, mess...

4. public relations: spin, pitch, public...

5. finance: pump and dump, dog, dead cat bounce...

Exercise 29.5

In the following sentences, replace the gobbledygook with plain English. As is often the case in jargon-filled writing, the meaning of these sentences is not clear. Figure out what you think the writer means, and then state that meaning clearly in your own words. Compare your revisions with our suggested answers on page 367.

1. To facilitate forward motion of the vehicle, disengage the hand-operated wheel-lock mechanism and exert a minimum of pressure on the accelerator pedal.

2. I am quite contented to dwell in a recently constructed building on the utmost perimeter of the local municipality.

3. His shrewd and intellectual spouse regularly crafted thoughtful journalistic pieces for the delectation of readers of the city's daily periodical.

4. Mariners in Halifax and other maritime regional zones are extremely cautious when it comes to anticipating potentially treacherous meteorological conditions in their nautical environments.

5. Michael Jordan played a role of considerable leadership in twice guiding the assembled collection of teammates known as the Chicago Bulls to consecutive NBA championships.

Slang

Slang is "street talk": non-standard language that indicates a close, informal relationship among those who speak it. The innumerable examples of slang range from *A-OK* to *zowie*. Slang changes so rapidly that most dictionaries don't even attempt to keep up with all the terms. Because slang dates so quickly and because it is understood by a limited group of people, you should avoid it in your writing. Unless you are quoting someone who has used slang, use standard written English.

If you're in doubt about a word, check your dictionary. The notation *sl.* or *slang* appears after slang words or after a slang meaning of a word. Some words — for example, *house, cool,* and *bombed* — have both a general meaning and a slang meaning. If the word in the sense in which you want to use it is not in your dictionary, then it may be current slang, too new to have been included. Taking the time to choose words and expressions appropriate to written English increases your chances of communicating clearly and of winning your readers' respect.

Exercise 29.6

The following are slang terms in current use. "Translate" them into general-level English words or phrases that would be appropriate in writing.

brownnoser	buzz	chillin'
cop-out	cushy	five-finger discount
rip-off	trashed	twisted

Exercise 29.7

List five of your favourite slang expressions and define each in a general-level English sentence.

30

Eliminating Wordiness

Wordiness is a problem that develops when a writer is trying to impress a reader. Keep in mind that nobody wants to read "fill" or "padding." Your writing should be as concise as you can make it and still convey your message clearly.

Here's an example of what can happen when, in trying to impress, you lose sight of the need to communicate. Does your writing ever sound like this?

> In my opinion, I feel very strongly indeed that the government of this country is basically in need of an additional amount of meaningful input from its electors, the people of Canada. For too long a period of time, the leaders of this nation in Ottawa have, rightly or wrongly, gone heedlessly off on their own course of action without the benefit of consultation or dialogue with the people, who, it stands to reason, are most willing and able to provide a distinct and clear path to follow into the future world of tomorrow.

By eliminating wordiness, you can make this into a clear statement that might convince your readers rather than irritate them.

The following are some of the worst offenders we have collected from student writing. In some cases, several words are used when one or two would do. In others, the wording is **redundant** (it says the same thing twice).

Wordy	Concise
a large number of	many
absolutely complete	complete
absolutely nothing	nothing
actual fact	fact
almost always	usually

Wordy	Concise
at that point in time	then
at the present time	now
circled around	circled
collect together	collect
completely free	free
continue on	continue
could possibly (*or* may possibly, might possibly)	could (*or* may, might)
dead bodies	corpses (*or* bodies)
disappear from view	disappear
due to the fact that	because
entirely eliminated	eliminated
equally as good	as good
exactly identical	identical
few and far between	rare
final conclusion	conclusion
for the reason that	because
having the same thing in common	sharing
I personally feel	I feel
in my opinion, I think	I think
in the near future	soon
in this day and age	now (*or* today)
new innovation	innovation
personal friend	friend
proceed ahead	proceed
real, genuine leather	leather
red in colour	red
repeat again	repeat
repeat the same	repeat
7:00 a.m. in the morning	7:00 a.m.
small in size	small
such as, for example	such as
surround on all sides	surround
take active steps	take steps
totally destroyed	destroyed
true fact	fact
very (*or* most, quite, rather) unique	unique

To avoid wordiness, eliminate clichés, repetition, redundancy, and unnecessary jargon from your writing.

Revise these sentences, making them more concise and understandable. Suggested answers are on page 367.

1. In this day and age, office typewriters are few and far between.

2. Will Celine Dion proceed ahead with a second embryo implant in the near future?

3. It's a true fact that many historical buildings in downtown Hamilton have disappeared from view.

4. Bryan Adams will repeat his tour again and appear live and in concert for two nights next week.

5. I personally feel this new innovation in manufacturing technology will at last bring real, genuine prosperity to the mining community.

6. Only once the frame is absolutely complete can the builder continue on with erecting the walls.

7. At 6:00 p.m. in the evening, the subway rattles by my kitchen window; the view at this time is exactly identical each night.

8. The new principal has promised to take active steps to eliminate completely the large number of graffiti sites in the school.

9. Caitlin's self-confidence was totally shaken when her new car, a lovely pale blue in colour, was maliciously and savagely attacked by vandals in Stanley Park.

10. The city told me that, in actual fact, there was next to nothing they could do about the raccoons that have gathered together in my back-yard.

Exercise 30.2

Revise the following paragraph by eliminating repetition, redundancy, clichés, and jargon. Then compare your revision with ours on page 368.

It's my personal belief that, at the present moment today, innumeracy is just as big a problem for Canadian society as is illiteracy. A large number of high school graduates do just as equally poorly on math tests as they do on reading tests. Due to the fact that computers have taken over so many of the basic calculating functions of everyday life, many people think that the need for math skills has been entirely eliminated in this day and age. However, no matter how automated our transactions may become, we will never be completely free of the need to perform basic, rudimentary calculations for the reason that cash registers and computers are not available and accessible everywhere. Here's an example of what I'm talking about: a personal friend reminded me of this true fact by telling me of his recent experience buying a popsicle at the Assiniboine Zoo. The young girl who was selling cold popsicles from a cart was unable to calculate together the cost of two fudgsicles. When she served the next person in line, she repeated her error again and returned back an extra toonie to the customer.

Although small in size, her mistakes illustrate the reason why I believe school boards need to take active steps to proceed ahead with changes to the school curriculum to emphasize basic math as a key survival skill.

31

Avoiding Abusages

Some words and expressions that appear in writing are simply incorrect. We've named these misused, misspelled, or non-standard expressions **abusages.** Usage mistakes occur when bad speech habits spill over into writing. Using them makes the writer appear ignorant to anyone who knows anything about the English language. Abusages are never good English, even in speech. But we hear them so often in daily conversation that, after a while, they become so familiar they begin to sound right. They aren't, and you need to be aware of the ones that are most likely to trip you up. The list of abusages that follows includes some of the worst offenders. You should add to it the abusages your instructors hate most. Go through the list carefully and mark the expressions that sound all right to you. Then memorize the standard English equivalent beside each one. These are the expressions you need to watch for when you edit your writing.

alot	There is no such word. Use *many, much,* or *a lot.*
alright	This is a misspelling of *all right.* Cf. *all wrong.*
anyways	Also, "anywheres" and "a long ways." There is no *s* on any of these words.
between you and I	A commonly misused expression for *between you and me.*
can't hardly **couldn't hardly**	Use *can hardly* or *could hardly.*

could of	Also, "would of," "should of," and so on. The helping verb is *have*. Write *could have, would have,* etc.
didn't do nothing	This, along with all other double negatives ("couldn't get nowhere," "wouldn't talk to nobody," and so on), is wrong. Write *didn't do anything* or *did nothing.*
irregardless	There is no such word. Use *regardless.*
irrevelant	This is a misspelling. Spell the word *irrelevant.*
***media* used as a singular word**	The word *media* is plural. The singular is *medium.* Write "TV is a mass medium. Print and radio are also examples of mass media."
off of	Use *off* alone: "I fell *off* the wagon."
***prejudice* used as an adjective**	It is wrong to write "She is prejudice against men." Use *prejudiced.*
prejudism	There is no such word. Use *prejudice.* "A judge should show no prejudice to either side."
***real* used as an adverb**	"Real sad," "real good," and "real nice" are wrong. Use *really* or *very,* or leave the word out.
reason is because	Use *the reason is that:* "The reason is that I don't use a deodorant."
suppose to	Also, "use to." Write *supposed to* and *used to.*
themself	Also, "theirself," "ourselfs," "yourselfs," and "themselfs." The plural of *self* is *selves: themselves, ourselves,* and so on. Don't use "theirselves," though; there's no such word in standard written English.
youse	There is no such word. *You* is used for both singular and plural. When waiting on tables, don't say "May I help youse?" to a group of English teachers if you want a tip.

Exercise 31.1

Correct the following sentences where necessary. Answers are on page 368.

1. There was alot of damage to the car, but the driver was alright.

2. I would of run farther but after a couple of miles I couldn't hardly breathe.

3. Jane decided to stay anyways even though many people at the meeting were prejudice against her.

4. Tony swore he didn't do nothing he wasn't suppose to when he visited his grandmother in Vancouver.

5. I find it real sad that more Canadians like youse and your friends are not running for political office.

6. Between you and I, there is still alot of prejudism against Aboriginal peoples.

7. Whenever people ask me why the Montreal Expos are struggling, I tell them the reason is because major league baseball has never done nothing to help them.

8. Irregardless of what his friends said, Fred believed he would of won the race if he had not fell off of his bike.

9. Television is the best media to study if you want to learn how average Canadians perceive themselfs.

10. I'd be happy to give you a lift to Kamloops; I am suppose to go to there anyways.

Exercise 31.2

Eliminate the 15 abusages from the following paragraph.

Dangerous sports are suppose to bring out the best in you. The reason for this is because people assume you will perform at your best when there is a risk that you might get hurt. I have a firm prejudism against activities that put me at personal risk, and anyways I hate the sight of blood—especially my own. Jumping off of a platform with a bungee cord tied around my feet is not my idea of a real good time, irregardless of how many people seem to enjoy this phenomena, searching out every available opportunity to practise the sport theirselves. I use to think I should be ashame of myself because I didn't ever do nothing that involved physical risk, so I bought a motorcycle. Driving it terrified me so much that I sold it after a week. Next, I tried scuba-diving, and for a while I enjoyed it alright, but because I could not bring myself to dive below three metres, my friends soon got bored with my lack of daring and stopped inviting me on their outings. Between you and I, the most dangerous things I do now are eat alot of butter and put cream in my coffee.

Appendixes

Readings

IN DEFENCE OF VIDEO GAMES
Brian Green

1   Video games have been blamed for everything from child obesity to the decline of the stock market. Journalists, politicians, teachers, parents, psychologists, television "experts," preachers, and miscellaneous other adults claim these games are immoral, dangerous, addictive, even evil. I suspect few of these critics have ever sat down at a console and tried to save the world from invading monsters, marauding spacecraft, villainous nasties, or savage terrorists. As an adult (alas!) and a teacher, I wish to register a vote of dissent against video bashing. In my observation, video games have considerable redeeming value: they teach useful skills, provide practical expertise, and even deliver positive social lessons.

2   Video games are not the mindless diversion television is. They demand skill, strategy, hand-eye co-ordination, and precision. Imagine combining the hands of a surgeon with the reflexes of a goalie and the mind of a chess grand master, and you'll begin to get a picture of the top game players. Most of the skills required seem to be genetically determined, but even the slowest and clumsiest of us could benefit from developing and augmenting whatever level of skill we have. On my favourite game I have twice achieved a score of 9,000. The fourteen-year old daughter of a colleague consistently racks up scores of 200,000 on the same game. I would not hesitate to put my life in her hands in any situation requiring manual dexterity, quick reflexes, and steady nerves.

3   Aside from honing mechanical and thinking skills, many video games have practical applications that go far beyond the entertainment value that first attracts players to them. The best games are enjoyable, effective, and relevant simulations of many workplace environments. Computer systems used to train

airline pilots, astronauts, designers, engineers, and even surgeons are nothing more than highly complex video games. Most computer programmers, software developers, and IT workers delight in games that employ the same technology on which their careers depend. At the elite level, video game contests, international leagues, and tournaments are sponsored by companies such as chip-maker Intel, peripherals giant Logitech, and many of the world's biggest and most progressive software companies. They know where the innovators and entrepreneurs in their businesses will come from.

4   In many ways, video games are socially useful as well. For example, there is the cathartic value of video violence. TV violence seems to stimulate aggression, possibly as a result of the viewer's passivity. In contrast, anyone who has pushed to the limit in a video game, scoring a "personal best" in the effort, feels only a sense of achievement and exhaustion. No energy is left over for a continuation of the carnage in real life. In addition, despite the apparent isolation of individual players, video games promote social interaction. As isolated as players may appear, they are part of a network of players who communicate both as opponents in the game and as allies against the machine. On-line bulletin boards, chat rooms, and Web sites are devoted to specific games whose participants discuss everything from strategy to optimum computer configuration to who's going to win an upcoming tournament. The tournaments themselves are becoming mainstream spectator sports, with up to 2,000 watching on site and 40,000 more taking in the action over the Internet.

5   I challenge any video game critic to devote a few hours getting to know the people who play video games and meet the programmers, inventors, pilots, technicians, and philosophers of tomorrow. The physical and intellectual skills of good players, as well as the friendly enthusiasm of the rest of us, will change your mind about our pastime. I predict that video games will eventually become televised sports attractions, and, unlike hockey or football, everyone can play on the same field and face the same challenges as the professionals we see on TV. Here's a concept: "Counter Strike" as an Olympic Event!

Green, Brian. "In Defence of Video Games." Reprinted with permission of the author.

CONSEQUENCES IN PARENTING
Nancy Marshall

1   Every parent's goal is to raise a loving and respectful child. However, many find this a difficult and stressful task. For example, what does a parent do when seven-year-old Sally refuses to eat her dinner? What can be done when Tommy, age ten, steals money from the neighbour's purse? There are two ways in which parents can handle situations like these. The most widely used method is punishment. Another way is to apply natural and logical consequences to guide the misbehaving child. This more recent method is often shunned by parents because they feel it takes too much effort and is ineffective. If parents use consequences in place of punishment, however, they can relieve much of their stress, gain the child's respect, and achieve excellent results.

2   A surprising amount of stress can be relieved by using consequences. The beauty of this alternative parenting style is that the children are responsible for their actions, not the parents. The example of Sally is not an uncommon one. Imagine the scenario: Sally's parents plead with her to eat, and she takes a bite or two. However, as soon as the pleading stops, so does Sally's eating. The dinner is a constant battle which soon turns into a power struggle between Sally and her parents. This very tiring and stressful experience can be avoided by using a natural consequence. The natural consequence of not eating is hunger. When dinner is over, Sally's mother simply says, "I guess you were not hungry. Remember there is no more food until morning." Then Sally's untouched plate is taken away. Of course, Sally complains later that night of hunger, but Sally's parents do not give in. They say, "I'm sorry you are hungry, but we don't eat again until morning." If the parent is persistent, Sally's hunger works as an effective stimulation and she begins to eat at regular meal times. This consequence required little effort from the parent, and the stress caused by an unnecessary power struggle was alleviated.

3   Not only do consequences help with anxiety, but children have more respect for the parent who does not feel the need to punish. Angry parents can get out of hand quickly in the heat of the moment. They may spank too hard or say something they do not mean. This causes hurt feelings in their children that can last a long time. Eventually, children think less of their authoritarian parents. Using consequences eliminates this possibility and allows parents to acknowledge their children's right to their own feelings. Ultimately, this is the key to gaining a child's respect. When the mother stated that Sally must not be hungry, she was acknowledging Sally's right to that feeling. This statement also reinforced that the child could fix her own problem. Sally was then given the chance to try again. In this way, she was treated as an equal. Children who are continually treated in a respectful manner will in turn treat their parents with the same consideration.

4   Along with increased respect, the parent also achieves outstanding results with the use of consequences. Natural and logical consequences remove the parental authority which is used to enforce punishment; therefore, the child is left with nothing to fight. Logical consequences were not needed in Sally's case, but can be . . . effective in other situations. Consider ten-year-old Tommy who steals from his neighbour. If punishment, such as spanking or a lecture, is used here, the child simply learns that if he does something wrong, he will be punished. Next time, he will remember not to get caught. When a logical consequence is used, however, such as returning the stolen item with an apology, the child learns that what he did was wrong. This technique is far more effective than a spanking because it is directly related to his misbehaviour. The goal here is to instill lasting values. Trying to impose them through punishment will have short-lived effects. When the parent uses consequences instead of punishment, the results are considerably more desirable.

5   Parenting can be quite difficult, and the temptation to punish will never disappear. [The] examples of Sally and Tommy suggest that, when parents use consequences, they can alleviate stress, gain respect, and achieve optimal results. It is also important for parents to remember that children are willing to learn from adults who treat them equally. When the punishment is removed, so is the authority children often fight against. With time, this impunity will ensure a loving, stable relationship between the parent and child.

Marshall, Nancy. "Consequences in Parenting." *Contest: Essays by Canadian Students.* Ed. Murray McArthur. 3rd ed. Toronto: Harcourt Brace, 1998. 190–91.

OF TOURISTS, TRAVELLERS, AND TRUE TRAVELLERS
Sue Sutton

1   A few months ago I met a young Australian woman at Kande Beach in Malawi. She had been travelling overland from London, and had spent four or five months in Africa. She had clearly "gone bush," as they used to say in colonial times. She asked me about a well-known beauty spot in the south of the country, and I told her it was not to be missed. Then she asked me if it was "touristy." Well, yes, I said, I supposed it was, at least as far as any place in Malawi could be called touristy. There might be up to 20 or 30 foreigners there at any given time. High as a kite, with that relaxed vagueness of the habitual smoker, she took another pull on her dagga cigarette, and dismissed the idea. She didn't want to be around tourists.

2   I'd encountered this attitude plenty of times before and forbore to ask this tourist-phobic traveller what distinguished her from them. It simply raises the frequent and, to my mind, pointless debate about the distinction between "tourists" and "travellers." Basically, it goes like this: Tourists wear inappropriate clothes (either too bright, too expensive and fashionable, or laughably colonial, "safari" style), have too much money and spend it in the wrong places, don't "care" about the culture in which they travel, and don't stay long enough to understand or help. Travellers, on the other hand, are more benign, tactfully grubby, and have found a deeper connection with the culture in which they are moving.

3   Some of those who fall into the narrow definition of "tourist" can certainly exert negative influences; it brings to mind the impact of Italian tourists on the Kenya coast town of Malindi. For a few months each year, hordes of visitors fill this small town. In flagrant disregard of the sensibilities of the largely Muslim community, the women practically burst out of the bodices of their impossibly short mini-dresses and sport tactlessly expensive jewellery. The men take as mistresses the lovely, desperately poor, local women, who are driven by extreme poverty to sell themselves, and treat them like chattel. Worse, a false economy has been created that makes the basics of the Swahili diet—including tomatoes—too expensive for the residents. It's simply not tactful to be throwing money around in a developing country, and in Malindi this is leading to increasing animosity and unrest.

4   It appears that, for many, being a traveller implies a kind of moral superiority, though based on what I've never been quite sure. Many so-called travellers I've met, like the Australian, disdain the company of tourists, will not speak to them, and will go out of their way to avoid areas where they might be found. I think perhaps there's an element of self-loathing in the self-dubbed traveller, who wishes to cleanse herself of the excesses and moral decay of her own culture and immerse herself in a society in which community, that elusive goal many

of us are so desperately seeking here in our own fragmented society, is the foundation that holds them together. Community is the key to their survival and security; in fact, it is practically all they can call their own. Bottom line: however shoestring the budget, the traveller has enough money—and even more important, that other expensive luxury, free time—to take a flight that will cost perhaps four times the average Kenyan's annual salary, carrying a sturdy backpack, the cost of which would feed an African family for months, filled with "essentials" like sunglasses, a good flashlight, sunblock, medicines and sturdy clothes that are far beyond the reach of the average African.

5   Tourists and travellers alike tend to take without giving much in return. The tourist may be looking for excitement, for the exotic and the perfect photo of a leopard, while the traveller may be on the road to "self-actualization" or some such inward-looking goal. In return for what can in either case be the experience of a lifetime, what can we offer? To share a meal, perhaps, or to share a few ideas. But while we may gain much by associating with the ordinary people of another country, the opposite is rarely true.

6   If distinctions are to be made, I think the true traveller finds herself, in the end, remarkably free of ego. The more you travel, the more you learn, and I think one of the key things to be learned from immersing oneself in an alien culture is that there is no point in being judgmental, either about one's own culture or someone else's. There is no good and bad, only different.

7   You cannot really don the primitive mantle. Those dissatisfied with the shallow materialism of the Western world will rarely find that the solution is to go off and live in a mud hut, however romantic the notion may be. You cannot unlearn your own culture. What you can do—and in many ways this is far more challenging—is go home, rich with the knowledge of other possibilities, and try to apply them to your own world.

Sutton, Sue. "Of Tourists, Travellers, and True Travellers." *Globe and Mail* 22 Mar. 1995: A22.

HERE KITTY, KITTY
Susan Luey

1   Among life's painful experiences—root canal, kidney stones, childbirth—bathing the family cat ranks with the worst. Cleaning a cat is not a chore to be undertaken lightly or routinely, and it should be performed only when the cat smells so bad that its owner must resort to one of two choices: bathe it or leave home. Some cats never reach this level of offensiveness, but fastidious owners might undertake the task as many as four times in the typical cat's lifetime. Those readers new to the process can learn much from the following instructions, and veterans of cat bathing may pick up a tip or two. Do not take this guidance lightly. You are about to enter battle.

2   Before embarking on the enterprise, it is wise to consider the participants' competitive advantages. On their side, cats have speed, agility, and complete disregard for human life. Your advantages are size, strength, and creativity, and you will need them all. Bathing a cat is a process with three distinct phases: preparation, the bath, and the aftermath.

3   You must prepare carefully for the event if you hope to avert disaster later in the process. To begin with, remove everyone except you and your pet from the war zone. This precaution is necessary both to ensure safety and to prevent recriminations later on when the cat tries to enlist sympathy from weak-willed family members (see "aftermath," below). Next, assemble your protective apparel. You will need impact-resistant ski goggles that can be tightly fitted over the face, and a helmet with earflaps. A football helmet will do but is cumbersome. Professionals prefer the leather flying helmets favoured by old-time pilots; these not only provide adequate protection but also allow for manoeuverability. A knee-length leather or heavy canvas waterproof coat, sturdy hip waders, and elbow-length gauntlets complete the ensemble. Fill a squirt gun or squeeze bottle with shampoo, stuff an old towel under your coat, and you are ready for combat.

4   As Wellington observed at Waterloo, choosing the ground is key to winning the battle. A tub with a sliding glass door is ideal for the encounter. An enclosed shower stall will do, but if things go horribly wrong, the stall provides little room for movement and scant avenue of escape. Never try to use a bath fitted with only a shower curtain. Once a cat's claws have sunk into the fabric of the curtain, they cannot be removed without the use of high explosives. When you've identified or constructed a suitable battle zone, climb into your combat gear, adjust the water temperature to a comfortable level (your comfort; it doesn't matter to the cat), and turn on the shower.

5   Typically, cats pay no attention to their owners unless they—the cats—want something. So, if this is your pet's first bath, she will have no suspicion of your intention, despite your protective garb, as you pick her up and cradle her

gently in your arms. Stroll casually about the house for a few minutes to lull the animal into a sense of security, and then, when she is purring contentedly, step into the tub and quickly slide the glass door shut. Let the bath begin!

6   There will be a split second of frozen disbelief during which you can get some water on the cat. From then on, it's a matter of keeping out of the way as she tries to use you as a shelter from the shower. The ensuing contest is the heart of the battle, and it is here that your stamina, strength, agility, and determination are tested. After a few frantic minutes, the cat should be at least damp, and you can use the squirt gun to apply shampoo. With your leather-gloved hands, massage the soap into your pet's fur whenever she sinks her claws into your coat or waders and is briefly immobile.

7   The world record for soaping and rinsing a cat in one bathing session is three applications. But this feat was accomplished by a trained professional in peak physical condition and should not even be attempted by the amateur. If you can get enough shampoo on the cat to produce a few bubbles of lather and then concentrate enough water on the animal to rinse some of it away, quit while you are ahead. Shut off the water and pull the towel out from under your coat. If you've been brisk, the towel will still be drier than the cat. By now, your pet will be firmly affixed to whatever part of your anatomy she can sink her claws into. With luck, she will be attached to an arm or a leg and can be towel-dried with relative ease. Never use a blow dryer for this procedure. Electricity in the presence of a saturated environment and an angry cat is a recipe for disaster. Once your pet is more or less dry, you can relax for a few moments. The physical phase of your combat is over—but the psychological war is about to begin.

8   For several days, your cat will avoid you. She will sulk, turn her back when you approach, seek allies among other family members, and hurl insults in cat language. She will attempt to repair the damage to her coat and dignity by incessant grooming, interrupting her toilette only to hiss or growl when she catches sight of you. This phase is temporary, however, and after several days or—at most—a few weeks, your pet will seem willing to resume normal relations. Do not be deceived. Felines do not forget. Beneath her purring exterior, your cat is dreaming of tortures that would make an Inquisitor queasy. And no matter how many years pass, the next time she sees you in helmet, waders, goggles, and gloves, she will remember. She will be ready.

Luey, Susan. "Here Kitty, Kitty." Reprinted by permission of the author.

DETERMINING PERSONALITY TYPE: THE WELLAND METHOD
Francine Letourneau

1   Humans have attempted to classify each other into personality types since they came out of caves and, for all we know, possibly even before that. Early religions believed that personality traits were determined by specific gods or goddesses. For example, someone with an aggressive, argumentative personality was thought to be controlled by Mars, the god of war. In the Middle Ages, astrologists maintained that the position of the planets and stars at the time of birth influenced the character and destiny of each person; humans were categorized according to which of the twelve celestial signs they were born under. More recently, the social sciences have developed several methods of sorting personality types. From Jungian theory to pop psychology, people can be classified by their response to various stimuli, their learning style, or their relationships with others. In this long and honourable tradition of classifying the characteristics of the human race, the citizens of Welland, Ontario, have a small but significant place.

2   Welland is bisected by its namesake canal. Until the 1970s, the portion of the Welland Canal that runs through the urban core was used by ships making the journey between Lake Ontario and Lake Erie, bypassing Niagara Falls. During peak season, the ships would steam through Welland at a rate of several an hour. All traffic crossing downtown Welland in an east–west direction was routed over one of three enormous steel lift bridges. When a ship approached, a siren sounded, traffic was halted, and the bridge over the canal was hydraulically raised between the steel towers on either side of the canal. The disruption to traffic flow in the centre of the city can only be imagined today. It was this setting that inspired the development of the Welland Method of determining personality type. Over a number of years, the citizens of Welland observed three characteristic responses to the sound of the siren and consequent interruption of traffic flow: work, wait, and wheel.

3   "Workers" were generally people who had to travel back and forth across the canal as part of their employment. They might be traveling from one office to another, from one campus of Niagara College to the other, or from a customer on one side to a client on the other. People in the Worker category could be easily identified: they always carried piles of paper on the passenger seat of their cars. At the siren's sound, Workers turned off the ignition, engaged the parking brake, and settled in to do some paperwork. Ambitious, dedicated, and efficient, Workers also tended to be well organized and in control. Assuming that they would be stopped by a raised bridge at least twice a day, typical Workers could, in the 15 to 20 minutes it took for each ship to pass and the bridge to be lowered, accomplish impressive amounts of work. Some insurance and real estate companies with clients on both sides of the canal were able to

close their offices during shipping season and count on their workers to get their paperwork done from the front seat of their cars.

4   "Waiters" were not dissimilar from Workers, but tended to be more laid back, less ambitious, not so driven to succeed. Waiters could be easily spotted: they were the drivers with a book tucked under the sun visor or a pillow behind the front seat. A Waiter could have the car in park, the ignition off, and be deeply engrossed in a novel before a ship was even in sight. Alternatively, a Waiter could pull out the pillow, place it on the passenger seat, and curl up for a power nap, relying on the good-natured honking of the car behind to advise when the bridge was back in place. Waiters, as might be expected, were calm, easy-going, and unruffled. Sometimes tending to overweight, they frequently carried snacks in the glove box to enjoy while reading. A quick reader could finish *The Ring Trilogy* in a summer, while a Waiter who opted to nap could catch up to an hour's extra sleep every day.

5   Unlike their two categorical cousins, "Wheelers" responded to the bridge siren the way thoroughbreds respond to the starting gate. Unable to shift focus the way Workers and Waiters did when their journey was interrupted, Wheelers would dash through side streets at high speeds, trying to get to the next canal bridge before it went up. Sometimes they would make it and cross in triumph, racing back the way they had come (but on the other side of the canal) to resume their interrupted trip. It didn't seem to matter to them that this detour often took longer than waiting for a ship to pass, or that Workers and Waiters were streaming across the bridge by the time Wheelers arrived on the other side. A truly tragic sight was the Wheeler who dashed upstream or down, only to arrive at the next bridge seconds after its siren had sounded. Committed Wheelers would speed on to the third bridge, while the less fanatic would either wait where they were or return in defeat to the first bridge—which, by the time they arrived, would again be functioning. Disorganized and inefficient, Wheelers nonetheless were energetic, enthusiastic, and optimistic. They were often thin and nervous.

6   When a new canal was dug to the east of downtown Welland and the towering lift bridges were stilled, the people of Welland were overjoyed at the prospect of easy travel across town. However, progress comes with a price, and the Welland Method of personality classification has gone the way of the buggy whip, the steam engine, and the typewriter—a victim of efficiency.

Letourneau, Francine. "Determining Personality Type: The Welland Method." Reprinted by permission of the author.

THE DIMENSIONS OF A COMPLETE LIFE[1]

Martin Luther King, Jr.

1   Many, many centuries ago, out on a lonely, obscure island called Patmos, a man by the name of John caught a vision of the new Jerusalem descending out of heaven from God. One of the greatest glories of this new city of God that John saw was its completeness. It was not partial and one-sided, but it was complete in all three of its dimensions. And so, in describing the city in the twenty-first chapter of the book of Revelation, John says this: "The length and the breadth and the height of it are equal." In other words, this new city of God, this city of ideal humanity, is not an unbalanced entity, but it is complete on all sides.

2   Now John is saying something quite significant here. For so many of us the book of Revelation is a very difficult book, puzzling to decode. We look upon it as something of a great enigma wrapped in mystery. And certainly if we accept the book of Revelation as a record of actual historical occurrences it is a difficult book, shrouded with impenetrable mysteries. But if we will look beneath the peculiar jargon of its author and the prevailing apocalyptic symbolism, we will find in this book many eternal truths which continue to challenge us. One such truth is that of this text. What John is really saying is this: that life as it should be and life at its best is the life that is complete on all sides.

3   There are three dimensions of any complete life to which we can fitly give the words of this text: length, breadth, and height. The length of life as we shall think of it here is not its duration or its longevity, but it is the push of a life forward to achieve its personal ends and ambitions. It is the inward concern for one's own welfare. The breadth of life is the outward concern for the welfare of others. The height of life is the upward reach for God.

4   These are the three dimensions of life, and without the three being correlated, working harmoniously together, life is incomplete. Life is something of a great triangle. At one angle stands the individual person, at the other angle stand other persons, and at the top stands the Supreme, Infinite Person, God. These three must meet in every individual life if that life is to be complete.

5   Now let us notice first the length of life. I have said that this is the dimension of life in which the individual is concerned with developing his inner powers. It is that dimension of life in which the individual pursues personal ends and ambitions. This is perhaps the selfish dimension of life, and there is such a thing as moral and rational self-interest. If one is not concerned about himself he cannot be totally concerned about other selves.

---

[1]"Dimensions" is a fairly challenging piece of reading because King uses a wide range of vocabulary. Don't let the unfamiliar words discourage you or throw you off track, however. If you read carefully, you'll notice that King frequently defines or explains difficult words as he uses them.

6   Some years ago a learned rabbi, the late Joshua Liebman, wrote a book entitled *Peace of Mind*. He has a chapter in the book entitled "Love Thyself
Properly." In this chapter he says in substance that it is impossible to love other
selves adequately unless you love your own self properly. Many people have
been plunged into the abyss of emotional fatalism because they did not love
themselves properly. So every individual has a responsibility to be concerned
about himself enough to discover what he is made for. After he discovers his
calling he should set out to do it with all the strength and power in his being.
He should do it as if God Almighty called him at this particular moment in history to do it. He should seek to do his job so well that the living, the dead, or
the unborn could not do it better. No matter how small one thinks his life's
work is in terms of the norms of the world and the so-called big jobs, he must
realize that it has cosmic significance if he is serving humanity and doing the
will of God.

7   To carry this to one extreme, if it falls your lot to be a street-sweeper, sweep
streets as Raphael painted pictures, sweep streets as Michelangelo carved
marble, sweep streets as Beethoven composed music, sweep streets as
Shakespeare wrote poetry. Sweep streets so well that all the hosts of heaven
and earth will have to pause and say, "Here lived a great street-sweeper who
swept his job well." In the words of Douglas Mallock:

> If you can't be a highway, just be a trail;
> If you can't be the sun, be a star,
> For it isn't by size that you win or you fail—
> Be the best of whatever you are.

When you do this, you have mastered the first dimension of life—the length of
life.

8   But don't stop here; it is dangerous to stop here. There are some people who
never get beyond this first dimension. They are brilliant people; often they do
an excellent job in developing their inner powers; but they live as if nobody else
lived in the world but themselves. There is nothing more tragic than to find an
individual bogged down in the length of life, devoid of the breadth.

9   The breadth of life is that dimension in which we are concerned about
others. An individual has not started living until he can rise above the narrow
confines of his individualistic concerns to the broader concerns of all humanity.

10   You remember one day a man came to Jesus and he raised some significant
questions. Finally he got around to the question, "Who is my neighbour?" This
could easily have been a very abstract question left in mid-air. But Jesus immediately pulled that question out of mid-air and placed it on a dangerous curve
between Jerusalem and Jericho. He talked about a certain man who fell among
thieves. Three men passed; two of them on the other side. And finally another
man came and helped the injured man on the ground. He is known to us as

the Good Samaritan. Jesus says in substance that this is a great man. He was great because he could project the "I" into the "thou."

11   So often we say that the priest and the Levite were in a big hurry to get to some ecclesiastical meeting and so they did not have time. They were concerned about that. I would rather think of it another way. I can well imagine that they were quite afraid. You see, the Jericho road is a dangerous road, and the same thing that happened to the man who was robbed and beaten could have happened to them. So I imagine the first question that the priest and the Levite asked was this: "If I stop to help this man, what will happen to me?" Then the good Samaritan came by, and by the very nature of his concern reversed the question: "If I do not stop to help this man, what will happen to him?" And so this man was great because he had the mental equipment for a dangerous altruism. He was great because he could surround the length of his life with the breadth of life. He was great not only because he had ascended to certain heights of economic security, but because he could condescend to the depths of human need.

12   All this has a great deal of bearing in our situation in the world today. So often racial groups are concerned about the length of life, their privileged economic position, their social status. So often nations of the world are concerned about the length of life, perpetuating their nationalistic concerns, and their economic ends. May it not be that the problem in the world today is that individuals as well as nations have been overly concerned with the length of life, devoid of the breadth? But there is still something to remind us that we are interdependent, that we are all involved in a single process, that we are all somehow caught in an inescapable network of mutuality. Therefore whatever affects one directly affects all indirectly.

13   As long as there is poverty in the world I can never be rich, even if I have a billion dollars. As long as diseases are rampant and millions of people in this world cannot expect to live more than twenty-eight or thirty years, I can never be totally healthy even if I just got a good check-up at Mayo Clinic. I can never be what I ought to be until you are what you ought to be. This is the way our world is made. No individual or nation can stand out boasting of being independent. We are interdependent. So John Donne placed it in graphic terms when he affirmed, "No man is an island entire of itself. Every man is a piece of the continent, a part of the main." Then he goes on to say, "Any man's death diminishes me because I am involved in mankind, and therefore never send to know for whom the bell tolls; it tolls for thee." Whenever we discover this, we master the second dimension of life.

14   Finally, there is a third dimension. Some people never get beyond the first two dimensions of life. They master the first two. They develop their inner powers; they love humanity, but they stop right here. They end up with the feeling that man is the end of all things and that humanity is God. Philosophically or theologically, many of them would call themselves humanists.

They seek to live life without a sky. They find themselves bogged down on the horizontal plane without being integrated on the vertical plane. But if we are to live the complete life we must reach up and discover God. H.G. Wells was right: "The man who is not religious begins at nowhere and ends at nothing." Religion is like a mighty wind that breaks down doors and makes that possible and even easy which seems difficult and impossible.

15   In our modern world it is easy for us to forget this. We so often find ourselves unconsciously neglecting this third dimension of life. Not that we go up and say, "Goodbye, God, we are going to leave you now." But we become so involved in the things of this world that we are unconsciously carried away by the rushing tide of materialism which leaves us treading in the confused waters of secularism. We find ourselves living in what Professor Sorokin of Harvard called a sensate civilization, believing that only those things which we can see and touch and to which we can apply our five senses have existence.

16   Something should remind us once more that the great things in this universe are things that we never see. You walk out at night and look up at the beautiful stars as they bedeck the heavens like swinging lanterns of eternity, and you think you can see all. Oh, no. You can never see the law of gravitation that holds them there. You walk around this vast campus and you probably have a great esthetic experience as I have had walking about and looking at the beautiful buildings, and you think you see all. Oh, no. You can never see the mind of the architect who drew the blueprint. You can never see the love and the faith and the hope of the individuals who made it so. You look at me and you think you see Martin Luther King. You don't see Martin Luther King; you see my body, but, you must understand, my body can't think, my body can't reason. You don't see the me that makes me me. You can never see my personality.

17   Plato was right: "The visible is a shadow cast by the invisible." And so God is still around. All of our new knowledge, all of our new developments, cannot diminish his being one iota. These new advances have banished God neither from the microcosmic compass of the atom nor from the vast, unfathomable ranges of interstellar space. The more we learn about this universe, the more mysterious and awesome it becomes. God is still here.

18   So I say to you, seek God and discover him and make him a power in your life. Without him all of our efforts turn to ashes and our sunrises into darkest nights. Without him, life is a meaningless drama with the decisive scenes missing. But with him we are able to rise from the fatigue of despair to the buoyancy of hope. With him we are able to rise from the midnight of desperation to the daybreak of joy. St. Augustine was right—we were made for God and we will be restless until we find rest in him.

19   Love yourself, if that means rational, healthy, and moral self-interest. You are commanded to do that. That is the length of life. Love your neighbour as you love yourself. You are commanded to do that. That is the breadth of life. But never forget that there is a first and even greater commandment, "Love the

Lord thy God with all thy heart and all thy soul and all thy mind." This is the height of life. And when you do this you live the complete life.

Thank God for John who, centuries ago, caught a vision of the new Jerusalem. God grant that those of us who still walk the road of life will catch this vision and decide to move forward to that city of complete life in which the length and the breadth and the height are equal.[2]

---

[2]King originally wrote "Dimensions" as a speech and later published it in written form. As King's piece demonstrates, the principles of organization we have explained in Unit 5 can be applied to oral presentations just as successfully as they can to writing.

King, Martin Luther, Jr. "The Dimensions of a Complete Life." *The Measure of a Man.* Philadelphia: Christian Educational Press, 1959.

APPENDIX B

List of Grammatical Terms

adjective A word that modifies (describes, restricts, relates to, makes more precise) a noun or pronoun. Adjectives answer the questions **What kind? How many? Which?** — e.g., the *competent* student; *five* home runs; my *last* class.

adverb A word that modifies a verb, adjective, or other adverb. Adverbs answer the questions **When? How? Where? Why? How much?** — e.g., Nino talks *fast* (*fast* modifies the verb *talks*); he is a *very* fast talker (*very* modifies the adjective *fast*); he talks *really* fast (*really* modifies the adverb *fast*). Adverbs often — but not always — end in *-ly*.

antecedent The word that a pronoun refers to or stands for. Literally, it means "coming before, preceding." The antecedent usually comes before the pronoun that refers to it — e.g., *Karen* believes *she* is possessed. (*Karen* is the antecedent to which the pronoun *she* refers.)

clause A group of words that contains a subject and a verb. If the group of words can stand by itself and makes complete sense, it is called an **independent clause** (or **principal clause** or **main clause**). If the group of words does not make complete sense on its own but is linked to another clause (depends on the other clause for its meaning), it is called a **dependent** or **subordinate clause.** Here's an example: The porch collapsed. This group of words can stand by itself, so it is called an independent clause.

Now consider this clause: When Kalim removed the railing with his tractor. This group of words has a subject, *Kalim,* and a verb, *removed,* but it does not make complete sense on its own. It depends for its meaning on *the porch collapsed;* therefore, it is a dependent clause.

colloquialism   A word or phrase that we use in casual conversation or in informal writing.

> Steve *flunked* his accounting exam.
> *Did* you *get* what the teacher said about job placement?
> I can't believe that *guy* is serious about learning.

comma splice   The error that results when the writer joins two independent clauses with a comma — e.g., The comma splice is an error, it is a kind of run-on sentence. (See Chapter 8.)

dependent clause cue   A word or phrase that introduces a dependent clause — e.g., when, because, in order that, as soon as. See p. 74.

modifier   A word or group of words that adds information about another word (or phrase or clause) in a sentence. See **adjective**, **adverb**, **dependent clause**, and Chapter 9.

noun   A word that names a person, place, or thing and that has the grammatical capability of being possessive. There are concrete nouns that are **proper** (Calgary, Beijing, Gaza, January, Sharon); **common** (woman, man, city, car, animal); and **collective** (group, audience, swarm, jury, committee). There are also **abstract** nouns (truth, softness, pride, confidence). Unlike their concrete cousins, abstract nouns refer to concepts, ideas, characteristics — things we know or experience through our intellect rather than through our senses.

object   The "receiving" part of a sentence. The **direct object** is a noun or noun substitute (pronoun, phrase, or clause) that is the target or receiver of the action expressed by the verb. It answers the question **what?** or **whom?** — e.g., John threw the *ball.* (John threw *what?*)

> He wondered where the money went. (He wondered *what?*)
> Munira loves Abdul. (Munira loves *whom?*)

The **indirect object** is a noun or pronoun that is the indirect target or receiver of the action expressed by the verb in a sentence. It is *always* placed in front of the direct object. It answers the question **to whom?** or **to what?**

> Doug threw *me* the ball. (Doug threw *to whom?*)
> Lisa forgot to give her *essay* a title. (Give *to what?*)

The **object of a preposition** is a noun or noun substitute (pronoun, phrase, or clause) that follows a preposition — e.g., after the *storm* (*storm* is a noun, object of the preposition *after*); before *signing the lease* (*signing the lease* is a phrase, object of the preposition *before*); he thought about *what he wanted to do* (*what he wanted to do* is a clause, object of the preposition *about*). Notice that what follows a preposition is always its object; that is why the subject of a sentence or clause can never be found in a prepositional phrase.

participle The form of a verb that can be used as an adjective (the *completed* work, the *weeping* willows) or as part of a verb phrase (am *succeeding*, have *rented*).

> The **present participle** of a verb ends in *-ing*.
> The **past participle** of a **regular verb** ends in *-d* or in *-ed*.
> For a list of **irregular verbs**, see pp. 125–27.

person A category of pronouns and verbs. **First person** refers to the person who is speaking (I, we). **Second person** refers to the person being spoken to (you). **Third person** is the person or thing being spoken about (he, she, it, they). Verb forms remain constant except in the present tense third-person singular, which ends in *-s*.

phrase A group of meaning-related words that acts as a noun, a verb, an adjective, or an adverb within a sentence. Phrases do not make complete sense on their own because they do not contain both a subject and a verb.

> Please order *legal-size manila file folders.* (phrase acting as noun)
> I *must have been sleeping* when you called. (verb phrase)
> *Sightseeing in Ottawa,* we photographed the monuments *on Parliament Hill.* (phrases acting as adjectives)
> Portaging a canoe *in this weather* is no fun. (phrase acting as adverb)

prefix A meaningful letter or group of letters added to the beginning of a word either (1) to change its meaning or (2) to change its word class.

> 1. *a* + moral = amoral
>   *bi* + sexual = bisexual
>   *contra* + diction = contradiction
>   *dys* + functional = dysfunctional
> 2. *a* + board (noun) = aboard (adverb, preposition)
>   *con* + temporary (adjective) = contemporary (noun, adjective)
>   *de* + nude = denude (verb)
>   *in* + put (verb) = input (noun)

Some prefixes require a hyphen, as here:
all-Canadian
de-emphasize
mid-morning

preposition A word that connects a noun, pronoun, or phrase to some other word(s) in a sentence. The noun, pronoun, or phrase is the **object** of the preposition.

> I prepared the minutes *of the union meeting.* (*of* relates *meeting* to *minutes*)
> One *of the parents* checks the children every half hour. (*of* relates *parents* to *One*)

prepositional phrase	A group of grammatically related words beginning with a preposition and having the function of a noun, adjective, or adverb. See the list on p. 62.
pronoun	A word that functions like a noun in a sentence (e.g., as a subject, or as an object of a verb or a preposition.) Pronouns usually substitute for nouns, but sometimes they substitute for other pronouns.

He will promote *anything that* brings in money.

Everyone must earn *her* badges.

There are several kinds of pronouns:

personal: *I, we; you; he, she, it, they; me, us; him, her, them*
possessive: *my, our; your; his, her, its, their*
demonstrative: *this, these; that, those*
relative: *who, whom, whose; which, that*
interrogative: *who? whose? whom? which? what?*
indefinite: all *-one, -thing, -body* pronouns, such as *everyone, something,* and *anybody; each; neither; either; few; none; several*

subject	In a sentence, the person, thing, or concept that the sentence is about—the topic of the sentence (see Chapter 6). In an essay, what the paper is about—the topic of the paper (see Chapter 23).
suffix	A letter or group of letters that is added to the end of a word (1) to change its meaning, (2) to change its grammatical function, or (3) to change its word class.

1. king + *dom* = kingdom
   few + *er* = fewer
   tooth + *less* = toothless
2. buy (base form) + *s* = buys (third-person singular, present tense)
   eat (base form) + *en* = eaten (past participle)
   instructor + *s* = instructors (plural)
   instructor + *'s* = instructor's (possessive singular)
3. your (adjective) + *s* = yours (pronoun)
   act (verb) + *ive* = active (adjective)
   active (adjective) + *ly* = actively (adverb)
   ventilate (verb) + *tion* = ventilation (noun)

Some words add two or more prefixes and/or suffixes to the base form. Look at antidisestablishmentarianism, for example. How many prefixes and suffixes can you identify?

tense	The different forms of the verb used to indicate past, present, or future time are called **tenses.** The verb ending (e.g., play*s*, play*ed*) and any helping verbs associated with the main verb (*is* playing, *will* play, *has* played, *had* played, *will have* played) indicate the tense of the verb.

There are simple tenses:	**present:** *ask, asks* **past:** *asked* **future:** *will ask*
and perfect tenses:	**present:** *have (has) asked* **past:** *had asked* **future:** *will (shall) have asked*

The simple and perfect tenses can also be **progressive:** am asking, have been asking, etc.

transition A word or phrase that helps readers to follow the text smoothly from one sentence to the next or from one paragraph to another. See Chapter 26.

verb A word or phrase that says something about a person, place, or thing and whose form may be changed to indicate tense. Verbs may make a statement, ask a question, or give commands. They may express action (physical or mental), occurrence, or condition (state of being). See Chapter 6.

> Wesley *hit* an inside curve for a home run. (physical action)
> Laurence *believed* the Blue Jays would win. (mental action)
> Father's Day *falls* on the first Sunday of June. (occurrence)
> Reva eventually *became* interested in English. (condition)

Some verbs are called **linking verbs:** they help to make a statement by linking the subject to a word or phrase that describes it.

> William Hubbard *was* Toronto's first black mayor. (*was* links *William Hubbard* to *mayor*)
> Mohammed *looks* tired. (*looks* links *Mohammed* and *tired*)

In addition to am, is, are, was, were, and been, some common linking verbs are appear, become, feel, grow, look, taste, remain, seem, smell, sound.

Another class of verbs is called **auxiliary** or **helping verbs.** They show the time of a verb as future or past (*will* go, *has* gone) or as a continuing action (*is* reading). They also show the passive voice (*is* completed, *have been* submitted).

voice Verbs may be **active** or **passive**, depending on whether the subject of the verb is *acting* (active voice) or *being acted upon* (passive voice).

> In 2003, the government *introduced* another set of tax reforms. (active)
> Another set of tax reforms *was introduced* in 2003. (passive)

APPENDIX C

Answers to Exercises

Answers for Chapter 1: Three Suggestions for Quick Improvement (pages 3 to 14)

Exercise 1.1
1. *license*. No, they are not interchangeable. *License* is a verb; *licence* is a noun.
2. *theatre*. Other words that end in *–er* and have alternative spellings are *centre* and *metre*.
3. Yes, *envelop* is spelled correctly, if the word is intended as a verb.
4. *Connection* is the preferred spelling of the word, which can also be spelled *connexion*.
5. *esthetic, realise, traveller, jewellery, behaviour*. The preferred spellings are *aesthetic, realize, traveller, jewellery,* and *behaviour*.

Exercise 1.2
1. potatoes
2. series
3. bases
4. deer
5. criteria
6. foci or focuses
7. heroes
8. curricula
9. species
10. phenomena

Exercise 1.3
1. relayed
2. keys
3. player
4. enjoyment
5. saying
6. entries
7. merciless
8. daisies
9. merriment
10. cursorily

The root words in 1 to 5 end in a **vowel** plus *y*; these words do not change spelling when you add an ending. The root words in 6 to 10 end in a **consonant** plus *y*; change *y* to *i* when you add an ending to such words.

Exercise 1.4

1. meth-od
2. im-ple-ment
3. rec-om-mend
4. res-o-lu-tion
5. re-verse

6. i-o-dine
7. ar-cha-ic
8. tel-ler
9. mis-un-der-stand-ing
10. in-tu-i-tion

Exercise 1.6

1. believer
2. producing
3. largely
4. accommodating
5. lateness

6. requirement
7. tolerated
8. hopeful
9. posturing
10. slicer

Exercise 1.7

1. boring
2. barely
3. recyclable
4. grading
5. inescapable

6. completeness
7. pollutant
8. enslavement
9. livable
10. writing

Exercise 1.9

1. planner
2. predicting
3. digging
4. nailed
5. popping

6. scanner
7. batting
8. drafting
9. gassed
10. tapped

Exercise 1.10

1. recurring
2. revealing
3. debtor
4. raining
5. outrunning

6. befitting
7. gripped
8. resetting
9. napped
10. regretted

Exercise 1.11

1. occurrence
2. existence
3. coherence
4. concurring
5. interfering

6. subsistence
7. difference
8. dependence
9. recurrence
10. insistence

Exercise 1.13

1. shield
2. chief
3. veil

4. yield
5. retrieve
6. reindeer

7. sieve

8. reign

9. receipt

10. niece

Exercise 1.14

1. friend, counterfeit

2. neither, foreign

3. beige, leisure

4. perceived, weird

5. conceivable, either

Answers for Chapter 2: Sound-Alikes, Look-Alikes, and Spoilers (pages 15 to 29)

Exercise 2.1

1. accept, except

2. complement, quiet

3. stationary, its

4. choose, courses

5. fourth, conscience

6. Who's, woman

7. two, their

8. hear, advice

9. dose, effects

10. our, dining

Exercise 2.2

1. morale, miners

2. led, women

3. piece, dessert

4. personnel, stationary

5. lose, minor

6. council, where

7. conscious, compliment

8. moral, it's, than

9. They're, later

10. Your, than

Exercise 2.3

1. Does, stationery

2. Lead, quite

3. lose, chose

4. forth, peace

5. personal, principal

6. Whose, advice

7. then

8. were, we're

9. latter

10. desert, affect

Exercise 2.4

Last summer, despite my mother's **advice**, I decided to **adopt** a puppy. There are so many cute dogs that I found it difficult **to** decide which breed to **choose**. Once I visited the pound, though, I made up my mind **quite** quickly. Lucky, a wiry little dog with **coarse**, curly fur, stole my heart.

Unfortunately, Lucky also stole gloves, socks, and almost everything **off** my desk **except** the pencil sharpener. Obviously, in his **past** life, he had been terribly neglected and, as a result, he did almost anything to attract attention. For a while, I tolerated his theft of **minor** articles, but when he ate a box of expensive **stationery**, I began to **lose** my **patience**.

I took Lucky to puppy school, but the training didn't have much **effect**. The trainer explained that, because dogs are pack animals, Lucky would try to play the **dominant** role unless I clearly demonstrated that I was pack leader. So, as a point of

principle, I made Lucky wait for his **dinner** until I had finished my **dessert**. When we **passed** someone we knew on the street, I made him **heel** while I chatted. Once a **week**, we devoted an **hour** to reinforcing his training.

Now Lucky has learned his **lesson** and behaves much better **than** he once did. Indeed, he has become such a wonderful companion that I really can't decide **who's** the luckier one—Lucky or me.

Exercise 2.5
1. Moments after **its** takeoff, the plane banked **too** sharply to the left.
2. I certainly won't **choose** the one **whose** application was late.
3. Please check with the **Personnel** Department before you hire legal **counsel**.
4. If he **does** that again, it will **affect** his chances for promotion.
5. The Canada **Council** for the Arts will announce its awards **later** this month.
6. When I receive a **compliment**, I feel self-**conscious**.
7. **Whose** turn is it to find the **complement** of the angle?
8. If you could remember these three simple rules, **then your** spelling troubles would be over.
9. **There** are many children who believe the tooth fairy will come if they **lose** a tooth.
10. My mother is **quite** a **woman**.

Answers for Chapter 3: Capital Letters (pages 30 to 34)

Exercise 3.1
1. Rowena spent two hours waiting in line to register for Introduction to Fashion Design.
2. When I worked at Swiss Chalet, I won the Employee of the Month Award two months in a row.
3. April and May, the beginning of spring, are my favourite months.
4. The Minister of Health plays a prominent role in the prime minister's cabinet.
5. Secret tunnels beneath Moose Jaw, Saskatchewan, once hid a number of Chicago gangsters, including Al Capone.
6. My wife never misses *Hockey Night in Canada*.
7. Charlottetown's *Anne of Green Gables* is one of the longest running plays in Canadian theatre history.
8. When my sister travelled to Rome, she read the *Vancouver Sun* every day on the Internet.
9. George has been the chief financial officer of Merman Enterprises for more than 12 years.
10. Reverend Mullen was very excited to speak to the bishop in person last fall.

Exercise 3.2
1. The Newcomers' Club welcomes immigrants from the south to the community.
2. The meeting will be held next Wednesday at the mayor's house on Clifton Avenue.

3. **Dr.** Thomas assured him that Grace Hospital was one of the best hospitals in New Brunswick for **o**rthopedic surgery.
4. Although I have never been very good at **m**ath, I'm doing very well in **Mr.** Johnson's computing class.
5. Karl phoned **P**ayroll **S**ervices to inquire about the unexpected deduction for dental insurance on his last pay cheque.
6. Timothy Findley, author of *The Piano Man's Daughter*, will be greatly missed by the literary community.
7. When he studied at Wycliffe College, Bishop Franklin developed a passion for Vietnamese food.
8. Rebecca has to use soy milk on her Cheerios now that she has been diagnosed with lactose intolerance.
9. The Hubble telescope floats above Earth and takes pictures of the moon.
10. My cousin and I plan to attend Caribana in Toronto next month.

Answers for Chapter 4: The Apostrophe (pages 35 to 44)

Exercise 4.1
1. can't
2. she'd
3. we'll
4. let's
5. she'll
6. wouldn't
7. we'd
8. they're
9. won't
10. he'll

Exercise 4.2
1. **I'd** like to see John, but **he's** not home today.
2. Yvette said **she'd** wash the dishes since **it's** her turn to do kitchen duty.
3. **Don't** you think we should find out if **he'll** be coming?
4. **Let's** help Johann and Chris think of some fresh ideas for the project **they're** starting.
5. The dialect in parts of Newfoundland **hasn't** changed much since the seventeenth century.
6. **There's** no one **who'd** hike the Bruce Trail with Scott.
7. **I'm** glad to learn that **you've** been given the job.
8. How are we supposed to read the map if **we've** lost the flashlight?
9. We finally realized our mistake: **we'd** entered the wrong password.
10. Terry **won't** go to the concert if her sister **can't** go too.

Exercise 4.3
1. children's
2. woman's
3. the Smiths'
4. computers'
5. Great Lakes'
6. photo's
7. babies'
8. strikers'
9. nobody's
10. Chris' or Chris's

Exercise 4.4

1. **Clara's** new dog is just starting to lose **its** puppy teeth.
2. **Biff's** favourite pastime is spending his **girlfriend's** money.
3. Our **college's** aim is to meet **students'** social needs as well as **their** academic goals.
4. The **Sorensons'** daughter is a **children's** entertainer in Vancouver.
5. **Bikers'** equipment is on special at Leather **Larry's**.
6. **Klaus's** feet are so small that he has to buy **women's** loafers.
7. **Calgary's** reputation as an affordable city is fading now that the **city's** housing costs are rising.
8. My **father's** intuition told me I should screen the **Web site's** images before letting my ten-year-old see them.
9. Virtue may be **its** own reward, but I won't refuse **your** offer of cash.
10. To **no one's** surprise, **Queen Elizabeth's** visit to Toronto attracted less attention than the **Pope's**.

Exercise 4.5

1. The Pittsburgh Penguins **wouldn't** have won the Stanley Cup without Mario **Lemieux's** goals.
2. Our **budget's** so tight this year that **we'll** be spending our vacation in the back yard.
3. "**Can't** you come back tomorrow?" begged **Gwen's** aunt.
4. The **CD's** surface was badly scratched, so its files could not be loaded into the computer.
5. Donald Sutherland, **who's** from St. John, New Brunswick, is one of **Canada's** most famous actors.
6. A **patient's** fears can be eased by a kind **nurse's** attention.
7. The **speaker's** topic was way beyond our **students'** understanding.
8. **You'll** notice that Key Porter **Books'** list of authors includes Pamela Wallin and Jean Chrétien.
9. **Isn't** it strange that **nobody's** heard from Sean since he left for Ireland?
10. *Due South's* hero, Paul Gross, put the **Mounties'** red uniform in **television's** limelight.

Exercise 4.6

1. The Fortress of Louisbourg is one of the **country's** largest historical **reconstructions**.
2. The Royal Ontario **Museum's collections** are internationally famous.
3. **Children's** wear and **women's** shoes have been moved to the second floor.
4. Peter's **life's** ambition was to travel across Nunavut with a team of **huskies**.
5. Despite what the **schools** have taught for **years**, Alexander Graham Bell was not the **telephone's** inventor.
6. **Apostrophes** can be difficult to place when you don't know the **rules** that govern their use.
7. Laura **Secord's** most famous legacy has been a chain of candy **stores**.

8. The required **texts** for this course are *The Bare **Essentials*** and ***Roget's Thesaurus***.
9. "**Victory's** mine!" claimed the wrestler, waving his **arms** and jumping up and down.
10. **Hedonists** are those who pursue pleasure for **its** own sake.

Exercise 4.7

Josh and Patricia plan to spend **their holidays** camping in one of **Banff's** beautiful parks. **They've** already purchased most of their equipment, including sleeping bags, tent, folding chairs, and a portable stove. They had intended to pack lightly, but already **it's** clear that **they'll** need a roof rack, if not a utility trailer, to carry all **their** gear. **Their** budget has been stretched to the limit, and they **haven't** even begun to shop for **supplies**. Clothing, food, and insect repellant will eat up **what's** left of their credit. **Canadians** who think that **camping's** a cheap vacation **haven't** spent much time in the **aisles** of Canadian Tire.

Answers for Chapter 5: Numbers (pages 45 to 51)

Exercise 5.1
1. List **three** good reasons why I should consider your request for promotion.
2. For the **first** time, Gus felt confident leading the class.
3. Having spent **four** summers on Prince Edward Island, I would feel very comfortable working in the Maritimes.
4. For every **two** books you purchase, you can buy a third one for **half** the regular price.
5. I paused for about 15 minutes to allow **12** goslings to cross the road.
6. **Seven** and **five** are my favourite numbers to choose in the lottery.
7. Between the ages of **fourteen** and **seventeen**, I lived in Taiwan.
8. At least **one-third** of the students on campus commute from the suburbs each day and another **one-quarter** live in residence.
9. Brandon, the **first** stop on our itinerary, is the **second** largest city in Manitoba.
10. It takes **43** muscles to frown, but only **17** to smile.

Exercise 5.2
1. On April **20th**, Beth will take possession of her new house at **18** Borden Lane.
2. At **eight** o'clock in the morning, I was awakened by the sound of winds blowing at **80** km/h.
3. The final product should measure **12** cm by 22 cm.
4. Remember that 1 teaspoon is equivalent to **5** ml and that **1** cup is equivalent to 250 ml.
5. Finally, at the age of **forty-two**, Dan was able to put a small down payment on his first home, a bungalow priced at **$60,000**.
6. In early **2002**, interest rates at the major banks dropped to less than **4** percent.
7. **Eighteen hundred** puppy mills in Quebec produce more than **900,000** sickly dogs each year.
8. The temperature in Yellowknife often falls below **–40°C** by **2:00** p.m.

9. Driving a car at **90** km/h uses about **20** percent less fuel than driving it at 105 km/h.
10. Petra's great-grandmother arrived in Lethbridge in **1915** when she was only **twenty-two** years old.

Exercise 5.3
1. The astrologist predicted that, over the next **three** years, Alden's chances of getting married would be **54%**, **33%**, and **22%**.
2. An adult polar bear can weigh up to **340** kg, or as much a mid-sized sedan.
3. More than **100 million** years ago, dinosaurs roamed Alberta's Badlands. The first fossils of these prehistoric beasts were discovered in **1884**.
4. **Nineteen** of the **twenty** candidates were under the legal driving age of **sixteen**.
5. In the **nineteenth** century, it was common for women to wear hoop skirts that measured between 2.7 and **4** metres in circumference.
6. For my **eighteenth** birthday, I received a **$2,000** cheque.
7. Karim is planning a party for his great-aunt, who will be **ninety-nine** on Wednesday. **Sixty** guests are expected to attend the celebration.
8. In 1998, over **2** million men and **3** million women attended Canadian theatres.
9. Hannah has a curfew of **10** p.m., but on her prom night she stayed out until **one** o'clock in the morning.
10. To assemble the workbench, you will need **32** four-cm nails.

Answers for Chapter 6: Cracking the Sentence Code (pages 55 to 69)

Exercise 6.1
1. <u>It</u> <u>lives</u>!
2. The <u>mummy</u> <u>lives</u> in a crypt.
3. The <u>crypt</u> <u>is</u> its home.
4. The cemetery's south <u>wall</u> <u>contains</u> the crypt.
5. In the movie, the <u>mummy</u> only <u>walks</u> at night during a full moon.
6. <u>Walking</u> alone in a cemetery during a full moon <u>is</u> not a good idea.
7. According to legend, the <u>mummy</u> never <u>goes</u> beyond the cemetery walls.
8. (<u>You</u>) <u>Believe</u> me. <u>It</u> <u>does</u>.
9. Some real Egyptian <u>mummies</u> <u>are</u> on display at the Royal Ontario Museum.
10. <u>Studying</u> them <u>provides</u> insight into ancient Egyptian life.

Exercise 6.2
1. Most <u>Canadians</u> <u>are</u> concerned about nutrition.
2. Specialty health-food <u>stores</u> <u>exist</u> in almost every town.
3. Even mainstream <u>stores</u> <u>offer</u> organic produce.
4. Many <u>people</u> <u>take</u> vitamin supplements.
5. <u>Demand</u> for vitamin-enriched foods <u>increases</u> each year.
6. Each year, our <u>consumption</u> of pasta and cereals <u>grows</u> as well.
7. But <u>we</u> also <u>eat</u> more fat-filled foods like butter and cream.
8. Every <u>Canadian</u> <u>eats</u> about 9L of ice cream every year.

9. This <u>number</u> <u>represents</u> a 7 percent increase over last year's figure.
10. <u>Lowering</u> our fat intake <u>is</u> an ongoing struggle for many of us.

Exercise 6.3
1. <u>grass</u> <u>waved</u>
2. <u>Hiking</u> <u>is</u>
3. <u>Kim</u> <u>is</u>
4. <u>Who</u> <u>dialed</u>
5. <u>(You)</u> <u>drive</u>

6. <u>gloves</u> <u>are lying</u>
7. <u>dog</u> <u>won</u>
8. <u>desk</u> <u>is</u>
9. <u>chocolates</u> <u>are</u>
10. <u>taverns</u> <u>were</u>

Exercise 6.4
1. <u>prairies</u> <u>have fostered</u>
2. <u>train</u> <u>could arrive</u>
3. <u>Bruce</u> <u>will have attended</u>
4. <u>should</u> <u>we</u> <u>try</u>
5. <u>Barb</u> <u>must have written</u>

6. <u>I</u> <u>have finished eating</u>
7. <u>You</u> <u>should try</u>
8. <u>Did</u> <u>you</u> <u>see</u>
9. <u>Peace</u> <u>will be achieved</u>
10. <u>Marvin</u> <u>had intended</u>

Exercise 6.5
1. <u>We</u> <u>ought to have registered</u>
2. <u>Ralph</u> <u>has been waiting</u>
3. <u>I</u> <u>have travelled</u>
4. <u>Suzy</u> <u>could have known</u>
5. <u>They</u> <u>had locked</u>

6. <u>is</u> <u>mother</u> <u>hiding</u>
7. <u>Kendra</u> <u>can attend</u>
8. <u>did</u> <u>you</u> <u>lend</u>
9. <u>friends</u> <u>are planning</u>
10. <u>You</u> <u>should explore</u>

Exercise 6.6
1. The <u>flock</u> ~~of Canada geese~~ <u>circled</u> overhead.
2. <u>John Irving</u> <u>is</u> the author ~~of *A Prayer for Owen Meany*.~~
3. <u>Millions</u> ~~of Canadians~~ <u>watch</u> American football ~~on television.~~
4. The <u>definition</u> ~~of high fashion~~ <u>varies</u> ~~from province to province.~~
5. A <u>trend</u> ~~in Vancouver~~ <u>is</u> not necessarily a fad ~~in St. John's.~~
6. ~~In her excitement,~~ <u>she</u> <u>sprang</u> ~~over the handrail.~~
7. Her <u>love</u> ~~for him~~ <u>has</u> not <u>waned</u> ~~for twenty years.~~
8. <u>Aren</u>'t <u>you</u> <u>concerned</u> ~~about the state of the environment~~?
9. <u>I</u> <u>appreciated</u> the honesty ~~of his response.~~
10. <u>He</u> <u>limped</u> slowly ~~through the door.~~

Exercise 6.7
1. The <u>stars</u> <u>shine</u> down ~~on Earth from light years away.~~
2. Twenty <u>minutes</u> ~~of aerobic exercise about three times~~ a week <u>keeps</u> me healthy.
3. The <u>crash</u> ~~of SwissAir flight 111 into the ocean off Peggy's Cove, Nova Scotia,~~ <u>reminded</u> all ~~of us of our mortality.~~
4. <u>Escape</u> ~~from the Kingston Penitentiary~~ <u>appears</u> to be nearly impossible.
5. The <u>party</u> <u>starts</u> ~~in the warehouse at 5 o'clock.~~
6. The <u>article</u> ~~concerning pet cemeteries~~ <u>is reprinted</u> ~~in tonight's paper.~~
7. <u>Several</u> ~~of the doctors~~ <u>were attending</u> the conference ~~for the first time.~~
8. The wild <u>roses</u> ~~of Prince Edward Island~~ <u>smell</u> sweeter than any other flowers.

9. <u>You</u> really <u>should see</u> the dentist ~~about that loose tooth~~.
10. ~~Of all the Canadian comedy shows on television,~~ *This Hour Has 22 Minutes* <u>is</u> the funniest.

Exercise 6.8

1. Most <u>tourists</u> <u>are willing</u> to try the local dishes, ~~except for cod tongues~~.
2. ~~By waiting on tables,~~ ~~(by) babysitting,~~ and ~~(by) borrowing from my friends~~, <u>I</u> <u>manage</u> to make ends meet.
3. ~~By lobbying the government for support~~, the <u>farmers</u> <u>should gain</u> greater subsidies.
4. The <u>parcel</u> ~~for the manager~~ <u>is waiting</u> ~~at the front desk~~.
5. ~~After cycling from one coast to the other~~, <u>Philippa</u> <u>wrote</u> a book ~~about her journey~~.
6. The journalist's obvious <u>bias</u> ~~in favour of the police~~ <u>made</u> his report unreliable.
7. ~~In *The Stone Diaries*~~, <u>Carol Shields</u> <u>includes</u> a great recipe ~~for lemon pudding~~.
8. The <u>forests</u> ~~of Temagami, in northern Ontario~~, <u>form</u> an unspoiled wilderness.
9. The <u>book</u> ~~behind the dresser~~ <u>was covered</u> ~~with mould and mildew~~.
10. ~~Despite its strong taste~~, <u>espresso</u> <u>contains</u> no more caffeine than regular coffee.

Exercise 6.10

1. The <u>Toronto Maple Leafs</u> and the <u>Montreal Canadiens</u> <u>are</u> traditional archrivals.
2. <u>Whistler</u> or <u>Lake Louise</u> <u>would make</u> an excellent vacation spot.
3. Neither <u>Geoff</u> nor <u>Sue</u> <u>was able</u> to attend the Roch Voisine concert.
4. ~~During World War II~~, many Canadian <u>women</u> <u>worked</u> ~~in munitions factories~~ and <u>nursed</u> ~~in military hospitals~~.
5. Both <u>women</u> and <u>men</u> <u>stand</u> to benefit ~~from the recent changes to parental leave policies~~.
6. <u>Shauna</u> and <u>Wes</u> <u>plan</u> to marry next July.
7. <u>(You)</u> <u>Measure</u> the ingredients carefully and <u>mix</u> them thoroughly.
8. Coal <u>miners</u> and <u>fishermen</u> <u>are seeking</u> retraining.
9. The <u>coyote</u> <u>stopped</u> ~~in its tracks~~, <u>stared</u> ~~at the small child beside the garbage dumpster~~, then <u>turned</u> and <u>loped</u> away.
10. <u>Students</u> ~~with good time-management skills~~ <u>can research</u>, <u>organize</u>, <u>draft</u>, and <u>revise</u> a first-class paper ~~by the deadline~~.

Exercise 6.11

    <u>Food</u> <u>fuels</u> our bodies. ~~In important ways,~~ <u>it</u> also <u>nourishes</u> our souls, <u>cements</u> relationships, and <u>provides</u> an outlet ~~for creative experimentation~~. <u>We</u> <u>use</u> food ~~for celebrating special events~~. <u>We</u> <u>share</u> food ~~with friends and even strangers~~. An essential <u>ingredient</u> ~~in any courtship~~ <u>is</u> dining together, whether ~~at a restaurant~~ or ~~at the home of one of the lovers~~. ~~In my family,~~ <u>we</u> <u>remember</u> history ~~according to certain meals~~. There <u>are</u> the cooking <u>disasters</u> ~~from the early years~~: "<u>(You)</u> <u>Remember</u> that soggy eggplant casserole? The <u>dog</u> <u>wouldn't</u> <u>touch</u> it." Then there <u>are</u> the more dramatic <u>catastrophes</u>, ~~like the flaming mushroom soufflé~~. That <u>incident</u> <u>required</u> Dad's prompt use ~~of the kitchen fire extinguisher~~. Finally, there <u>are</u> the extraordinary culi-

nary <u>labours</u> ~~of love~~. ~~For a special wedding gift~~, <u>Dad</u> <u>gave</u> Mom a triple-layer wedding cake ~~of his own making~~. ~~On my brother's second-birthday~~, <u>Mom</u> <u>stayed up</u> all night and <u>baked</u> a choo-choo train birthday cake, complete ~~with a caboose~~. ~~After my sister's first chess championship~~, <u>Mom</u> <u>cooked</u> a special Chinese meal ~~from scratch~~. <u>Cooking</u> together, <u>eating</u> together, and <u>cleaning</u> the kitchen together <u>form</u> important rituals. ~~Without them~~, <u>we</u> <u>would be</u> hungry not just ~~for physiological nourishment~~ but also ~~for a sense of human community~~.

Answers for Chapter 7: Solving Sentence-Fragment Problems (pages 70 to 80)

For exercise 7.1, we have made up complete sentences to give you an idea of how fragments can be changed to sentences. Many different sentences can be made out of a fragment; just be sure each of your sentences has a subject and a verb.

Exercise 7.1
1. F <u>I am</u> happy to hear from you.
2. F The <u>choir is</u> large enough to fill the room.
3. S
4. F <u>We would like</u> to talk about Tuesday's meeting.
5. S
6. F <u>We stopped</u> in Winnipeg on the way to Saskatchewan.
7. F The <u>boys have been driving</u> for three days.
8. F The <u>acrobats were juggling</u> on the corner.
9. F <u>Stella left</u> the party feeling too tired to drive.
10. F <u>It is</u> not a problem.

Exercise 7.2 (suggested answers)
__F__ For the seventh year in a row, the <u>Buskers' Festival</u> <u>is taking</u> over the downtown area. __F__ There <u>are</u> <u>acrobats</u>, <u>jugglers</u>, <u>mimes</u>, and <u>musicians</u> from all over the world. __F__ <u>Streets</u> in the business district <u>have been</u> magically transformed into a strolling circus. __S__ [You] <u>Try</u> to take in at least a couple of events. __F__ <u>I</u> especially <u>recommend</u> the sword swallower from London. __S__ Also entertaining <u>is</u> the <u>unicyclist</u> from Spain. __F__ [You] <u>Be</u> careful to watch your valuables in the crowds. __F__ <u>Pickpockets</u> <u>are</u> as fond of the buskers as everyone else.

Exercise 7.3 (suggested answers)
__F__ Canadian singers <u>Shania Twain</u> and <u>Celine Dion</u> <u>have</u> a lot in common. __S__ Although Shania sings country music and Celine records pop songs, both are successful superstars. __S__ Yet, despite the millions of records they have sold and the luxurious lifestyles their stardom provides, neither woman is a diva. __F__ <u>Both</u> <u>come</u> from humble backgrounds and <u>are</u> still close to their families. __F__ Shania <u>was</u> a surrogate mother for her orphaned brothers and sisters. __F__ Celine <u>keeps</u> in touch with her family in Quebec. __F__ Finally, <u>both</u> <u>are</u> new mothers who took maternity breaks from their musical careers.

Exercise 7.4
1. F Although
2. F Until
3. F As soon as
4. F Provided that

5. F Whoever	8. F Where
6. F After	9. F Before
7. F Since	10. F Because

Exercise 7.5

1. F Before	6. F Although
2. F Which	7. S
3. F After	8. F Whoever
4. S	9. F who
5. F Even if	10. F Unless

Exercise 7.7

Although Canada enjoys a temperate climate compared to the rest of the world, complaining about the weather is a favourite national pastime **that** is popular from coast to coast. **Whereas** Vancouver urbanites groan about the rainy weather, Saskatchewan farmers lament the prairie drought. **Unless** Ottawa has an abnormally mild winter, Ottawa's citizens complain **about** the frigid temperatures and the nearly impassable snowdrifts. **Even though** we Canadians enjoy outdoor sports and activities and are known as hardy folks, we're seldom content **with** whatever the weather brings us. **Whether** it's cold or hot, we compensate for our vulnerability **by** grumbling about Mother Nature's unpredictability.

Exercise 7.8 (suggested answers)

People say that pets and their owners tend to look alike **after** a while. There is some truth to this generalization**, as** far as I can see. Reflecting on my own experience**,** I can think of several uncanny resemblances **between** pets and owners. For example, Fluffy the long-haired tabby cat **resembles** my Aunt Ruby with her permed hair. My neighbour, Joe Maxwell, **has** a Rottweiler that is as surly and overweight as he is. Then there is Sheena Lougheed's toy poodle, **which is** high-strung, fussy, perfectly groomed, and whiny. **The dog is the** mirror image of Sheena, **especially** when they both wear red ribbons in their hair.

Exercise 7.9 (suggested answers)

My cousin, Jack, used to fix Automatic Teller Machines (ATMs) for CIBC **when** he was in college. He liked the job **because** he said it gave him a feeling of prestige. Wearing a beeper was part of the job**, so** he felt important**, as if** he were a surgeon or a firefighter on call. The job had its drawbacks, however**, particularly** the odd hours. Some weekends Jack had to work the 4 p.m. to 12 a.m. shift. This made it hard for him to make a Saturday night date**, let** alone enjoy one uninterrupted. Not many young women have the patience to put up with leaving a movie halfway through to report to a repair site **and** watch Jack and his partner fiddle with the insides of an ATM for an hour **or** more. The job presented certain risks, too. Whenever Jack opened up an ATM**, he** put himself in potential danger **by** exposing thousands and thousands of dollars. He worked with a partner**, of course, but** neither of them carried a gun**, only** a pager and a cell phone **to** communicate with security guards. Despite the excellent pay**, I** never applied to work with Jack. For me, **the job offered** too much responsibility and too little social life.

Answers for Chapter 8: Solving Run-on Sentence Problems (pages 81 to 91)

Exercise 8.1 (suggested answers)
1. Sir John A. MacDonald is on the ten dollar bill, **and** Sir Wilfred Laurier is on the five dollar bill.
2. I have had many manicures, **but** I have never had a pedicure.
3. **Although** Russell de Carle has a solo album, he still sings with Prairie Oyster.
4. Natalie prefers pickles, onions, and tomato on her hamburger. **She** doesn't like mayonnaise, mustard, or ketchup.
5. Yan plans to travel to Montreal this summer, **and** she hopes to see Quebec City on the way
6. Dwight has lived in Punkeydoodle Corners, Ontario, all his life. **He** never understands why people laugh when he tells them the name of his hometown.
7. correct
8. Zachary will be going to college if he is accepted. **His** parents have more than enough money.
9. Harry Houdini was in Montreal in October 1926 and was punched by a student. **He** died in Detroit two weeks later. **Some** biographers believe his death was caused by the injury he sustained in Montreal.
10. Kenny bought me a dozen roses; I didn't tell him I'm allergic to flowers.

Exercise 8.2 (suggested answers)
1. I love soccer. **I** feel like Pele every time I'm on the field.
2. Francis asked me to a movie, **but** I couldn't go because my cousin had just flown in from the Yukon.
3. Quarterback Doug Flutie went to the NFL. **Many** Canadians remember him for having led the Calgary Stampeders and the Toronto Argonauts to Grey Cup victories.
4. The rules of CFL and NFL football are different, **and** I don't understand either game.
5. correct
6. **When** she smelled the flowers, she smiled happily; then she sneezed loudly.
7. Tomorrow we will pay off our mortgage. **Then** we can finally afford to buy some furniture.
8. Don't tell Chris where his wife has gone; she is at the mall buying his birthday gift.
9. Yasmine and David are getting married in the United Church, even though they are Jewish, **because** no synagogues are available that day.
10. **After** my brother's friends spilled red wine all over my white carpet, it was ruined.

Exercise 8.3 (suggested answers)
1. When our team wins, we always do our special cheer. **Some** other teams think we are crazy.
2. correct

3. Sally left the bank because Quebecor offered her a management position. **She** loves her new job.

4. Vowing to make her the happiest woman in the world, Shane asked Lana to marry him, **and** she agreed.

5. The Taxpayer Action Movement wants Jean Chrétien to retire; I'd like him to go to the moon.

6. Frances thought her interview had gone very well; however, she wasn't offered the job.

7. **Although** there are some advantages to having a friend for a boss, there are more disadvantages.

8. The most important thing I've learned as a manager is that success depends on teamwork. **Unless** team members play the same game, the business may fail.

9. During filming of the movie, the actor worked under a pseudonym, **so** the credits of the movie don't even list him as playing the lead character.

10. After I woke up late for work, I decided to call in sick. **An** hour later, I went to the mall and ran into my boss.

Exercise 8.4 (suggested answers)

The most popular tourist attraction in Derby Line, Vermont, is a theatre in which audiences sitting in the United States can watch performances in Canada. This seemingly impossible feat is the result of the theatre's unique location. The building straddles the border between Vermont and Quebec. A black stripe painted on the floor marks the official dividing line between the two countries. Constructed early in the last century, the building is divided not only geographically but also functionally; it is a library as well as a theatre. The name of this unusual structure is the Haskell Free Library and Opera House. The library is on the ground floor, **and** the theatre is upstairs. Most of the building, including the library and the stage, is in Quebec, **but** the entrance to the building is in Vermont.

A Canadian woman, Martha Stewart Haskell, built the structure as a tribute to her American husband. Over the past 100 years, some famous troupers have performed on its stage. The first "name act" to appear was the Columbian Minstrels, who opened the theatre in 1904. Recently renovated, the Haskell Free Library and Opera House continues to provide its cross-border patrons with full library services **and** first-rate theatrical performances.

Exercise 8.5 (suggested answers; deleted words and phrases indicated by ***)

1. A recent study *** in *The National Post* claims that women have better *** verbal skills than men. I *** want to say to the authors of that study, "D'oh."

2. Our supervisor recently held a meeting *** to discuss *** our department's lack of productivity. She told us that we would continue to have **daily meetings** until she finds out why we are not working **more efficiently**.

3. There are two *** reasons for my dissatisfaction with my car: the *** rusting of the *** undercarriage and *** the *** disintegration of the electrical system.

4. I look back with *** nostalgia on winters in the small Manitoba town where I grew up with *** softly falling snow, the *** excitement of the year's first snow-

ball fight, and the crunch of snow beneath my boots on *** cold prairie mornings. These memories prove that the mind recalls *** pleasant experiences and forgets *** painful ones *** as we age.

5. Following a high-speed chase and the arrest of the car's driver, the police learned that the vehicle *** had been stolen. They added *** theft to the reckless-driving charge, and the driver had to spend the night in jail. There he realized the seriousness of his situation and *** demanded his right to call a lawyer.

Exercise 8.6 (suggested answers; deleted words indicated by ***)

One popular *** Canadian pastime that is seldom mentioned in the media *** is poking fun at the regional accents that distinguish one part of the country from another. Since their dialect is particularly distinctive, Newfoundlanders have long been the target of this game; however, anyone who has travelled across Canada *** quickly learns that each region *** of the country has its own characteristic linguistic features. Sometimes these features are determined by provincial or territorial borders, **but** at other times linguistic regions transcend political and geographical boundaries. For instance, *** many people in the Atlantic provinces *** tend to pronounce vowel sounds with a Maritime twang, **so that** "light" sounds like "loight" ***. They also tend to soften the "th" sound in words such as "brother" or "other," which are *** commonly pronounced as "brudder" and "udder."

Sometimes regional speech *** variations go beyond matters of pronunciation ***; such differences produce what is called a regional dialect. In speech, for instance, many Newfoundlanders use verbs differently than do speakers of standard English. They say "I wants to go shopping" instead of "I want to go shopping." Natives of the Miramichi Valley use another distinctive construction; they say "youse" instead of the standard second person plural, "you."

Pronunciation, slang, and grammatical constructions differ *** across Canada, **and** we should be proud of our rich, diverse regional dialects.

Answers for Chapter 9: Solving Modifier Problems (pages 92 to 102)

Exercise 9.1
1. Wearing his best suit, Sylvester bathed the dog.
2. Every week I write a letter to my boyfriend who lives in England.
3. The blaze was put out by the Riverview Fire Department before any damage was done.
4. Shelley did not arrive until almost three o'clock in the morning.
5. You will find a parking lot with an elevator in the next block.
6. With your books closed, tell me what you have read.
7. She ate only one piece of toast this morning.
8. Elizabeth said she would drop off her job application to Esso on her way to school.
9. Some people never go to restaurants unless they are Chinese or Italian.
10. After almost driving over me, my sister was grounded for a week.

Exercise 9.2

1. He kicked the ball barely ten metres.
2. A mechanic who looked slightly younger than my car was the only employee working in the garage.
3. At the end of the term, my instructor told me I would get my marks by mail. *Or:* My instructor told me I would get my marks by mail at the end of the term.
4. Using his new binoculars, Harry caught sight of a moose and her two calves.
5. With a screwdriver, I was able to loosen the clamp that held the broken cable in place.
6. Nearly six hundred thousand Canadian men get a vasectomy each year.
7. In Wales, Pedro married a woman with a title and a vast fortune.
8. Penny thought her daughter, dressed in her Kelly Osbourne costume, looked perfect for the Hallowe'en party.
9. The football practices have been organized as a fitness program for players who are not playing with a team in the summertime.
10. Claire arrived in a summer hat with her golden retriever.

Exercise 9.3

1. Leaving the theatre, we were surprised to find it had gotten dark.
2. Reading a novel, Emma cuddled her dog on her lap.
3. Swerving to miss the cyclist, we hit the tree.
4. Before taking a grammar quiz, you should review dangling modifiers.
5. After find a four-leaf clover, I put it into my diary to be pressed and dried.
6. Hanging in the Avenida Art Gallery, the new show is by photographer Frank Buchwitz.
7. After criticizing both my work and my attitude, my supervisor fired me.
8. Not having practised beforehand, we performed dismally.
9. Hoping to miss the rush hour traffic, I had the car warmed up and ready to go by 7:00 a.m.
10. Driving down the Trans-Canada Highway, I was sickened by the road kill.

Exercise 9.4

1. Before vacuuming the floor, you should dust the furniture.
2. Setting the oven on high, I cooked the chicken quickly.
3. Before calling you, I had already started watching *Chicago*.
4. After changing the tire, you should release the jack.
5. Having decided on pizza, we should decide whether to order beer or soft drinks.
6. Having completed the beginning, you should focus on the ending, the second most important part of the essay.
7. Staring into the black night, I was terrified by the wolf's howl.
8. Pulling out of the driveway, I smelled the lovely fragrance of the rose border.
9. While taking a bath, I was startled when a mouse jumped on the counter.
10. Littering on the road, the bicycle campers were stopped by the Mounties.

Exercise 9.5
1. When we left the theatre, it had gotten dark.
2. As Emma was reading a novel, her dog cuddled on her lap.
3. When I swerved to miss the cyclist, I hit the tree.
4. Before you take the grammar quiz, you should review dangling modifiers.
5. After I found a four-leaf clover, I put it in my diary to be pressed and dried.
6. The photographs that are hanging in the Avenida Art Gallery are by Frank Buchwitz.
7. After she had criticized both my work and my attitude, my boss fired me.
8. Because we had not practised beforehand, our performance was a dismal failure.
9. Since we hoped to miss the rush-hour traffic, the car was warmed up and ready to go before 7:00 a.m.
10. As I was driving down the Trans-Canada Highway, the road kill sickened me.

Exercise 9.6
1. Before you vacuum the floor, you should dust the furniture.
2. Because I had set the oven on high, I cooked the chicken quickly.
3. Before I called you, I had already started to watch *Chicago*.
4. After you have changed the tire, release the jack.
5. Now that we have decided on pizza, our next decision is whether to order beer or soft drinks.
6. When you have completed the beginning, you should focus next on the ending, the second most important part of the essay.
7. As I stared into the black night, I was terrified by the wolf's howl.
8. As I pulled out of the driveway, I noticed that the rose border smelled lovely.
9. While I was taking a bath, a mouse jumped on the counter.
10. Because they were littering on the road, the bicycle campers were stopped by the Mounties.

Exercise 9.7 (suggested answers)
1. Just before I left Shoppers Drug Mart, my cell phone rang.
2. The mosquitoes became annoying while I was sitting on the back porch.
3. While I was watching *Royal Canadian Air Farce*, the television suddenly went off.
4. Startled by the telephone, Derek cut his chin with the razor.
5. While the batter was swinging away from the pitch, a ball hit her.
6. When I was four, my mom taught me to drive a tractor.
7. While I was sitting outside the Swiss Chalet, my brother drove by and waved.
8. Bryan Adams is acclaimed from Vancouver to Halifax for his skillfully choreographed performances, his sensitive lyrics, and his original compositions.
9. As a college student constantly faced with new assignments, I sometimes find the pressure intolerable.
10. Being horribly hung over, I concluded sadly that the only problem with a free bar is knowing when to quit.

Exercise 9.8 (suggested answers)

1. Marilyn plans to prepare for her guests an olive and onion appetizer soaked in vodka.
2. Above my desk, hanging by a blue ribbon, is a photo of my baby.
3. Because their dog is allowed to run freely, we are concerned that it may be run over.
4. She gave the customer the oranges wrapped in newspaper.
5. Being from Nova Scotia, Joseph and Karyn miss the smell of the sea.
6. Seth was rejected by nearly every girl in Guelph.
7. Riding home on the subway, I had my wallet stolen.
8. Because Biff had obviously drunk too much, I drove him to his apartment, made him a pot of coffee, and called his mother.
9. While walking to school, three children were injured by a falling tree.
10. I told my mother I had attended almost all my classes this term.

Answers for Chapter 10: The Parallelism Principle (pages 103 to 111)

Exercise 10.1

1. The minimum requirements for survival are food and shelter.
2. I like to run in Waterton Lakes National Park, hike along the Bruce Trail, and swim in English Bay.
3. Elsie wants both love and freedom.
4. Carefully and gracefully, Bonita descended the stairs in her satin gown.
5. We can either drive to Summerside or fly to Tucson.
6. Haley spent the day watching the whales and visiting the tourist shops.
7. I opened my eyes and discovered I had a cast on my arm, a brace on my leg, and a big headache.
8. A teacher's main responsibilities are to educate students and ensure their safety.
9. If I can't be an RCMP officer, I want to be a chef or a comedian.
10. The best thing I ever did was get married and have children.

Exercise 10.2

1. Our team is quick, strong, and skilful, despite its losing record.
2. This term, our art class includes drawing, painting, and sculpting.
3. While our guests chatted about the Sarah Harmer concert, Lauren and I made the salad, grilled the hamburgers, and set the table.
4. The most common ways to catch a cold are to share someone else's food or drink, to be sneezed on, and to fail to wash your hands.
5. You can invite the boys to the taping of *Gabereau* by phoning or emailing them.
6. I have to complete three projects for my literature classes: write a research paper on T.S. Eliot, read three Canadian novels, and act in a Shakespeare play.
7. Thursday night the Hamilton Chamber of Commerce hosted a dinner attended by trustees, managers, and employees.
8. Kwok is a good leader: charismatic, fearless, principled, and articulate.
9. The literal meaning of the word "flog" is "to beat." Figuratively, it means to promote something, sell something aggressively, or sell illegally.

10. Caring for pigs not only requires a lot of attention but also is expensive and tiring.

Exercise 10.3 (suggested answers)

1. Chinese	Canadian	American
2. brush	rinse	floss
3. sensitive	responsive	approachable
4. original	functional	ingenious
5. valueless	meaningless	uninteresting
6. hot chocolate	bedtime story	back rub
7. achieve my career goal	find true love	travel the world
8. handsome	witty	kind
9. being a pharmacist	being a doctor	being a nurse
10. efficient	prompt	organized

Exercise 10.5 (deleted words indicated by ***)

One of the frustrating things about living in Canada is that there is little choice about which airline to use when you want to see friends, **visit** relatives, or **make** a business trip. As a sales representative for a national company, I often have to travel within Canada, **to** the United States, and **to** Hong Kong. Ever since Air Canada became a monopoly, I have often found myself swearing under my breath when faced with their limited flight options. It's true that a few discount airlines, such as WestJet and Jetsgo, are now available, but their schedules tend to be erratic. For instance, a budget airline might fly from Regina to Calgary only on Tuesday mornings and **Thursday afternoons**. But these flights are often delayed because of low priority on the runways.

As a business traveller, I need an airline I can count on because I have appointments to keep and deadlines **to meet**. Also, budget airlines do not provide cell phones at every seat, and **they do not** offer seats wide enough to fit my large frame. Furthermore, in-flight service is hardly existent. I'm used to being offered food, beverages, headsets, and *** a choice of reading materials. Budget airlines provide none of these things. Instead, you have to bring your own lunch, *** **magazines**, and newspapers. I'm already carrying a laptop, a briefcase, *** my sample case, and a carry-on! How am I supposed to add lunch to this burden, let alone reading material?

I will, however, give budget airlines credit for one thing: they don't lose my luggage as often as Air Canada does, even when I check in late or **forget** to label one of my bags.

Answers for Chapter 11: Refining by Combining (pages 112 to 120)

Exercise 11.1
1. Rapunzel pulled up her hair when the prince was in the tower.
2. The new Thai restaurant is popular and inexpensive.
3. I enjoy many aspects of small-town life, but I miss Vancouver's coffee shops.
4. The supervisor hired Roger for the forestry job, even though there were better qualified candidates.

5. Although Kate Nelligan has never played a major Hollywood role, she is a well-established actor.
6. Kim Campbell came to power as prime minister in 1993, just when the backlash against feminism was in full swing.
7. Based in Nova Scotia, the Mermaid Theatre is a puppeteer troupe that tours Canada and the United States.
8. The Calgary Stampede is an exciting event that draws thousands of spectators every year.
9. Obviously enjoying Paula's peculiar brand of humour, the audience frequently interrupted her performance with applause.
10. Even though the value of the Canadian dollar makes vacationing in Canada a real bargain for Americans, not many of them choose to spend their holidays here.

Exercise 11.2 (suggested answers)
1. If Fred is not at Castle Frank station, we should call the restaurant where he works.
2. Although most people like chocolate, Inez does not because she is allergic to it.
3. Holding hands, the two lovers walked up and down Lovers' Lane until it was time for them to part for the night.
4. When the clock in the Peace Tower had struck six times, we took off our skates and went home.
5. Margot cannot come to class today because she has a toothache and has to see her dentist.
6. The famous Canadian painter Tom Thomson was an enthusiastic canoeist who disappeared mysteriously during a canoeing trip.
7. Please serve something besides pickerel so that those of us who hate it can still enjoy our dinner.
8. The loon's call suddenly echoed, startling the tourist, who ran inside the hotel.
9. Terence can register for classes in the fall providing he pays his tuition on time and passes all his current courses.
10. The Northern Lights, whose scientific name is *aurora borealis*, danced across the sky like fireworks.

Exercise 11.3 (suggested answers)
1. The Canada Games, which were first held in 1967, are held every two years in a different city and create great national pride.
2. The Miramichi River in northern New Brunswick is famous for its salmon. It attracts fly fishers from all over the world.
3. Writer's block, the inability to generate ideas on paper, can be a paralyzing experience that is difficult to overcome. Strategies to overcome writer's block include freewriting, dictating into a tape recorder, or asking questions of your topic.
4. Prince Edward Island is now connected to Nova Scotia by the 12.9-km Confederation Bridge. As a result, the island, which could formerly be reached only by ferry, is much more accessible than it used to be.

5. The World Wide Web is a boon to researchers because it provides a wealth of information rapidly and is accessible 24 hours a day. Since not all Web sites offer reliable information, however, it is important to note the source of a site and to evaluate its content.

6. The children's book *Harry Potter* has sparked the imaginations of millions of young readers and become an international phenomenon. The book's author has even given a public reading at Toronto's Skydome. Although *Harry Potter* has been critically acclaimed, it has also been denounced by some religious conservatives, who claim the book encourages Satanism.

7. Margaret had several errands to complete, so she walked to the bank, deposited her pay cheque, and walked home. Then she discovered that she had left her wallet at the automatic teller machine. She returned to the bank and asked a teller about her wallet. When the teller returned it, Margaret gave him a big hug.

8. Cross-cultural communication can be challenging because, for one thing, cultures do not agree on the use of hand gestures. American President George Bush discovered that a polite signal in one culture can be offensive in another culture. On a visit to Australia, he gave the "V" for victory sign with his pointer and middle fingers, not realizing that Australians consider this an obscene gesture.

9. The study of a musical instrument teaches self-discipline, listening skills, and history. In addition, it provides people with entertainment, creative inspiration, and a sense of accomplishment. If more people studied musical instruments, their quality of life would be enhanced.

10. It has been an unbearable day. Everything has gone wrong: the maid is on vacation; the chef is ill; the Rolls is in the shop; my tailor has cancelled this afternoon's appointment; and I'm even out of champagne. On the financial front, the news is no better: the stock market is down, and my accountant tells me I have to pay taxes again this year. Life is hardly worth living.

Answers for Chapter 12: Choosing the Correct Verb Form (pages 123 to 130)

Exercise 12.1

1. bit, bitten
2. eaten, ate
3. forgave, forgiven
4. hid, hidden
5. wrote, written

6. lay, lain
7. told, told
8. shook, shaken
9. laid, laid
10. struck, struck

Exercise 12.2

1. I would have **come** on time if I had **known** you were serving dinner.
2. The dealer at Casino Niagara **dealt** me a lousy hand, but I **won** anyway.
3. My aunt had already **given** her daughter the family home; in her will, she also **left** her a car, several valuable paintings, and her jewellery.
4. The front doorbell **rang** twice; you could have **cut** the tension with a knife.
5. Margie could have **drunk** another bottle of beer if she hadn't **eaten** the rest of the pizza.

6. Jared could never have got as far north as Edmonton if he hadn't **met** a friendly truck driver in Lethbridge.
7. At the Camp Berwick reunion, we **sang** all the old camp songs, **raised** our mugs of cocoa to toast absent friends, and **swore** eternal friendship by the campfire.
8. When I was four or five, my grandfather first **told** me the story of his journey from Nigeria to Canada, many details of which have **stuck** in my memory.
9. Near the end of term, it occurred to us that if only we had **gone** to class and **done** the homework, we could probably have passed the course.
10. Capital punishment is no longer **practised** in Canada, but in some states of the U.S., you can be **hanged** if you have **broken** certain laws.

Answers for Chapter 13: Mastering Subject–Verb Agreement (pages 131 to 144)

Exercise 13.1
1. ringing
2. anyone
3. keyboarding
4. many
5. you
6. sailing
7. Susan
8. dishes
9. results
10. dreams

Exercise 13.2
1. The <u>rivers</u> <u>empty</u> into Hudson's Bay.
2. New <u>Canadians</u> <u>appreciate</u> meeting other people who share the same cultural background.
3. My <u>grandparents</u> <u>give</u> me peppermint candies whenever I visit **them** in the nursing home.
4. The latest <u>albums</u> from The Tragically Hip <u>are selling</u> quickly.
5. The <u>sailor</u> <u>misses</u> Canadian bacon and maple syrup.
6. The bald <u>eagle</u> <u>is</u> a rare bird.
7. <u>She</u> <u>talks</u> constantly during a movie.
8. All <u>provinces</u> <u>send</u> **delegates** to the conference.
9. Our <u>supervisors</u> <u>want</u> us to take a more positive approach to customer service.
10. <u>Both</u> the latecomers <u>were</u> **unable** to talk **their** teacher into letting **them** write the exam.

Exercise 13.3
1. answers
2. is
3. influences
4. recall
5. represents
6. supervises
7. interests
8. sign
9. is
10. endangers

Exercise 13.4
1. isn't
2. is
3. costs
4. irritates
5. keeps
6. occurs

7. promises
8. demonstrates

9. form
10. offer

Exercise 13.5

1. finishes
2. makes
3. finds
4. visits
5. is

6. happens
7. dares
8. lives
9. saves
10. is

Exercise 13.6

1. wants
2. offers
3. matches
4. is
5. speaks

6. wears
7. wakes up
8. has served
9. runs
10. influences

Exercise 13.7

1. loves
2. are
3. is scheduled
4. argue
5. brush

6. leave
7. sings
8. plays
9. prefers
10. is

Exercise 13.8

1. seems
2. holds
3. is
4. drags
5. hurl

6. equals
7. takes
8. was
9. crawls
10. is

Exercise 13.9

1. No one who **cares** about the environment will use plastic or Styrofoam cups.
2. After each of the couples **has paid** the fees, the mass wedding can begin.
3. As the mayor passed the crowd that **was** gathered in front of the bank, he raised his hand and waved.
4. There **are** no good reasons for rejecting this application.
5. The amount of federal government resources directed towards job creation **is** enormous.
6. The rust problem, not the broken water pump or the faulty brakes, **was** what made me decide to sell the car.
7. Did you interview everybody who **lives** within 2 km of the tar ponds?
8. Val Grabove, together with two or three part-time instructors, **is** planning to offer a course in winter wilderness camping.
9. The scarcity of jobs in small communities **causes** widespread depression.
10. Seven years **is** a long time to spend in a jail cell.

Exercise 13.10

Although most jobs now **require** the use of computers, the digital revolution does not seem to be improving our overall quality of life. Since a desktop computer, complete with headphones for voice-activated functions, **exists** in every office, work should be becoming simpler. However, neither increased efficiency nor improved employee morale **has resulted** from computer use. Rather, each worker's tasks **have** become more complex. In the past, for example, an invoice or two purchase orders **were** necessary to complete a request for supplies. The process, including online confirmation, now **requires** five separate documents. The obvious results of this complication **are** frustration and curses. Everybody, including the supervisors, **is** fed up with the extra workload. When our division **implements** a new computer system next month, I expect at least two of my coworkers to quit. Fifteen hours of training **is** needed to learn the new system, and that is more time than any of us **has** to waste.

Exercise 13.11

Canada's national luge team **practises** at the luge track in Calgary, Alberta. Luge, like bobsledding, **is** a relatively new sport for most Canadians. Because there **are** few places in the world where an athlete can train for the luge, the number of lugers in the world, let alone in our country, **remains** small. Membership in this elite group of athletes **requires** nerves of titanium. Eighty kilometres per hour **is** the beginning speed on a luge track. Moreover, not the luge's speed, which can reach 150 kilometres per hour, but the layout of the track **presents** the real breathtaking challenge of the sport. Anyone who **experiences** vertigo should steer clear of the luge's twisting track. One of the curves in the Calgary track, called the "Kriesel," **requires** lugers to endure G forces greater than 4 Gs. Only serious daredevils, such as jet pilots or skydivers, **qualify** for this demanding sport.

Exercise 13.12

1. singular
2. plural
3. singular
4. singular
5. singular
6. singular
7. singular
8. singular
9. singular
10. singular

Answers for Chapter 14: Keeping Your Tenses Consistent (pages 145 to 149)

Exercise 14.1

1. Steve Nash plays for the Dallas Mavericks and **is** arguably Canada's best basketball player.
2. I used to listen to Peter Gzowski on CBC Radio before I **went** to my afternoon classes at the college.
3. James gets up at six o'clock and **goes** to work in an office downtown.
4. I have been very unhappy since my cat died, but I still get up every morning and **eat** breakfast.
5. William went to Winnipeg for his vacation every summer and **stayed** with his best friend, Omar.
6. correct

7. George and Martha are best friends who **love** to go hiking together in the mountains on warm, sunny days.
8. We were very excited when the Canadian men's hockey team **won** the gold medal at the 2002 Olympic games in Salt Lake City.
9. correct
10. Nabil still likes to play cricket with his friends from Canada even though most of them **don't** understand any of the rules.

Exercise 14.2
1. Jay went to the movies every night while his friends **stayed** at home and **studied.**
2. International studies consistently rank Canada as one of the best places in the world to **live.**
3. correct
4. Many students the reporter interviewed liked to listen to country music, but few **were** aware of great singers and songwriters from Canada's past, such as Hank Snow and Gene MacLellan.
5. I knew I would be late for my meeting in Vancouver when a snow storm **delayed** my flight from Calgary.
6. Marcella visited her grandmother every week even though she **had** to travel more than two hours to reach the nursing home.
7. My friends and I think most Canadian politicians serving in parliament today **are** greedy and dishonest.
8. correct
9. When the new neighbours refused to turn down the music at their party, my dad **called** the police.
10. After the movie *Titanic* was released, thousands of tourists **came** to Halifax to visit a memorial to the victims of this famous maritime disaster.

Exercise 14.3
I sometimes think that life *was* much simpler forty or fifty years ago. For example, it **seems** to me that food was a lot less complicated. There **were** simply not as many nutritional concerns for us to worry about every day. We just drank our milk and **ate** our vegetables; we **didn't** bother with reading low-fat cookbooks and counting every calorie. Eating meat **was** not a political statement, and dessert was a treat to be enjoyed, not a substance you **had** to analyze. Also, we **knew** nothing about Mad Cow Disease, so we cooked our burgers medium-rare and **gobbled** them without anxiety. Without worrying about pesticides, we bought plenty of farm-fresh produce when it **was** in season. Because genetically modified foods were developed much later, we thought that Frankenfood **was** the stuff of science fiction, not standard grocery fare. We never imagined that even basic foods, such as milk, **would become** controversial. Neither did we realize that scientists **would** one day **grow** new varieties of grain in test tubes. Certainly, we **could not have predicted** the mammoth health food industry that would develop. I remember that, when I was a youngster, "granola" was an exotic food, wheat germ **sounded** like a contagious disease, and the word "organic" **applied** to a branch of chemistry.

Answers for Chapter 15: Choosing the Correct Pronoun Form (pages 150 to 157)

Exercise 15.1

1. In the end, both of **us** were disappointed.
2. As a result of her persistence, the team leader nominated **her** for a special company award.
3. Years ago, **he** and his uncle ran a hotel on the shore of Lake Superior.
4. Grandmother knit new angora sweaters for my cousin and **me**.
5. I can get along with Adam and Janna, but I can't work with **them**.
6. **We** skiers like to see a snowstorm arrive in the Rockies.
7. Jacob was afraid the instructor wouldn't believe **him** when he said that neither of **us** had checked our answers against the textbook.
8. When Francesca gets here, **she** and I are planning to go shopping at the West Edmonton Mall.
9. It is difficult to choose between **her** and **him**.
10. If the managers approve the recommendation **we** team leaders have made, **we** and **they** will exchange shifts.

Exercise 15.2

1. **He** and George take the same photography class.
2. Neither Jody nor **I** managed to get to the bank before it closed.
3. For once, there was no one in front of Bob and **me** in the bookstore line-up.
4. Will Shirley and **he** visit the Arctic again next summer?
5. We want you and **her** to correct the errors the interns made on the spreadsheet.
6. Sheldon and **I** are going to be your trainers for the next month.
7. I think Franz and **she** would make a good team.
8. If the decision were up to you and **me**, we would get the new office furniture.
9. **We** and our partners agreed to expand, but only if it was **they** who raised the extra capital.
10. One thing is clear to **us** parents: those who say they sleep like a baby do not have one.

Exercise 15.3

1. Stan trusts his psychologist more than he trusts **me**.
2. correct
3. All of **us** put more work into the class project than did Ursula or **he**.
4. Finally, I have found a lab partner who works as hard as **I** [do].
5. Because she grew up in Digby, Kyla enjoys scallops more than **I** [do].
6. Tristan thinks that, as the oldest in the family, he should use the family car more than **I** [do].
7. Although I generally trust friendly people, I dislike salespeople who smile as much as **he** [does].
8. The entrance to the secret garden was as high as **he** [was], but not as wide as **I** [am].

9. Few Canadians know as much **he [does]** about the occult experiences of William Lyon Mackenzie King.
10. The real difference between Diana Krall and **me** is style, not skill.

Exercise 15.4

In my family, everyone is over two metres tall except **me**. This means that everyone, including my youngest brother, is taller than **I [am]**. Both **he** and my younger sister play on the high school basketball team, while my older brother stars on his college team. As for **me**, I can hardly shoot the ball high enough to get it in the hoop, even when I stand on my tiptoes. Whether on or off the basketball court, **we** vertically challenged folk face many difficulties. The world, it seems, is made for my siblings, not **me**. Each time I struggle to reach a book on a high library shelf, or roll my shirtsleeves up to prevent them from dragging in my soup, I wish that I were as tall as **they [are]**.

Recently, however, by exploring my family history, I learned that that being overly tall has disadvantages. One of my family's nineteenth-century ancestors, Anna Swan, known as the Giantess of Nova Scotia, was so tall that **she** and her husband had to have their carriage, their furniture, and even their church pew specially made. Although she had hoped to become a teacher, Anna felt such a misfit at the Truro Normal School (teacher's college) that she decided to make her living as a "freak" in P.T. Barnum's shows. Here she met other extraordinary mortals like **her**—one of whom became her husband, the giant from Kentucky, Martin van Buren Bates. The two giants lived quietly in Seville, Ohio, where they were active and well-liked members of the community. Tragically, though, Anna's tall life was not a long one. Both Anna and her husband suffered from health problems, but the giant spouse who died first was **she**, at the early age of forty-two.

Answers for Chapter 16: Mastering Pronoun–Antecedent Agreement (pages 158 to 171)

Exercise 16.1
1. Jim Cuddy is a singer-songwriter **who** truly depicts his soul in his music.
2. I would love to own any car **that** had the name Ferrari on it.
3. Are you sure that Colleen Jones is the reporter **who** became a curling champion?
4. My second wife was a woman **[whom]** I met on a blind date.
5. The book report, **which** was due on Wednesday, has not yet been handed in.
6. Successful farmers understand the climate and know the crops **that** they are raising.
7. It was Trent McCleary **who** was severely injured in the Canadiens-Flyers game in Montreal in January 2000.
8. My aunt is the one **who** drove the car **that** ended up in the creek after the wedding.
9. I cannot stand people **who** are always late.
10. Students **who** try their best will succeed more often than students **who** never have to try.

Exercise 16.2

1. her	6. it
2. a	7. a
3. his or her	8. a
4. who, her	9. a
5. its	10. his *or* her

Exercise 16.3 (suggested answers)

1. It's not every day that someone **sacrifices sleep** to serve you breakfast in bed.
2. Do you think anyone will send copies of **the** photos to me?
3. **No family loves its neighbours** as much as the Joneses love the Guptas.
4. Cooking is a great activity for anyone who wants to show off **creativity** as well as **project management skills.**
5. Everyone who has been to Winnipeg Beach Provincial Park **says it's one** of the most beautiful places to spend the summer.
6. Everyone **must be seated** before class begins.
7. **Dancers** must consult their partners in choosing the music and costumes for **the** competition next fall.
8. **When we are children, we rush** towards adulthood; once we grow up, **we wish we had our** childhood back.
9. **People who eat** peanut butter and pickle sandwiches should have their **heads** examined.
10. **If you do not attend the party, your membership in the club will be cancelled.**

Exercise 16.4 (suggested answers)

1. Each time the newborn grabbed her mother's hand, **the woman** smiled.
2. Donald **returned his dad's ring** yesterday.
3. Figure skating is my least favourite sport although I've owned **a pair of skates** for several years.
4. As a child, Wanda was a gifted musician, **and** she practised **the piano** at least four hours every day.
5. I did not see the girls' dance recital **because I was out of town.**
6. What did Susan say to her mother before **her mother** hung up the phone?
7. At our church, **the minister and her husband** ensure everyone is looked after.
8. That Charles would be Joe's neighbour never occurred to **Joe.**
9. Upset, I slammed my drink on the table and broke **the glass.**
10. When Jane and Tory met, **Jane thought Tory** was a bit odd.

Exercise 16.5 (suggested answers)

1. The culprit must be someone **who** is left-handed.
2. Each of the televisions had **its** pros and cons, but the Sony was the one for me.
3. Katrina is the only person I know who can play the piano while **juggling.**
4. Mona can't figure out why Margaret hasn't called her since Margaret's birthday.

5. A diplomat is someone **who** can tell you to go to hell in such a way that makes you feel grateful to be on your way.
6. Cycling is Mohammed's favourite pastime, but he had to sell three of **his bikes** to get some cash.
7. Each committee chair knows exactly what **the** duties are for next year.
8. Watching TV requires little mental or physical effort, and we all need more **exercise**.
9. **Each of us** should live every day to its fullest and reach for **our** dreams; that is how **we** will find true happiness.
10. Last year my brother taught me how to ski, but I have yet to buy any **skis** of my own.

Exercise 16.6 (suggested answers; deleted words indicated by ***)
1. Before **she takes** any medication, a pregnant woman should consult **her** physician.
2. Anyone **who** has finished one hundred math problems in three minutes can't possibly have all the correct answers.
3. I have gone hunting four times, and I have never shot **a duck (deer, pheasant, etc.)**.
4. When Mrs. Tomak saw Ayat and Mary yesterday she thought she must have been mistaken about **Mary's** trip to her parents' home in Egypt.
5. Lack of exercise will cause anyone to lose *** tone and flexibility.
6. I am sure every teacher will be there even though **teachers** aren't required to be at the hockey games.
7. Opportunities are everywhere, as long as **you** know where to look.
8. When Ben and Tom returned from the tour of the CBC building, **Ben** said he would think of pursuing a career in journalism.
9. Every acting student must pick **a** favourite play or movie as one of this year's projects.
10. A woman who marries a man **who** has been married before is doing **her** best to be ecologically responsible….

Exercise 16.7 (suggested answers; deleted words indicated by ***)
Anyone **who** visits Toronto notices the CN Tower as a prominent feature of the skyline. As one approaches the city from the air, **one** can see it pointing upwards like a silver needle from the shore of Lake Ontario. A visitor can see the famous structure from many vantage points downtown. As one emerges from the St. George subway station, **one** can see it clearly past the Bata Shoe Museum, even though **the Tower** is still a twenty-minute walk away. Everyone **who** walks down University Avenue or Spadina Avenue has a clear view of the Tower, and every tourist **who** strolls along the harbourfront can't help but notice it.
The CN Tower stands as a symbol of Toronto's industrial and economic importance, but anyone **who** travels to the city should know that Toronto is also home to much natural beauty: there are many lush ravines and tranquil green spaces. For pic-

nickers, there are many beautiful city parks where one can have **a** choice of peaceful picnic spots. For families with small children, there are plenty of great playgrounds to visit. For cyclists, there are numerous bike trails *** to try. Moreover, anyone **who** enjoys waterside walks can visit the Don River, Grenadier Pond, or the boardwalk along Lake Ontario.

Everyone **who** visits Toronto should spend some time in High Park, my favourite green space in the city. The park is most beautiful in May, when the ornamental fruit trees are in bloom. One can walk along the park paths and delight in the billows of pink blossoms. Even someone **who** has grown up in the Niagara region or the Okanagan Valley would have to agree that the sight is spectacular. In addition to its fruit trees, High Park also offers the visitor **a** choice of several other attractions, including a large playground, a duck pond, and a tiny train **that** takes children on a ride around the park. No one should miss the park's summer theatre festival, which features plays by Shakespeare performed in a natural amphitheatre. Go early, though, to get a seat, since everybody in the city throngs to the park for **the** free entertainment.

Answers for Chapter 17: Maintaining Person Agreement (pages 172 to 179)

Exercise 17.1

1. you want
2. you
3. you don't
4. he
5. you will

6. we
7. he or she studies
8. you
9. you have
10. her

Exercise 17.2

Students who manage full-time careers while **they're** in college may do better at **their** academic work than those who do nothing but study. Because **they** have a steady job, students who work full-time benefit from a stable lifestyle and may actually be more dedicated to **their** classes. **They** may be better able to concentrate, partly because of the ability to apply some of **their** work skills, such as the ability to manage projects, to **their** studies. The challenge of balancing job responsibilities with academic commitments motivates **them** to do **their** best at both work and at school. College students with full-time jobs also tend to appreciate **their** education more than the students who do not work during **their** college years. They can see the direct relevance of **their** class work to the tasks **they face** in the workplace. Working students make many sacrifices to attend college, so they know they must perform well to prove to **themselves** that **their** education is worth all the hard work **they do**.

Exercise 17.3 (suggested answers; deleted words indicated by ***)

1. It's hard for Canadians to accept that **they** will always live in the shadow of America.
2. Baking a cake is not difficult to do *** as long as you have the right ingredients, a functioning oven, and confidence.

3. **You** would be a hypocrite if you preached against fashion *faux pas* and then showed up at a classical music performance wearing an orange skirt with a green and purple blouse.

4. The emotional turmoil that results from breast cancer can affect a woman's physical health as well as **her** psychological well-being.

5. Beer is good for **you**, even better for you than red wine.

6. If **you put** on a smile and a confident attitude, then you might win the partner of your dreams.

7. **You** should talk to someone about what's bothering **you**, so **you** can get help if necessary.

8. After graduation night, the partying and lack of sleep made it hard ***** to stay** awake.

9. One cannot be convicted of a crime ******* without a fair trial.

10. It's difficult to ******* cope without **a** loved one when your heart has been broken.

Exercise 17.4 (suggested answers; deleted words indicated by *******)

How can **you** prevent frostbite? Frostbite usually affects areas that are exposed to the cold, such as **your** cheeks, nose, ears, and chin. **Your** extremities (**your** hands and feet) are at higher risk than the rest of **your** body. In order to avoid freezing **your** skin, **you** must prepare **yourself** before venturing outdoors in winter weather. For best insulation, **you** should dress in loose, warm layers of clothing. A hat is essential since much of **your** body heat escapes from the top of **your** head. Another important way to prevent frostbite is to avoid getting ******* wet.

If, in spite of **your** precautions, **you develop** frostbite, [**you** must] take care to prevent permanent skin damage. [**You** should] Thaw the affected skin slowly by wrapping it in warm clothes or soaking it in warm water. If **you have** ever had frostbite, **you know** that thawing the skin is a painful process. [**You**] **Do** not try to speed up thawing by applying direct heat, since **you** can cause blisters that way. [**You** should] Never rub ice or snow on frozen skin, no matter what **your** grandmother says. When **your** skin is pink, and **you** feel normal sensation return to the area, the skin has been successfully thawed. **You** should then wrap the affected area and seek medical attention as soon as possible.

Exercise 17.5 (deleted words indicated by *******)

A. Second-person

Mike Weir said, "Sometimes the hardest thing to do in golf is wait." You have to wait on the tee, wait in the fairway, and wait—ever so patiently—for **your** success. Because **you** spend so much time waiting, **you** are often tempted to give up. However, Weir is a good example of someone who trained himself to wait patiently for success. He won the Ontario Junior Championship in 1988. As a golf fan, **you** will agree that his road to international fame has been lengthy. **You** can use Weir as a role-model by striving to match his patience, endurance, and confidence. Weir proved that patience pays off when he won the Masters in 2003 and became the first Canadian man to win a major tournament. If **you** have that same attitude, then surely **you** can make it as a successful golfer, too. If **you** are young and have a positive attitude, then **you** can make it from the local to the national junior golf tournaments, all the way to the PGA. **You** just have to do one thing: wait.

B. Third-person

Mike Weir said, "Sometimes the hardest thing to do in golf is wait." **One has** to wait on the tee, wait in the fairway, and wait—ever so patiently—for ******* success. Because **they** spend so much time waiting, **golfers** are often tempted to give up. However, Weir is a good example of someone who trained himself to wait patiently for success. He won the Ontario Junior Championship in 1988. **Golf fans will agree** that his road to international fame has been lengthy. **Amateur golfers** can use him as a role-model by striving to match his patience, endurance, and confidence. Weir proved that patience pays off when he won the Masters in 2003 and became the first Canadian man to win a major tournament. If **they** have that same attitude, then surely **others** can make it as successful golfers, too. If **they** are young and have a positive attitude, then **they** can make it from the local to the national junior golf tournaments, all the way to the PGA. **They** just have to do one thing: wait.

Answers for Chapter 18: The Comma (pages 183 to 191)

Exercise 18.1
1. The five largest cities in Canada were once Montreal, Toronto, Quebec, Ottawa(,) and Hamilton.
2. correct
3. I want my wedding to be unusual, but I can't decide whether the bridesmaids should wear black, brown(,) or olive dresses.
4. Heather is a well-rounded student; she does well in mathematics, English, history(,) and science.
5. correct
6. My favourite bands are The Tragically Hip, Blue Rodeo(,) and the Matthew Good Band.
7. Brushing my teeth, combing my hair(,) and putting in my contacts are automatically part of my morning routine.
8. My favourite animals are llamas, chimpanzees(,) and zebras.
9. Do you think crop circles are the work of aliens, humans(,) or gods?
10. I enjoy listening to country music, rap(,) and jazz.

Exercise 18.2
1. Sandra, a recovering alcoholic, has been sober for twelve years.
2. Coach Quarles, my favourite teacher, taught us the value of determination.
3. correct
4. *The Enchanted Echo*, published in 1944, was Al Purdy's first collection of poetry.
5. The medical examiner, a man of his word, promised the family he would respect the widow's privacy.
6. Dr. Kozey, the town's newest dentist, just moved here from Gimli.
7. Despite his lead roles in *Double Jeopardy* and *Thirteen Days*, Bruce Greenwood has not achieved the fame that Harrison Ford has.
8. correct
9. Do you know Anne Murray, the former physical education teacher from Nova Scotia?

10. My father's favourite song, believe it or not, is "Snowbird."

Exercise 18.3

1. We can't see our children, nor can we hear them.
2. Please pay attention, for the lesson today will be on the exam.
3. correct
4. This is my first full-time job, so I don't want to mess it up.
5. Dave and Angus are moving to Inuvik, and Mel is moving to Corner Brook.
6. correct
7. correct
8. The deer ran across the road, and I just missed it.
9. Either you are Denver's wife, or she has a twin.
10. Michelle doesn't see Chloe very often, yet the two of them are always in touch.

Exercise 18.4

1. Daddy, why is the sky blue?
2. Walking slowly across the beam, I made it to the other side without looking at the water below.
3. correct
4. Until I received a raise, I didn't think I was appreciated at work.
5. No matter how long I practice, I can never seem to play that song very well.
6. Touched by the toast, the bride fought back her tears.
7. When our boss talks about improving productivity, she is never talking about herself.
8. When the first leaves fall from the trees, I prepare myself for another school year filled with new faces, old memories, and new challenges.
9. Although Jed is originally from Medicine Hat, he calls Regina his home.
10. Where the little one-room schoolhouse had stood for 100 years, a Canadian Tire now stands.

Exercise 18.5

1. Hot, sunny(,) and muggy days are what the weather reporter predicts for this week.
2. Inside, the children are laughing at their principal.
3. Despite the news of his disappearance, Faye remained confident her son's life was not in danger.
4. As their wedding anniversary approached, the couple began to look at travel brochures.
5. I loved John Irving's novel *A Prayer for Owen Meany*, but I did not enjoy *Simon Birch*.
6. One of my favourite bands, Blue Rodeo, played in Halifax in February.
7. After class today, I plan to deliver applications to CTV, CBC(,) and the BBC.
8. You can't believe everything you read, everything you hear(,) or everything you see.
9. Surprisingly, David Foster has produced as many albums as Quincy Jones.
10. Foster has produced albums for such well-known artists as Chicago, Celine Dion, The Corrs(,) and Michael Jackson.

Exercise 18.6

1. Acadians, the French-speaking settlers from Nova Scotia and New Brunswick, became known in Louisiana as Cajuns. (rule 2)
2. After being diagnosed with Hepatitis C, Pamela Anderson started to speak out about the need for health research. (rule 4)
3. Maya, you aren't colouring inside the lines! (rule 4)
4. We won the first game, but we lost the second and third. (rule 3)
5. Trevor laughs like a chicken, walks like a duck(,) and sings like a turkey. (rule 1)
6. If you know what you are doing, driving a vehicle with a manual transmission isn't difficult. (rule 4)
7. The Apple Blossom Festival, which takes place every May, brings in thousands of tourists. (rule 2)
8. If you enjoy running through the woods, swimming in the lake(,) and cycling through the mountains, you might consider competing in a triathlon. (rule 4, rule 1)
9. On Wednesday evening, the budget committee will meet to elect a new chair for the next fiscal year. (rule 4)
10. When my family moved to Victoria from Labrador City, I felt as if I had moved from one country to another. (rule 4)

Exercise 18.7

Ringette, first played in 1963, is a Canadian game that started in North Bay, Ontario. Designed with girls in mind, ringette is similar to ice hockey. Players use a straight stick, rather than one with a curved blade, to manipulate a rubber ring and score goals. In the beginning, most ringette teams were in Ontario and Quebec. By the 1970s, however, the sport had established itself in all regions of Canada. Today, ringette is a popular pastime with girls and women, but it also appeals to boys and men. There are over 50,000 ringette players in Canada, and this number continues to grow. The ringette community now boasts 9,000 coaches, 2,866 trained referees(,) and many thousands of volunteers. The volunteers run ringette organizations from British Columbia to Newfoundland, taking care of countless administrative details, including registration and fund-raising.

Exercise 18.8 (deleted punctuation indicated by ***)

Since Confederation, Quebec has produced many remarkable federal leaders, including two of our most famous prime ministers, Sir Wilfred Laurier and Pierre Trudeau. According to a nineteenth-century rumour, *la belle province*, then known as Lower Canada, may also have produced an American president. Chester Arthur was running *** for president *** in 1881 when the Democrats paid a lawyer, Arthur Hinman, to investigate his past. Hinman alleged *** that Arthur was born in Dunham, Quebec, and moved to Fairfield, Vermont, his official birthplace, as an infant. Hinman's theories have since been discredited, but they created a controversy during Arthur's presidency, which lasted from 1881 to 1885. In 1884, Hinman created a temporary scandal when he printed his claims in a pamphlet titled "How a British Subject *** Became President of the United States."

Answers for Chapter 19: The Semicolon (pages 192 to 200)

Exercise 19.1

1. correct
2. incorrect
3. correct
4. incorrect
5. correct
6. incorrect
7. incorrect
8. incorrect
9. correct
10. incorrect

Exercise 19.2

1. incorrect
2. correct
3. incorrect
4. correct
5. incorrect
6. incorrect
7. incorrect
8. correct
9. incorrect
10. correct

Exercise 19.3

2. The weather was beautiful; **it was** perfect for the wedding.
4. The bride stumbled in the aisle when the heel of her shoe broke.
6. I wanted to attend the reception at the Saint Mary's Boat Club; however, my fear of boats prevailed, and I did not go.
7. The bride and groom bought many things at the last minute: candles for the reception tables; flowers and candelabra for the ceremony; ribbon, fabric, and satin hearts for the decorations; and, finally, a lacy garter for the bride.
8. The minister encouraged the couple to recite traditional vows; instead, they wrote their own.
10. The flower girls wore white; the bridesmaids wore yellow.

Exercise 19.4

1. We should get in bed early tonight, for we have to be up by 6:00 a.m.
3. Cigarette prices are outrageous; still, my parents continue to smoke.
5. Due to the widespread drought, forest fires have been a serious problem this summer.
6. If you need any help renovating your home, Ty would be glad to help.
7. Nikita bought a dress and make-up; Chelsea bought a purse and a wallet; Kara bought a watch, a school bag, and a pair of shoes; but Jess bought a car.
9. I wanted an exciting adventure, so we went to the Calgary Stampede.

Exercise 19.5

1. When I was four years old, my parents told me I was adopted; ever since then, I have wondered who my biological parents are.
2. My brother has two children; I have seven children; my younger sister has only one child; and my older sister, who is not married, has none.
3. Michelle, who is from Chicoutimi, and Niko, who is from Bathurst, speak French at home, but at work they speak mainly English.

4. Brant couldn't afford a diamond ring for Anne-Marie; therefore, he bought her a cubic zirconia.
5. When I take a long time at a task, I am slow; when my boss takes a long time, he is thorough.
6. When James graduated from Sheridan College, he went to California to work in an animation studio; as a result, his family lost touch with him.
7. There will be plenty of time for you to watch television later, but right now I need you to clean the bathroom.
8. *Anne of Green Gables*, by L.M. Montgomery, is the story of a little red-haired orphan from Prince Edward Island. First published in 1908, it is one of the best-selling Canadian books of all time.
9. I collect autographs of famous people; for example, I have signatures from Kurt Browning, Mike Myers(,) and Catriona Le May Doan.
10. The comforter is blue and yellow plaid; we chose the curtains and wall colour to complement it.

Exercise 19.6
1. Marwan and Dahlia did not want a big wedding ceremony, so they eloped to Las Vegas instead.
2. Art Linkletter is 90 years old; however, he doesn't look a day over 70.
3. When Mary Jane and Mary Anne go out together in public, people always confuse them; after all, they are identical twins.
4. I wondered why Sparky was limping; unfortunately, he had a splinter in his paw.
5. At the beginning of the school year, I am always faced with the same problems: buying new school supplies, registering for my courses, buying new clothes(,) and making new friends.
6. The idea of a voyage to the moon was once science fiction; now, there is talk of sending a spacecraft to Pluto.
7. We have continually adjusted the budget by decreasing expenditures and increasing revenue; this careful monitoring has produced higher net income.
8. Running the red light at 100 km/h, Ian crashed into a truck; fortunately, no one was hurt.
9. Please leave the books on the counter; I'll sort through them later.
10. There is much debate over who actually invented the baseball glove; nevertheless, Canadians are convinced that the true inventor is Art Irwin, from Toronto.

Exercise 19.7
1. I have read about the seven wonders of the world; I think the CN Tower should be included.
2. Alex Trebek hosts *Jeopardy!* on television; I wish I could be a contestant on that show.
3. The twins took a train trip to Alberta; they were exhausted by the end of the long ride.
4. My mother is going back to school; she has already bought her books and a backpack.

5. I can't believe Satchel called me yesterday; I thought he was planting trees in British Columbia.

6. Timothy Eaton established a chain of Canadian department stores; he started a mail-order business in 1884.

7. Angus McAskill, the Cape Breton giant, was not unusually large at birth; as an adult, however, he measured a startling 2.36 metres tall.

8. The toboggan is a sled designed by Aboriginal peoples for work, not pleasure; today, it is most commonly used by children.

9. There are many famous Bobbys in hockey: Bobby Hull was famous for his slap-shot, Bobby Orr for speed, and Bobby Clarke for his tough attitude.

10. Klondike ice-cream bars are named for the place where gold was first discovered during the Yukon Gold Rush; the lucky explorers who started the rush to the Klondike were George Carmac, Skookum Jim(,) and Tagish Charley.

Exercise 19.8

In Winnipeg's Assiniboine Zoo, you can see a statue of the original bear cub who inspired the children's stories about Winnie-the-Pooh, Piglet(,) and the rest of the animals from the Hundred Acre Woods. Some people think that Winnie-the-Pooh was created by Walt Disney; actually, he was the brain child of British author A.A. Milne. During the First World War, Milne and his young son, Christopher, used to visit a bear cub named Winnie at the London zoo. The bear itself was a visitor; a Canadian soldier, Captain Harry Colebourn, had adopted the cub as a pet in Ontario in 1914 and brought it with him overseas. Because he hailed from Winnipeg, Colebourn gave the cub the name of his hometown. When he was called to the front, he left the cub with the London zoo. Thanks to Captain Colebourn's bequest to the zoo, generations of children have grown up reading about the adventures of the fictional bear, Winnie-the-Pooh; watching the Disney cartoons and movies about his adventures; wearing his image on shirts, hats, socks, and sleep-wear; and dressing up in his likeness for costume parties and Hallowe'en night.

Answers for Chapter 20: The Colon (pages 201 to 205)

Exercise 20.1

1. incorrect	6. incorrect
2. correct	7. correct
3. correct	8. incorrect
4. incorrect	9. incorrect
5. incorrect	10. correct

Exercise 20.2

1. correct

2. Although the famous athlete had won many prizes, he was proudest of one par-ticular achievement: the Citizen of the Year award, from his home town in Saskatchewan.

3. The contents of my grandfather's desk drawer included the following items**:** a bag of barley sugar candy, a stapler, three pencils, and a pocket watch.
4. As we drove through the Rockies, our cousin from Austria harped on one topic**:** the spectacular beauty of the Alps.
5. Two items remain on the agenda**:** the bake sale and the bottle drive.
6. Petula calls herself an omnivore, but there is one food she will not eat**:** haggis.
7. I was surprised to discover that Katie is related to one of Canada's most famous painters**:** A.J. Casson.
8. The premier gave a catchy slogan to his budget-cutting measures**:** The Common-Sense Revolution.
9. Clearly, there was only one thing to do**:** open the mysterious package.
10. correct

Exercise 20.3
1. The new federal law is harsh and unfair.
4. Two reasons for the bankruptcy are overspending and bad investments.
5. Consider this example**:** John Turner.
6. Don't forget to invite Sarah, John, and Yvor.
8. Several factors contributed to the project's success, including Jan's computer skills and Gary's rapid editing.
9. One more tool was needed**:** the screwdriver.

Answers for Chapter 21: Quotation Marks (pages 206 to 212)

Exercise 21.1
1. "The steak and eggs are delicious**,**" said Ian.
2. correct
3. Frustrated with his reading assignment, Ben asked his instructor**,** "Is Margaret Atwood really one of Canada's best authors?"
4. The *World Guide to Beer* describes Labatt's Blue as "another sweetish pale lager."
5. "Mt. Royal College has a good public relations program**,**" said Nancy.
6. In his poem "A Road Not Taken," Robert Frost explains how he chose his particular path in life: "I took the one less traveled by/And that has made all the difference."
7. correct
8. The front-page headline of today's **Daily News** is "Shooting Foiled."
9. I'm not sure if my favourite song is "Somewhere Over the Rainbow" or "Follow the Yellow Brick Road."
10. Bert asked Jim**,** "Why were you late for work today?"

Exercise 21.2
1. "After fourteen years in Nova Scotia," said Dan**,** "I am finally applying for Canadian citizenship."
2. correct

3. correct
4. "Why in the world," asked Yosef, "would you gamble away $5,000?"
5. correct
6. The monument to Samuel de Champlain quotes from his journal: "As for me, I labour always to prepare a way for those willing to follow."
7. Did Led Zeppelin sing the old Hank Snow song, "I'm Moving On"?
8. "I wish I were as wealthy as you," said Ashley, wondering why her debt load was so high.
9. After recording his voice on a wax cylinder for an Edison phonograph, Peter Jennings said, "This is something you get to do only once in your life."
10. I will never forget two of my mother's sayings: "Never ask yourself a question," and "Never give yourself an answer if you do."

Answers for Chapter 22: Question Marks, Exclamation Marks, and Punctuation Review (pages 213 to 221)

Exercise 22.1
1. Rosa inquired whether the Chateau Frontenac would charge her for an additional night's stay.
2. Does it make any difference to you if we bring our Duck Tolling Retriever with us when we visit?
3. I often wonder if there is life on other planets.
4. Should you decide to purchase this dishwasher, I will give you a free box of detergent as a bonus.
5. How can anyone possibly eat an entire lobster without making a mess?
6. Please tell me whether I can get my money back if I return these shoes before Saturday.
7. When the Blue Jays make it to the finals again, do you think Trisha will finally agree to watch a baseball game with us?
8. Whatever happened to the University of Winnipeg jacket Dad bought in 1972?
9. The pressing question that remains is whether the new premier will change the carpet in the legislature buildings.
10. Did you know that Manitoba's Golden Boy, the province's symbol of hope and prosperity, is over 5 m tall?

Exercise 22.2 (suggested answers)
1. Please pour me a drink. That salsa is hot!
2. I'm shocked. After nine years of dating, Blair finally proposed to Camilla.
3. "More, More!" screamed the crowd at the Barenaked Ladies concert.
4. Leave this house at once. (or !) I never want to see you again!
5. The War of 1812 called forth feats of extraordinary bravery.
6. You've torn a hole in my shirt!
7. "Help! I'm drowning!" came a cry from the lake.

8. I was astonished by the latest figures describing child poverty in Canada**.** They indicate that one out of five children lives in desperately poor circumstances**.**
9. Don't look back**!** It's gaining on us**!**
10. I can't endure this torture any longer**.** I'm leaving**!**

Exercise 22.4 (deleted words indicated by ***)
1. **"**Wait for us**!"** we cried, as their boat headed toward the rapids**;** unfortunately, we were too late to take the plunge.
2. Every day on the guided wilderness hike includes a new adventure, such as *** canoeing, rock climbing**(,)** and eagle watching.
3. I didn't know if I would be able to meet Wendy at Green Gables**,** so**,** after much discussion, we decided to meet at the ice-cream parlour in downtown Cavendish.
4. Our accounting instructor was surprised to learn that most of us had never before heard of debits or credits**;** in fact**,** many of us had never even balanced a chequebook.
5. The visiting Texan wondered why Canadians were so slow to boast about their many accomplishments**.**
6. **"**Don't forget to take your gloves**,"** my mother advised.
7. Even though the audience at The Pantages Theatre was shouting **"**Bravo**!",** the actor had no choice *** but to follow the two police officers off the stage and into the paddy wagon.
8. According to the recipe, this cake requires two eggs**;** however**,** I'm sure we could substitute one egg and two egg whites.
9. Sharon Pollock's play ***Blood Relations*** creates two possible portraits of the accused murderer Lizzie Borden**:** a dutiful nineteenth-century daughter and an outraged feminist rebel.
10. **"**Tell me a little about yourself**,"** the interviewer asked. **"**What makes you think you can handle this job**?"**

Exercise 22.5
  Although we usually work well together, Chantal and I had a hard time deciding on a figure to carve for this year's Winterlude ice-carving competition. At first, we both favoured a Walt Disney design, such as Mickey Mouse, Pluto**(,)** or Winnie-the-Pooh. We soon realized, however, that there was a crucial flaw common to all these ideas**:** none of them involved a Canadian theme.
  We flipped through popular magazines, we quizzed our friends**(,)** and we even searched the Internet to try to find a Canadian alternative, but we had no luck. Everywhere we looked, we seemed to be surrounded by American images.
  Chantal finally had an idea. **"**Why don't we carve an ice statue of Louis Riel**?"** she said. **"**He's a Canadian hero.**"**
  "That's too complicated,**"** I protested. **"**What about a Canadian beaver**?"**
  "That's too boring,**"** was Chantal's response.

We argued back and forth about the design for days; we were both so annoyed that we were almost ready to withdraw from the competition. In the end, we settled on a compromise that reflected humorously on our own frustration: a tableau featuring a baffled-looking beaver surrounded by a jeering gang of Disney characters.

Exercise 22.6 (deleted punctuation indicated by ***)

My cousins from Alberta, Jeff and Janet, decided to spend their summer vacation touring British Columbia. They wanted to experience the full flavour of local hospitality, so they chose to stay in a bed and breakfast in each town they visited. To their surprise, they discovered that staying in a quaint bed and breakfast can involve some unexpected adventures.

In Victoria, Jeff and Janet slept on a hundred-year-old bed that was so saggy it gave them both terrible backaches; no matter how much they tossed and turned, they could not find a comfortable position. In Whistler, they discovered an additional guest in the turn-of-the-century converted stable loft they had rented: a green-eyed Siamese cat that was accustomed to sleeping at the foot of the bed. In Kelowna, they were startled awake at 8 a.m. by their exuberant host, who delivered them an unannounced breakfast in bed.

After hearing about my cousins' experiences, I wonder why anyone would opt to stay in a bed and breakfast. Because I am someone who values privacy, I can't imagine a more nerve-wracking way to spend my vacation. I guess Jeff and Janet have a more flexible sense of humour than I do; they took all these unexpected incidents in stride. When I asked them whether they regretted their choice of accommodation, they told me that *** all their future travel plans would include bed and breakfasts.*** "We've never had so much fun!" they declared enthusiastically.

Answers for Chapter 23: Finding Something to Write About (pages 225 to 238)

Exercise 23.1

1. Not specific
2. Not specific
3. Not significant
4. Not single
5. Not significant
6. Not single
7. Not supportable
8. Not specific
9. Not single
10. Not specific; not supportable without significant research

Exercise 23.2

1. Possible, but too broad. You could make the topic more significant by applying one or more limiting factors to it. For example, "How predatory mites and spiders protect organic wheat farms."
2. Not significant, and it's hard to imagine how you could make it so.
3. Not specific. What about it? Also not supportable without significant research.
4. Possible, but the subject needs to be limited. You might, for example, discuss the role of the Métis in the Red River Rebellion.

5. Possible, but the topic needs to be more specific. Try applying one or more limiting factors. You could perhaps discuss "How to prevent electrical damage to your motherboard," or "How to avoid catching an e-mail virus."
6. Not specific. Limit the topic to make it more supportable. For example, "Three tax strategies the government should use to decrease the national deficit."
7. Possible. Make the topic more specific by identifying two or three typical obstacles and by focussing on one province (e.g., B.C., Quebec).
8. Possible, but too broad. Focus on one particular kind of Internet piracy and apply one or more limiting factors to that topic. For example, "The impact of Internet piracy on the rock music industry."
9. Possible, but too broad. Choose one or two specific women to discuss.
10. So broad it has lost significance as a meaningful subject for a paper. Try limiting it to one kind of pollution that has not been widely written about, e.g., noise pollution.

Exercise 23.6
1. high cost of cigarettes (overlaps with "financial savings")
2. leash and clicker (specifies equipment rather than a part of the training process)
3. lack of contact with instructor and lack of contact with peers (overlap with "lack of motivation due to isolation")
4. depression in adolescents (unrelated to main topic; belongs to larger topic of depression in general)
5. take a half-hour lunch break (not significant and unrelated; a lunch hour is not a responsibility)
6. risk of radiation (a subtopic of "cold fusion")
7. hydroelectric power (unrelated to the subject; it is the kind of energy produced by water sources)
8. decrease in tourism (part of "economic downturn")

Exercise 23.8

Subject	Order	Main Points
1. How to send an e-mail message	chronological	_1_ start e-mail program
		_3_ enter name of recipient and subject of message in spaces provided
		_2_ click on "New Document" icon to start a new message
		_5_ click on "Send" icon to send message
		_4_ type body of message

Subject	Order	Main Points
2. Differences between amateur and professional figure skating	climactic	_3_ amateur skaters focus on the judges; professional skaters focus on the audience _2_ amateur skaters are not paid; professional skaters are paid _1_ amateur skaters must include mandatory elements in their programs; professional skaters have more artistic licence
3. How to prepare for a job interview	chronological	_1_ visit the company's Web site _4_ dress carefully _2_ prepare answers to standard interview questions _3_ ask a friend to role play the interview with you
4. How the Olympic Games benefit Canadians	logical	_1_ they provide role models of active, goal-oriented achievers _3_ they enhance the profile of amateur sport in Canada _2_ they encourage young people to pursue their dreams
5. Negative effects of pesticides	logical	_3_ pesticides cause deformity and death in birds _2_ pesticides kill the bugs that birds eat _1_ pesticides release toxic chemicals into the air and ground
6. Why affirmative action policies are necessary	chronological	_1_ they place members of visible minorities in positions of power _3_ they foster the development of a more egalitarian society _2_ they create powerful role models for future generations of visible minority groups

7. and 8. Decide on your own climactic arrangements for these questions. Be sure you can explain your choices.

Answers for Chapter 24: Writing the Thesis Statement (pages 239 to 246)

Exercise 24.1

1. Although each region of the country has its own local symbol, the universal Canadian symbols are the maple leaf, the beaver, and the moose.
2. According to the Conference Board of Canada, among the skills most desired by today's employers are the ability to listen carefully, speak clearly, and write effectively.
3. People with chronic indigestion may actually be suffering from one of three ailments: lactose intolerance, complex carbohydrate intolerance, or irritable bowel syndrome.
4. In order to find prosperity in the twenty-first century, Canada must abandon its dependence on a resource-based economy, cultivate a spirit of entrepreneurship, and encourage immigration.
5. International travel has expanded my horizons in several ways: it has exposed me to the ways of other cultures, it has taught me foreign languages, and it has made history a living experience for me.
6. Learning a musical instrument benefits a child in several important ways, including the development of self-discipline, listening skills, and hand-eye coordination.
7. Because they lack a strategic plan, personnel, or funding, many young companies falter in the early growth stage.
8. The elderly, children, and asthmatics form the main population groups that suffer from air pollution.
9. Youth organizations that encourage leadership in young people include Scouts, Junior Achievement, and Boys and Girls clubs.
10. Margaret Laurence's *Stone Angel*, Margaret Atwood's *Robber Bride*, and Michael Ondaatje's *In the Skin of a Lion* are three of the most critically-acclaimed Canadian novels.

Exercise 24.2

1. The reunion episode of *The Beachcombers* was touching, funny, suspenseful, and tragic.
2. Young creatures of any species appeal to us because they are small, vulnerable, affectionate, and cuddly.
3. Dan's favourite uncle is tall, wealthy, good-natured, and generous.
4. A successful investigative journalist requires relentless curiosity, rapid writing skills, the stamina to work long hours, and keen interviewing skills.
5. Gina lost 12 pounds by exercising daily, eating less, increasing her water intake, and giving up ice cream.
6. Antoinette uses the World Wide Web to access her bank accounts, order her groceries, play online bingo, and buy her work uniforms.
7. To be an effective manager, you must maintain open lines of communication, allow free exchange of ideas, encourage input from subordinates, and create opportunities for advancement.

8. In order to encourage an entrepreneurial spirit in school children, we need to make entrepreneurship part of the curriculum, encourage experiential learning, allow children to make mistakes and learn from them, and profile the achievements of successful Canadian entrepreneurs.

Exercise 24.3

1. not parallel
2. parallel
3. not parallel
4. not parallel
5. parallel
6. not parallel
7. parallel
8. not parallel
9. not parallel
10. not parallel

Exercise 24.4 (suggested answers)

1. Frequent causes of failure in college are lack of responsibility, lack of discipline, and lack of basic skills.
3. As a person ages, time moves more quickly, the body moves more slowly, and the teeth decay.
4. I can't decide whether to take a certificate program in computing, accounting, or dental hygiene.
6. Daycare, parental leave, and work equity are not just women's issues.
8. There are two important questions about the high-technology field: will it remain a fast-track industry, and what role will Canada play in it?
9. No matter how hard I search, I cannot seem to find the hospitality, generosity, or community spirit that I remember from my childhood in Newfoundland.
10. Organizational behaviourists teach that managers assume three different corporate roles: they are *disseminators* when communicating their goals; they are *negotiators* when they lead working groups; and they are *figureheads* when they represent the company to outside agencies.

Exercise 24.5

1. Under the "Skills" section of his résumé, George highlighted his abilities as a bilingual writer, listener, and speaker. (overlap)
2. Pierre Trudeau will always be remembered as one of Canada's most influential prime ministers because he was intelligent, progressive, and provocative. (parallelism and relevance; Trudeau's pirouette is an example of his ability to be provocative, not a separate main point)
3. We hope that the new provincial Minister of Health will establish wellness clinics, fund nurse practitioners, and legislate midwifery. (parallelism and significance)
4. His dedication to physical fitness is so extreme that he exercises for three hours a day and follows a strict diet he obtained from a Tibetan monk. (parallelism and overlap)
5. Even though it is a dead language, Latin is worth learning because it teaches the history of the English language and improves one's ability to recognize problems with English grammar. (parallelism, significance)

Answer for Chapter 25: Writing the Outline (pages 247 to 250)

Exercise 25.2 (suggested answer)

Attention-getter: Video games have been blamed for everything from child obesity to the decline of the stock market. . . .

Thesis statement: Video games have considerable redeeming value: they teach useful skills, provide practical expertise, and even deliver positive social lessons.

I. Topic sentence: Video games demand high-level skills.
   A. Description of skills involved
      1. Comparison of skills with those of a surgeon, a goalie, and a grand chess master
      2. Skills are inborn, but anyone can improve his/her ability
   B. Example: author's personal best score compared to that of fourteen-year-old player
   C. Concluding statement: author would trust his life to colleague's daughter

II. Topic sentence: Video games have practical applications.
   A. The best games are simulations of various working environments
      1. Examples: systems used to train pilots, astronauts, designers, engineers, surgeons
      2. Workers in these fields enjoy games based on technology that they use in the workplace
   B. At the elite level, huge corporate sponsors support contests, leagues, and tournaments
      1. Examples: Programmers, software developers, and IT workers love games based on the technology with which they work every day
   C. Concluding statement: Big companies know that elite-level games will produce future innovators and entrepreneurs

III. Topic sentence: Video games are socially useful.
   A. Example and contrast: the violence of video games is cathartic, unlike TV violence
   B. Video games promote social interaction
      1. Players may appear isolated, but they are in fact part of two communities
         (a) opponents in the game
         (b) allies against the machine
      2. Examples of communication among players: bulletin boards, chat rooms, Web sites
   C. Concluding statement: tournaments are becoming mainstream spectator sports
   Summary: Challenge to critics to get to know some players and discover their physical, intellectual, and social skills. These people will be tomorrow's high-tech experts, inventors, and philosophers.

Memorable statement: Prediction that video games will become televised attractions in which everyone can compete with the professionals. Example: "Counter Strike" as an Olympic event.

Answers for Chapter 26: Writing the Paragraphs (pages 251 to 264)

Exercise 26.1

paragraph 3:

topic sentence

"Workers" were generally people who had to travel back and forth across the canal as part of their employment. They might be traveling from one office to another, from one campus of Niagara College to the other, or from a customer on one side to a client on the other. People in the Worker category could be easily identified: they always carried piles of paper on the passenger seat of their cars. At the siren's sound, Workers turned off the ignition, engaged the parking brake, and settled in to do some paperwork. Ambitious, dedicated, and efficient, Workers also tended to be well organized and in control. Assuming that they would be stopped by a raised bridge at least twice a day, typical Workers could, in the 15 to 20 minutes it took for each ship to pass and the bridge to be lowered, accomplish impressive amounts of work. Some insurance and real estate companies with clients on both sides of the canal were able to close their offices during shipping season and count on their Workers to get their paperwork done from the front seat of their cars.

supporting sentences

conclusion

paragraph 4:

topic sentence

"Waiters" were not dissimilar from Workers, but tended to be more laid back, less ambitious, not so driven to succeed. Waiters could be easily spotted: they were the drivers with a book tucked under the sun visor or a pillow behind the front seat. A Waiter could have the car in park, the ignition off, and be deeply engrossed in a novel before a ship was even in sight. Alternatively, a Waiter could pull out the pillow, place it on the passenger seat, and curl up for a power nap, relying on the good-natured honking of the car behind to advise when the bridge was back in place. Waiters, as might be expected, were calm, easy-going, and unruffled. Sometimes tending to overweight, they frequently carried snacks in the glove box to enjoy while reading. A quick reader could finish *The Ring Trilogy* in a summer, while a Waiter who opted to nap could catch up to an hour's extra sleep every day.

supporting sentences

conclusion

paragraph 5:

topic sentence

supporting sentences

conclusion

<u>Unlike their two categorial cousins, "Wheelers" responded to the bridge siren the way thoroughbreds respond to the starting gate.</u> Unable to shift focus like Workers and Waiters when their journey was interrupted, Wheelers would dash through side streets at high speeds, trying to get to the next canal bridge before it went up. Sometimes they would make it and cross in triumph, racing back the way they had come (but on the other side of the canal) to resume their interrupted trip. It didn't seem to matter to them that this detour often took longer than waiting for a ship to pass, or that Workers and Waiters were streaming across the bridge by the time Wheelers arrived on the other side. A truly tragic sight was the Wheeler who dashed upstream or down, only to arrive at the next bridge seconds after its siren had sounded. Committed Wheelers would speed on to the third bridge, while the less fanatic would either wait where they were or return in defeat to the first bridge— which, by the time they arrived, would again be functioning. <u>Disorganized and inefficient, Wheelers nonetheless were energetic, enthusiastic, and optimistic. They were often thin and nervous.</u>

Exercise 26.7

1. Series of steps
2. Examples, specific details
3. Definition
4. Comparison and quotation
5. Examples
6. Specific details
7. Definition, examples, details
8. Examples and quotations
9. Extended example
10. Extended example

Exercise 26.10 (suggested answers)

I never knew my great-grandparents, but my generation has a lot in common with theirs. They grew up in the 1930s, when jobs were scarce; the job market today is almost as difficult as it was during the Great Depression. When he was my age, my great-grandfather had to hitch a train ride from a dried-up farm in Saskatchewan all the way to Cape Breton to find a job as a miner. He worked the night shift in the mine for subsistence wages, without job security, sick pay, or pension. Now, my cousins from Cape Breton are making great-grandpa's journey in reverse; they are so poor that they're moving to Alberta to look for work in the oil fields. The work there is hard, but the wages are much better than the Employment Insurance they've been drawing in Sydney. I'm thinking of following them next year, once I graduate. On the other hand, I might start my own business here in Antigonish, if I can raise enough capital. Like our great-grandparents, my peers and I will probably have to do without the social safety net, including public health care and the Canada Pension Plan, that our parents and grandparents could count on. It seems clear that members of Generation Y will have to pay their bills without much government help, so the sooner I start making my own fortune the better.

Answers for Chapter 27: Revising Your Paper (pages 265 to 273)

Exercise 27.1

What attracts Canadians to the country life? Could it be the slower pace and closer ties to neighbours? A recent survey conducted by Angus Reid for the Royal Bank of Canada suggests that country residents are more attached to **their** communities **than** urban residents. In response to the survey, urban residents said there was a **28 percent** chance that they would move to a small town or country setting; however, only **13 percent** of rural respondents **reported** any chance of moving to the city. One of the survey's most interesting findings was that there was no significant difference **between older and younger Canadians** in their attitude to where they lived. **This finding** appears to contradict the myth that young people **can't** wait to leave small communities for the bright lights of the big city or that their parents are counting the days until they can flee the urban hustle for the country calm. **Surprisingly, the survey concluded that, on average, regardless of where they live or what their ages, Canadians stay in one community for twenty-five years.**

Answers for Chapter 29: Cutting Out Clichés, Jargon, and Slang (pages 280 to 286)

Exercise 29.5 (suggested answers)
1. To move the car, release the brake and press gently on the gas pedal.
2. I am quite happy to live in a new house on the edge of town.
3. His clever wife regularly wrote thoughtful articles for the city newspaper.
4. Sailors in Halifax and other maritime regions are very cautious about watching for storms.
5. Michael Jordan led the Chicago Bulls to two NBA championships in a row.

Answers for Chapter 30: Eliminating Wordiness (pages 287 to 291)

Exercise 30.1 (suggested answers)
1. Today, few offices have typewriters.
2. Will Céline Dion proceed with a second embryo implant soon?
3. Many historical buildings in downtown Hamilton have disappeared.
4. Bryan Adams will repeat his tour and give two live concerts next week.
5. This innovation in manufacturing technology will bring prosperity to the mining community.
6. Once the frame is complete, the builder can erect the walls.
7. At 6:00 p.m., the subway rattles by my kitchen window; the view is identical each night.
8. The new principal promised to eliminate graffiti in the school.
9. Caitlin's self-confidence was shaken when her new car was attacked by vandals in Stanley Park.
10. The city told me that there was nothing they could do about the raccoons that have gathered in my backyard.

Exercise 30.2 (suggested answer)

Today, innumeracy is as big a problem for Canadian society as is illiteracy. Many high school graduates do just as poorly on math as they do on reading tests. Because computers have taken over so many calculating functions, many people think that math skills are no longer needed. However, no matter how automated our transactions may become, we will never be free of the need to perform basic calculations, for computers are not available everywhere. Here's an example: a friend recently bought a popsicle at the Assiniboine Zoo from a girl who was unable to calculate the cost of two fudgsicles. When she served the next person, she repeated her error and returned an extra toonie to the customer. Although small, her mistakes illustrate why I believe that our school boards need to change the curriculum to emphasize basic math as a key survival skill.

Answers for Chapter 31: Avoiding Abusages (pages 292 to 296)

Exercise 31.1

1. There was **a lot** of damage to the car, but the driver was **all right**.
2. I would **have** run farther, but after a couple of miles, I **could hardly** breathe.
3. Jane decided to stay **anyway** even though many people at the meeting were **prejudiced** against her.
4. Tony swore he **didn't do anything** he wasn't **supposed** to when he visited his grandmother in Vancouver.
5. I find it **really** sad that more Canadians like you and your friends are not running for political office. (*Or:* I find it sad that...)
6. Between you and **me**, there is still a lot of **prejudice** against Aboriginal peoples.
7. Whenever people ask me why the Montreal Expos are struggling, I tell them the reason is **that** Major League Baseball has never done **anything** to help them.
8. **Regardless** of what his friends said, Fred believed he would **have** won the race if he had not **fallen off** his bike.
9. Television is the best **medium** to study if you want to learn **about** how average Canadians perceive **themselves**.
10. I'd be happy to give you a lift to Kamloops; I am **supposed** to go there **anyway**.

Index

Credits